MAINE'S
JUBILEE COOKBOOK

Published for Maine's Sesquicentennial

Published By
Down East Books
Camden/Maine 04843

COMPILED AND EDITED
BY
LOANA SHIBLES
AND
ANNIE ROGERS

COVER DESIGN
BY
FLORA CULLEN

SKETCHES
BY
ANNA CROCKETT

Thirteenth Printing

International Standard Book Number: 0-89272-096-4

DOWN
EAST BOOKS   CAMDEN/MAINE

The Foods of the State of Maine

The history of food and the development of dishes peculiar to the State of Maine is a long and interesting one. It has all developed from the plain, down to earth "Mainer's" interest in filling his belly with whatever was at hand.

From the beginning the native was able to take the bounty of nature, add a little seasoning and common sense and come up with food fit for the Gods. The earliest settlements of this country were started on our coast and it stands to reason that our ancestors use of the wild foods were the first to be eaten on these shores. Add to this the teaching of our Maine Indians and you find that the origins of some of our dishes and cooking methods go back for centuries. Our cooks have shown a great deal of ingenuity in developing a whole heritage of good eating.

The history of food is tied to the sea as the first settlements were along the bays, inlets and islands along our coast. The first evidence of food that we have is attested to by the enormous oyster shell heaps along some of our tidal rivers. These tasty shellfish, long since disappeared from our shores, and the clams that are with us still, were consumed by the millions by the ancestors of the Indians who greeted the first visitors to these shores. Our modern day clambake originated from their methods of cooking these shellfish. An open fire was built and allowed to burn down to live coals over which was placed a layer of wet seaweed. The shellfish were placed on this and covered with another layer of wet seaweed and the whole thing was allowed to steam away until done.

The Indians also fished with spears and used brush weirs to trap schooling fish in the shallows along the coast. They passed on a great deal of skill and experience in harvesting the sea to our early colonists.

ANNA CROCKETT

Clara's Fried Lobster

Meat from a 1 pound lobster for each person
¼ cup (or more) of cream

3 tablespoons of butter or oleo for each serving

Cut the cooked lobster meat in small pieces, about 1 inch cubes. Melt the butter in frying pan, add the lobster pieces. Cook over medium heat, stirring constantly and adding more fat if necessary. Cook until all meat becomes pink. Add ¼ cup of cream at a time and as cream is absorbed, add more, simmering until a little cream remains.

Serve with baked potatoes, asparagus, and green salad. You will have a meal worthy of royalty.

Submitted by Margaret F. Stevens, Old Town, Maine

Baked Spanish Lobster

5 tablespoons butter
1 cup bread crumbs
½ cup ground pecans
2 small onions, minced
2 hard cooked egg yolks
2 sprigs parsley, minced
½ teaspoon salt

⅛ teaspoon pepper
½ teaspoon Accent
⅛ teaspoon thyme
½ cup cooked mushrooms
1 teaspoon lemon juice
2 cups lobster meat

Melt butter, add crumbs and fry to a golden brown; saving some crumbs for top. Mix together the nuts, onion, egg yolks, parsley, salt, pepper, Accent, thyme and mushrooms. Add to the fried crumbs. Mix well and cook over low flame 5 minutes. Spread in greased casserole, cover with lobster and sprinkle with the lemon juice. Cover with the following sauce:

6 tablespoons butter
3 tablespoons flour
1½ cups scalded milk
½ teaspoon salt

¼ teaspoon Accent
Dash pepper
3 tablespoons sherry

Melt butter, add flour, blend well. Add milk slowly. Cook until smooth and thickened, stirring constantly. Add salt, Accent, pepper and sherry. Pour over lobster, sprinkle thickly with remaining buttered crumbs and bake in hot oven 450 degrees for 10 minutes or until crumbs are nicely browned.

Submitted by Mrs. Gavin H. Watson, East Sullivan, Maine

Deviled Lobster

1 cup thin cream
2 tablespoons butter
2 tablespoons flour
½ cup milk
½ teaspoon dry mustard

Salt — paprika — Accent
4 slices bread, cubed (crust removed)
3 pounds lobster in shell

Cook lobster, remove from shell and cut in bite-size pieces. Make the white sauce with the cream, milk, butter and flour. Add the mustard and seasonings. Mix lobster and crumbs together in a buttered baking dish. Pour the white sauce over lobster and sprinkle with buttered crumbs. Bake at 350 degrees for 35 minutes.

Submitted by Charlotte Lancaster, Dover-Foxcroft, Maine

Lobster Casserole

1½ cups lobster meat
1 cup soft bread crumbs
1 egg, well beaten
1 cup milk

1 tablespoon lemon juice
2 tablespoons melted butter
1½ teaspoons salt

Mix all ingredients together. Place in a greased casserole and bake for one hour at 325 degrees.

Submitted by Mrs. Ivy Chatto, Rockland, Maine

Lobster Newburg

2 cups cubed lobster meat
2 tablespoons butter
½ cup sherry
2 tablespoons brandy
3 egg yolks, slightly beaten

½ cup thin cream
½ teaspoon salt
Pepper and nutmeg to taste
6 slices of toast

Cook lobster in butter 3 minutes, add liquors and cook 1 minute longer. Mix egg yolks and cream, add to lobster and cook just until thick, stirring constantly. The sauce will curdle if overcooked. Remove from fire, season with salt and pepper. Add nutmeg if desired. Serve at once on toast, saltines or in patty shells. Approximate yield — 6 servings.

Submitted by Mrs. Doris W. Pratt, Castine, Maine

Shrimp Exotica

1½ pounds of de-veined, cooked shrimp
1 No. 2 can sliced pineapple, drained (reserve syrup)
2 cups water
1 cup long-grain rice
3 chicken bouillon cubes
¼ cup cooking oil
1½ cups cubed cooked ham
¼ cup chopped onion
1 clove garlic, crushed or minced
1 medium-sized green pepper, cut in strips
2 tablespoons of chopped preserved or crystallized ginger
2 teaspoons soy sauce
2 teaspoons curry powder
½ teaspoon salt

Reserve 5 or 6 whole shrimp for garnish. Cut remaining shrimp into pieces. Set aside. Cut 4 pineapple slices into pieces and set aside.

Bring 2 cups of water to boil in a deep sauce pan. Add the bouillon cubes, and when dissolved, add the rice gradually, so boiling does not stop.

Cover pan tightly, reduce heat, and simmer 15 to 20 minutes until rice kernel is soft when pressed between fingers.

Heat ¼ cup cooking oil in a large skillet. Add ham, onion, and garlic. Heat thoroughly, turning with a spoon.

Blend together 2/3 cup of the reserved pineapple juice, ginger, soy sauce, curry powder and salt. Add this mixture and the green pepper to the skillet. Heat thoroughly. Add rice, shrimp, and cut-up pineapple· pieces. Toss until mixed. Heat well. Serve on a warm platter. Garnish with the whole shrimp and pieces of pineapple.

Submitted by· Doris Emery, Eastport, Maine

Curried Shrimp Creole

2 pounds cleaned and peeled shrimp
¼ pound butter
3 tablespoons flour
1 quart canned whole tomatoes
2 large onions, diced
2 large green peppers, diced
1½ teaspoons of Worcestershire sauce
2 tablespoons curry powder (more if you like it hot)
Season with salt and pepper

In a saucepan saute the onions and peppers until onions turn yellow. Add flour to make a paste. Add tomatoes, reserving liquid to thin. Add shrimp and curry powder. Simmer 30-35 minutes. Serve with Chutney on or with rice and a tossed salad.

Submitted by Mr. David Heilner, Dover, Mass.

Shrimp Chowder

¼ pound salt pork
1 small onion
3 medium-sized potatoes
¼ teaspoon salt

2 cups milk
2 cups shrimp
Butter the size of a walnut
Dash of pepper

Fry the salt pork in a kettle, add the onion, cut in small pieces. Cook until the onion is soft. Add the potatoes, cut in cubes or sliced. Add salt. Cover with water and cook until potatoes are done when tested with a fork. Add the milk, shrimp, butter and pepper. Simmer gently for 5 to 10 minutes and serve hot. Fresh or frozen shrimp may be used.

Submitted by Mrs. Jennie B. Teel, Port Clyde, Maine

Shrimp Pie

1 can shrimp, cut up
1 heaping cup peas
1 cup cold diced baked
  potato
2 tablespoons of butter

2 tablespoons flour
2 cups milk
Salt and pepper to taste
1 tablespoon prepared mustard
Bread crumbs

Make a white sauce with the butter, flour and milk. Season to taste and add a tablespoon of prepared mustard. Arrange the shrimp, peas, and potato in layers in a buttered casserole with white sauce and bread crumbs on top. Bake at 350 degrees for ½ hour.

Submitted by Mrs. Eva MacDougal, Bowdoinham, Maine

Shrimp Creole

2 cans shrimp, drained
2 cups raw white rice
2 cups diced onions
2 cups diced celery
1 1/3 cups minced green
  pepper

½ cup Wesson oil
4 teaspoons of salt
5 cups canned tomatoes
2 tablespoons flour
3 tablespoons water
Dash pepper

Boil the rice in salted water until tender (about 20 minutes). Drain and keep hot. Meanwhile, cook celery, onion and green pepper in Wesson oil in a skillet over low heat for 15 minutes, or until tender. Stir occasionally. Add salt, pepper and tomatoes. Make a smooth paste of flour and water. Add to the sauce. Cook 5 minutes longer, stirring constantly. Add shrimp. Heat to boiling. Serve on rice. Serves 12.

Submitted by Mrs. O. S. Allen, Rockland, Maine

Shrimp and Scallops Gruyere

¾ cup plus 2 tablespoons butter
¾ cup flour
3 cups milk
12 ounces Swiss Gruyere cheese
¼ teaspoon garlic powder
3 teaspoons plus ½ teaspoon salt
¼ teaspoon pepper

¼ teaspoon Accent
¼ teaspoon dry mustard
2 teaspoons plus 1 teaspoon lemon juice
1 pound raw scallops
½ pound mushrooms, sliced
1 pound cooked, cleaned shrimp
2 tablespoons diced green pepper

Make a white sauce with the ¾ cup butter, ¾ cup flour and the 3 cups of milk, in top of double boiler. Cut the cheese in pieces and add to sauce, stirring until melted. Mix together garlic powder, 3 teaspoons salt, pepper, Accent, dry mustard and 2 teaspoons lemon juice. Add to the white sauce.

Poach the scallops for about ten minutes in water to cover and to which has been added the 1 teaspoon lemon juice and ½ teaspoon salt. Add ½ cup of this broth (scallops have been cooked in) to the white sauce.

Saute the mushrooms in the 2 tablespoons of butter and add to the white sauce. Drain the scallops and add with the shrimp to the sauce. Heat for 15 minutes. Garnish the top with the green pepper which has been sauted in a little butter.

Serve with rice or in baked frozen patty shells. Wilted cucumbers make a fresh tasting accompaniment.

Submitted by Mrs. Kermit K. Bailey, Caribou, Maine

Shrimp Noodle Casserole

1 can frozen shrimp soup
1 (6 oz.) can evaporated milk
½ cup shredded cheddar cheese
1/3 cup mayonnaise
¼ teaspoon salt

¼ cup dry sherry or cooking wine
1 can shrimp, drained
4 ounces medium noodles, cooked and drained
½ cup crushed potato chips

Combine soup and evaporated milk. Heat to the boiling point. Remove from heat. Add cheese, mayonnaise and salt. Blend in the wine. Add shrimp and cooked noodles. Put in a casserole and bake uncovered for 25 minutes, at 350 degrees. Put crushed potato chips on top and cook for 10 minutes longer.

Submitted by Mrs. Percy Van Note, Saint George, Maine

Baked Cheese-Shrimp Custard

7 slices of bread
3 tablespoons of softened
  butter or margarine
½ pound American cheese
2 cans shrimp or 1 pound
  fresh shrimp
3 eggs, well beaten

½ teaspoon salt
½ teaspoon paprika
2½ cups of bottled milk
  or
1¼ cups evaporated milk and
  1¼ cups water

Remove crusts from bread; spread bread with butter and cut into 1 inch squares. Cut cheese into thin slices. De-vein the shrimp. Alternate layers of bread, shrimp and cheese in a greased 2 quart casserole. Combine the beaten eggs, salt, paprika and milk. Pour over the mixture in the casserole. Bake in a 350 degree oven for 1 hour or until silver knife inserted in center comes out clean. Serves 4 to 5.

Submitted by Mrs. Ada B. Bates, Orono, Maine

Scallop and Shrimp Casserole

1 pint scallops, sliced in halves
1 cup of large raw shrimp
3 cups soft bread crumbs
½ cup butter, melted

1 teaspoon salt
¼ teaspoon pepper
1 tablespoon celery seeds
1 cup cream

Arrange in a greased 11 x 7 baking dish, the scallops and shrimp, mixed. Pour over the mixture ½ cup of cream. Combine and sprinkle over scallop-shrimp mixture, the bread crumbs, butter, salt, pepper and celery seeds. Pour over this, the rest of the cream (it should come ¾ of way up on scallop-shrimp mixture). Bake at 375 degrees for 30 to 40 minutes. Sprinkle with paprika.

Submitted by T. Niedermann, NE-9, Cushing, Maine

James Pease's Method of Cooking Shrimp

1 pound shrimp
1 biscuit tin

Remove the heads from about 1 pound of shrimp and place on a biscuit tin. Preheat the oven to 450 degrees. Place the shrimp in the hot oven and cook for 4 minutes. Remove from the shell.

Frozen shrimp may be used, just let thaw and cook the same way. Dump the frozen shrimp out on the biscuit tin to thaw.

Fresh shrimp can be cooked this way without the shell, but shrimp are much firmer and brighter colored especially if cooked in the shell.

Submitted by James Pease, St. George, Maine

Sweet and Sour Shrimp

1 pound fresh shrimp (raw)
1 cup rice, uncooked
3 tablespoons cooking oil
1 small can sliced pineapple
½ green pepper, sliced
1 onion, sliced
½ cup diced celery
1 tomato, cut in junks

1 cup pineapple juice and
  vinegar
1 cup water
1 cup sugar
½ teaspoon salt
2 tablespoons cornstarch
1 tablespoon soy sauce
3 tablespoons cooking oil

BATTER

1 egg
1 tablespoon water

4 tablespoons flour
1 teaspoon baking powder

I use my stainless steel double boiler to make this recipe. Cook the rice in the bottom of the double boiler. Put 3 tablespoons of oil in the top of double boiler over low heat. Drain the can of pineapple slices, save the juice in a cup and fill with vinegar to use later. Dredge the pineapple slices in flour and brown lightly in the oil in top of double boiler. Cut the pineapple slices in inch size pieces and add the green pepper, onion, celery and tomato. Add the cup of pineapple juice and vinegar to the vegetables. Add the 1 cup of water also and turn up the heat a little higher.

Mix together the sugar, salt, cornstarch, and soy sauce in a bowl with enough water to make a paste. Add this paste to the vegetables, stirring constantly. When thick, remove from heat and set top of double boiler over the rice in the bottom of double boiler. Keep warm.

Put 3 tablespoons of oil in frying pan to fry shrimps. Mix the ingredients for the batter in a bowl. Stir and beat with a fork. Dip shrimps into the batter a few at a time, and fry a few at a time. Add the fried shrimp to the vegetable mixture in top of double boiler. Stir and mix well. Serve on the rice.

Rice can be placed in a casserole dish and vegetable mixture poured over it, for serving. Soy sauce goes well with this dish.

Submitted by Mrs. Athleen Pease, St. George, Maine

Shrimp Espanol

1 tablespoon of green bell
peppers (fresh or dried)
1 teaspoon onion powder
2 tablespoons of water
3 tablespoons cooking oil
2 cups cooked or canned
tomatoes
1 can (8 oz.) tomato sauce
¼ teaspoon celery seed

⅛ teaspoon cracked bay leaf
⅛ teaspoon garlic powder
1 tablespoon chopped parsley
¼ teaspoon oregano
2 teaspoons of Mei Yen
seasoning (optional)
2 pounds of cleaned, cooked
shrimp

Crush the peppers. Mix with onion powder in the 2 tablespoons of water to rehydrate. Saute for 3 or 4 minutes in the oil. Add tomatoes and tomato sauce, celery seed, bay leaf and garlic powder. Crush oregano and stir into sauce with parsley and Mei Yen. Simmer over very low heat for about two hours. Just before serving add the shrimp. Heat thoroughly. Can be served over rice.

Submitted by Margaret Graves Salameda, Los Altos, California

Scalloped Scallops

1 pint of scallops
½ cup butter
1 cup cracker crumbs

½ cup soft bread crumbs
2/3 cup cream or top milk
Salt and pepper to taste

Wash and pick over scallops. Melt butter and add the crumbs. Mix well. Put a layer of crumbs in buttered baking dish, add half of the scallops, half of the cream, salt and pepper. Repeat, and cover with buttered crumbs. Bake in a 350 degree oven until crumbs are brown, about 25 minutes. Serves 4 to 6.

Submitted by Mrs. Louise Griffee, Millinocket, Maine

Baked Scallops

1 pound of scallops
2 eggs, beaten

Flour
Milk

Dip the scallops in the beaten egg, roll in flour and re-dip in egg. Bake in a foil-lined pan in a small amount of milk, in a 400 degree oven for 15 minutes. Serves 3.

Submitted by Mrs. Irving L. Dunton, Jr., Salisbury Cove, Maine

Along about the fifteenth and sixteenth centuries, the countries of northern Europe and Portugal had fishing fleets off our coast. They set up factory settlements on the offshore islands for salting the fish they caught and at the end of the season would depart for home with a fine cargo in the holds of their ships. Most of these fish were probably slack-salted and some of it may have been dried. The reports that these early fisherman brought home must have had a lot to do with arousing the interest of these countries in settling and exploiting these shores. Early explorers waxed eloquent on the beauty and plenty that existed along the coast.

ANNA CROCKETT

Scalloped Scallops

1 pint scallops
1 cup mushrooms (chopped)
1 onion (chopped)
4 tablespoons butter
4 tablespoons flour
1 cup cream
½ cup scallop liquid

Parboil scallops, drain (save ½ cup of the liquid) and cut scallops in slices. Melt the 4 tablespoons of butter. Add the onion and mushrooms and cook for 5 minutes. Add the liquids, cream and scallop liquid. Add the flour (in paste). Cook until thick. Place scallops and creamed mixture in a buttered baking dish. Cover with butter and crumbs. Bake at 350 degrees until crumbs are brown, about 30 minutes.

Submitted by Mrs. Otis A. Ward, Bar Harbor, Maine

Mussel Stew

4 doz. mussels, steamed
1 cup broth
1 qt. milk
Salt to taste
Pepper to taste
1 tbsp. butter
1 tbsp. chopped parsley

Steam the mussels, shell out. Add the mussels to the cup of broth which has been thoroughly strained. Add the milk, salt and pepper, and butter. Bring to the boiling point. Sprinkle with parsley and serve immediately.

Submitted by Mrs. Wallace Lindquist, Camden, Maine

Oyster Soup

1 quart oysters
1 quart cold water
1 quart milk
2 tablespoons butter
2 tablespoons flour
1 teaspoon salt
¼ teaspoon pepper

Place the oysters in strainer and drain away the liquid. Pick over to remove shells. Pour the cold water over them. Bring the milk to scalding point, thicken with the flour and butter blended. Add the oysters and water, salt and pepper. Bring to a boil and serve at once. Do not allow soup to boil, or the oysters will become hard.

Submitted by Mrs. Ella Gray, Hampden Highlands, Maine

Oyster Soup

2 quarts oysters
1 quart milk
2 tablespoons butter

1 cup hot water
Salt and pepper to taste

Strain all of the liquid from the oysters. Add the hot water to liquid from the oysters and heat. When nearly to boil, add the seasonings, then the oysters. Cook about 5 minutes (do not boil) until they "ruffle." Stir in the butter, cook one minute and pour into the tureen or serving dish. Heat the milk to boiling and stir into the oysters. Serve at once.

Submitted by Mrs. Ada M. Spencer, Bradley, Maine

Scalloped Oysters

1 pint oysters, very little liquid
1 can mushroom soup (undi-luted)

1½ cups oyster crackers or your favorite cracker
¼ lb. butter (can use half margarine)

Heat mushroom soup, melt butter. Line casserole dish with crumbs, then layer of oysters, add pepper (no salt as soup is salty) then layer of soup, then repeat. Add a layer of crumbs over top. Bake at 425 degrees for 35 minutes. Never have more than two layers.

Submitted by Hester Pullen, North Anson, Maine

Oyster Toast

1 quart oysters
Salt and pepper

1 tablespoon butter (heaping)
Buttered toast

Place oysters in a saucepan in their own liquid. Bring to boiling and cook three or four minutes. Add seasonings to taste and the butter. Serve on buttered toast.

Submitted by Mrs. Ann Watkins, Casco, Maine

Casino Oysters

1 pint oysters
½ cup minced green pepper
½ cup cooked bacon, minced

1 tablespoon lemon juice
Pepper

Drain the oysters, arrange on a greased oven-proof platter. Sprinkle with the green pepper, bacon and lemon juice. Bake in a hot 450 degree oven for 10 to 15 minutes. Serve hot.

Submitted by Mrs. Elizabeth Shyne, Rockland, Maine

Clam Souffle

2 cups milk
2 cups cracker crumbs
2 cans minced clams (juice included)
¼ cup minced onion
Salt and pepper to taste
4 eggs beaten

Pour milk over the crackers and let set for ½ hour. Add the remaining ingredients, folding in the eggs last. Pour into a greased baking dish and bake in a 350 degree oven for 45 minutes or until knife comes out clean. This recipe is easy to cut in half for the smaller family. Very good.

Submitted by Mrs. Evelyn Lucas, Morrill, Maine

Clam Chowder With Dumplings

1 pint shucked clams (raw)
6 potatoes, sliced
1 medium onion, chopped
Salt and pepper to taste
2 tablespoons pork fat
½ can evaporated milk
2 cups flour
2 teaspoons baking powder
½ teaspoon salt
½ teaspoon sugar
Water enough to mix dough thoroughly

Cook clams, potatoes, onion and seasonings with water to cover in a kettle until partly done. Mix flour, baking powder, salt, sugar and water to make the dumpling dough, then spoon dough by spoonfuls into the clam chowder. Cover and cook 10 minutes. Add the milk and pork fat and some butter if you wish. Set on low heat until ready to serve. Makes about 6 servings.

Submitted by Mrs. Iola E. Beal, Stonington, Maine

Fried Clam Cakes

1 pint clams
or
2 cans minced clams
1 egg
¼ cup milk
1 teaspoon salt
¼ cup clam liquid
1 heaping cup flour
1 rounded teaspoon baking powder

Remove black sections from fresh clams and put through the food chopper. Mix beaten egg, milk, salt, clam liquid and flour to which baking powder has been added. Add to the clams and beat well. Drop in deep fat or fry flat as pancakes, about 5 minutes. Makes 12 puffs or cakes. Serve hot.

Submitted by Etta B. Beverage, North Haven, Maine

Clam Dip

½ cup minced clams (save juice)
1 clove garlic or garlic powder
2 packages cream cheese, 3 ounce size
1 tablespoon Worcestershire sauce
1 tablespoon clam juice
1 tablespoon lemon juice
½ teaspoon salt

Blend with electric mixer. Chill. Serve with saltines or potato chips.

Submitted by Sharon Melia, Sangerville, Maine

Clam Puffs

6 slices bread, cubed
1½ cups grated American cheese
2 cups cooked clams (if large, cut up)
2 eggs, slightly beaten
1 cup milk
Dash Worcestershire sauce
1 tablespoon onion juice
or
1 teaspoon onion powder
2 drops Tobasco sauce
1 teaspoon minced parsley
Salt and pepper to taste

In a 2 quart greased casserole, place half of the bread cubes, a layer of grated cheese, all of the clams, the rest of the cheese, and the bread cubes. Add salt and pepper.

Mix the eggs, milk, Worcestershire sauce, onion, Tobasco and parsley flakes. Pour over the clam mixture in baking dish. Bake at 325 degrees for one hour. Will make 3 to 4 generous servings.

Submitted by Mrs. Ernest E. Haskell, Freeport, Maine

Clam Corn Casserole

1 can clams (7 ounce)
3 eggs, beaten
1 cup cream style corn
½ cup cracker crumbs
1 tablespoon melted butter
1 tablespoon minced onion
2 tablespoons chopped pimiento
½ teaspoon salt
Dash cayenne
Milk

Drain liquid from clams in a cup and fill cup with milk. Combine with beaten eggs. Add remaining ingredients and pour into a greased casserole. Bake in a moderate oven, 375 degrees, until firm, about 45 minutes. Serves 6.

Submitted by Mrs. Thomas G. Powell, Mechanic Falls, Maine

Clam Cakes

2 cups clams, chop, drain,
   save juice
½ cup rolled cracker crumbs
2 tablespoons flour
1 teaspoon baking powder

1 teaspoon salt
⅛ taspoon pepper
1 teaspoon sugar
2 eggs, well beaten
½ cup clam juice

Mix eggs and juice. Sift dry ingredients over crumbs, add clams and mix well. Let set a few minutes. Add a little more juice if needed. Drop by large spoonfuls into a fry pan of hot fat, does not need to be deep fat. Cook until golden brown on both sides.

Submitted by Mrs. Shirley B. Hobbs, Alfred, Maine

Minced Clam Drops

½ package soda crackers (about
   2 ounces)
1 can minced clams
1 egg

2 tablespoons milk
½ teaspoon milk
½ teaspoon baking powder
Salt and pepper to taste

Crumb crackers finely. Add clams. Beat egg and milk together and add to the clams and crumbs. Add baking powder, salt and pepper. Drop by spoonfuls into hot frying pan which has ½ cup of oil or shortening melted in it. Turn and cook until nicely browned.

Submitted by Mrs. Richard Audet, Poland Spring, Maine

Codfish Balls

1 cup mashed potatoes
½ cup shredded codfish
1 egg, beaten

⅛ teaspoon pepper
Egg and crumbs

Pick apart the codfish (this is the old-fashioned salt cod) and freshen in cold water for a few minutes. Drain well. If the fish is very salty and dry, it may be parboiled. Mix hot unseasoned potatoes with codfish, add beaten egg and pepper. Beat well, shape and roll in fine crumbs, dip in egg and more crumbs and fry in hot shortening.

Tiny individual codfish balls may be fried and served on toothpicks for before-dinner appetizers.

Submitted by Mrs. Clarence W. Spiller, Bridgton, Maine

Crabmeat Cobbler

½ cup shortening
½ cup chopped green pepper
½ cup chopped onion
½ cup flour
1 teaspoon dry mustard
½ teaspoon Accent
1 cup milk

1 cup shredded cheddar cheese
1 can crabmeat
1½ cups drained tomatoes
  (canned)
2 teaspoons Worcestershire
  sauce
½ teaspoon salt

BISCUIT TOPPING

1 cup flour
2 teaspoons baking powder
½ teaspoon salt

¼ cup shredded cheese
2 tablespoons shortening
½ cup milk

Melt the ½ cup shortening, add the green pepper and onion. Cook until tender, about 10 minutes. Blend in the ½ cup flour, mustard, Accent, milk and cheese. Cook stirring constantly until cheese melts and mixture is very thick. Add crabmeat, tomatoes, sauce and salt. Blend well and pour into a 2 quart casserole. Cover with biscuit topping. Sift together the 1 cup of flour, baking powder, and salt. Add cheese, cut in the shortening until mixture resembles coarse meal. Add milk and mix only until flour is dampened. Drop by rounded teaspoons on top of crabmeat mixture in casserole. Bake in a 450 degree oven 15 to 20 minutes.

Submitted by Mrs. Winfield L. Chatto, Rockland, Maine

Crabmeat Rolls

1 cup sharp cheese
1 cup or 1 can crabmeat
3 hard-cooked eggs
2 teaspoons chopped onion
2 teaspoons chopped sweet
  pickle

2 teaspoons chopped green
  pepper
2 teaspoons chopped stuffed
  olives
½ cup mayonnaise
12 hot dog rolls

Mix ingredients, fill rolls and wrap in foil. Can be stored in refrigerator. Bake in 350 degree oven 25 to 30 minutes.

Submitted by Mrs. Virgil Dorr, Otter Creek, Maine

Baked Flounder

1 3-pound flounder
1 large onion
1 tablespoon butter
Bay leaf
Thyme
Salt
Pepper
1 cup milk

½ tablespoon flour
1½ tablespoons butter
½ cup strained tomato juice
¼ teaspoon salt
1 teaspoon lemon juice
1 egg yolk
1 teaspoon prepared mustard

Wash the fish and place on a platter on rack to drain. In a baking pan place the finely chopped onion, the tablespoon of butter cut in small pieces, the bay leaf and sprig of thyme. Rub the fish with salt and black pepper and place it in the baking pan. Pour over it a half cup of hot water. Cover the pan and bake. When the water begins to boil, turn the fish very carefully so as not to break it and let the other side cook. When done, remove the fish carefully to the dish in which you plan to serve it. Cover with a sauce made as follows: In a double boiler, melt the 1½ tablespoons of butter. Blend in the flour and seasonings. Add the milk and tomato juice. Cook until thick, then pour on the beaten egg yolk (while the sauce is still hot). Add the lemon juice and pour over the fish. Serve all very hot. (Lukewarm fish is dreadful.)

Submitted by Mrs. Leola Peaslee, North Edgecomb, Maine

Salmon-Rice Casserole

¼ cup butter or margarine
½ cup chopped celery
2 tablespoons chopped onion
2 tablespoons flour
1 teaspoon salt
⅛ teaspoon pepper
2 cups milk
2 cups cooked rice

1 (1-pound can) salmon
(drained, boned, flaked)
½ cup processed American
cheese, coarsely shredded
1/3 ounce can mushrooms,
drained
¼ cup chopped parsley
(optional)

Melt butter over low heat. Add celery and onion and cook slowly until tender. Blend in flour and seasonings. Add milk, stirring constantly; cook until sauce is smooth and thickened. Blend sauce with remaining ingredients. Pour into buttered two-quart casserole. Bake in slow oven 300 degrees until heated through, 25 to 30 minutes. Makes 6 servings.

Very good served with a green vegetable, fruit salad and buttered rolls.

Submitted by Ruby E. Johnson, Lubec, Maine

Salmon Curry

1 pound can salmon
¼ cup chopped onion
3 tablespoons butter
3 tablespoons flour
1½ teaspoons curry powder
½ teaspoon salt

¼ teaspoon ginger
Dash pepper
2 cups salmon liquid and
  milk
3 cups cooked rice

Drain salmon, reserving liquid. Break salmon into large pieces. Cook onion in butter until tender. Blend in flour and seasonings. Add salmon liquid gradually and cook until thick, stirring constantly. Add salmon, heat. Serve over rice. Tuna fish (packed in water) may be substituted for salmon.

Submitted by Mrs. Betty Pelletier, Old Town, Maine

Stuffed Salmon Slices

½ inch slices of salmon
  needed for meal

Slices of salt fat pork
Flour, salt and pepper

STUFFING

1 cup bread crumbs
¼ cup melted fat
¼ tsp. salt
⅛ tsp. celery salt

⅛ tsp. pepper
1 tsp. lemon juice
¼ cup water

Mix stuffing ingredients in order given. If a dry filling is desired, omit water.

Arrange half the number of slices in a baking pan on thin slices or strips of salt fat pork. Cover with the stuffing mix, cover with remaining slices of salmon. Sprinkle with flour, salt and pepper. Surround with leftover boiled potatoes, cut into fourths lengthwise. Arrange strips of salt fat pork on top and bake in a moderately hot oven about 30 minutes or until done. Garnish with lemon and parsley.

Submitted by Mrs. Mae Hatch, Howland, Maine

Mixed Shellfish au Gratin

½ cup butter
½ cup flour
1 quart milk, scalded
½ teaspoon salt
½ teaspoon dry mustard
½ cup sherry
1 teaspoon monosodium glutamate

2 teaspoons Worcestershire Sauce
½ pound diced lobster
½ pound crabmeat
½ pound shrimp
½ pound scallops (diced)
½ cup grated cheese
Cracker meal
Paprika

Combine flour and butter. Brown over low heat, stirring constantly. Add the quart of scalded milk and let come to a complete boil. Stir until smooth. Add the seasonings and the wine. Arrange the shellfish in a casserole or individual shells and cover with the sauce. Sprinkle with grated cheese, cracker meal and paprika. Brown lightly in 400 degree oven for 15 minutes. Serves 8. This is one of my favorite seafoods dishes. I have used it for luncheons many times.

Submitted by Mrs. Albert Levenseler, Rockland, Maine

Gravy Fish

2 pounds haddock, ready to cook
1 teaspoon salt
1 tablespoon vinegar or lemon juice
2 tablespoons butter
1 tablespoon finely chopped onion

2 tablespoons flour
⅛ teaspoon paprika
½ teaspoon salt (more to suit taste)
2 cups whole milk
1 egg, beaten
¾ cup mild cheese, grated fine

Place haddock in a cheesecloth bag. Place in a kettle and just cover with hot water. Add 1 teaspoon of salt and the vinegar (or lemon juice). Simmer fish very gently about 25 minutes. Remove fish to serving dish and carefully flake, removing bones and skin. To prepare the sauce, melt butter in saucepan, add onion, cook over low heat until tender. Stir in flour, paprika, salt, and slowly add the milk.

Stirring constantly, bring to a boil over medium heat. When it boils, remove from heat, add the beaten egg. Return to heat for 2 minutes. Remove and add the grated cheese. Stir to dissolve cheese and gently fold in the fish.

Submitted by Mrs. Mary Sprowl, Liberty, Maine

Seafood Thermidor

1 can sliced mushrooms
  (4 ounces)
1 tablespoon butter or margarine
1 cup diced cooked lobster
1 can frozen, condensed, cream
  of shrimp soup (10 ounces)

¼ cup milk
½ teaspoon dry mustard
Dash cayenne pepper
Grated Parmesan cheese
Paprika

Brown the mushrooms in butter, add the lobster, cook a few minutes. Stir in the soup, milk, mustard, and cayenne. Heat slowly. Stir often until soup is thawed. Spoon the lobster mixture into 3 individual baking dishes. Sprinkle the top with Parmesan cheese and paprika. Bake in a 400 degree oven until nicely browned, about 15 minutes.

Submitted by Mrs. Sara C. Wilson, Rockland, Maine

Fish Salad

4 cups cooked haddock, flaked
1 cup chopped celery
¼ cup chopped green pepper
¾ cup chopped sour pickle
  (pressed dry)
1/3 cup salad oil
¼ cup lemon juice

¼ cup chili sauce
2 tbsp. grated onion
½ tsp. white pepper
1 tbsp. Worcestershire Sauce
2 tsp. paprika
1 tbsp. parsley

Toss together the haddock, celery, green pepper and sour pickle. Combine the remaining ingredients for the dressing. Add to the salad. Chill thoroughly. When serving, garnish with egg slices and olives.

Submitted by Mrs. Eleanor Clark, Thomaston, Maine

Baked Haddock

2 pounds haddock fillets
Butter
1 grated onion or onion
  powder

1 egg, beaten
½ cup cracker crumbs
1 can frozen shrimp soup

Place fillets in a greased baking dish, dot with butter. Mix the remaining ingredients and add to the fish. Bake at 400 degrees for about one hour. This is delicious.

Submitted by Mrs. Raymond Rice, Stonington, Maine

Fish Shanty Fish Loaf

2 cups cooked, flaked fish
  (preferably haddock)
1½ cups soft bread crumbs
½ tsp. baking powder
2/3 cup finely chopped celery
1/3 cup finely minced onion

1 tbsp. minced pimiento
1 tbsp. finely chopped green
  pepper
1 cup milk
1 tbsp. lemon juice
Salt and pepper

Mix all ingredients lightly. Pour into a buttered bread tin. Bake at 350 degrees for 1 hour. Serve with desired sauce, such as a butter sauce with capers added. Frozen shrimp soup heated, undiluted, makes an excellent sauce; or your own favorite cream sauce for a fish loaf. Serves 6.

Submitted by Miss Dorothy Chandler, North Anson, Maine

Baked Fish, Cheese Dressing

Haddock fillets (number required
  for the meal)
1 small onion
4 tbsp. butter

½ cup soft bread crumbs
½ cup grated cheese
¾ cup milk
Salt and pepper

Arrange the pieces of fish in a buttered baking dish. Slice the onion and saute in the butter (do not burn) until tender. Add the bread crumbs, grated cheese and seasoning. Toss lightly with a fork until well browned. Spread over the fish. Pour the milk around the fish and bake for 30 minutes in a 350 degree oven.

Submitted by Cora M. Dorney, Belfast, Maine

Fish Turbot

3 to 4 pounds of haddock
4 tablespoons butter
4 tablespoons flour
1 teaspoon salt

2 cups milk
1 tablespoon grated onion
1 tablespoon pimiento
Bread crumbs

Boil haddock in salted water until it flakes. Make a thick white sauce with the butter, flour, salt and milk. Add the grated onion and pimiento, cut in small pieces. In a buttered casserole put flaked fish and white sauce in alternate layers, having sauce on top. Cover with bread crumbs. Bake at 350 degrees 45 minutes. Serve hot.

Submitted by Mrs. Lillian Reed, Northeast Harbor, Maine

Maine Chowder

1 medium onion, chopped
¼ pound salt pork, sliced thin
4 cups sliced potatoes
1 tsp. salt
¼ tsp. black pepper

2 cups water
1 pound haddock
1 can whole kernel corn
1 can evaporated milk

Fry salt pork until lightly browned, add onion and saute until clear. Add potatoes, salt, pepper and water. Simmer for 15 minutes. Add haddock and simmer 15 minutes longer or until fish and potatoes are tender. Stir in the can of corn (do not drain) and the can of milk. Heat to boiling. DO NOT BOIL. Serves 6.

Submitted by Mrs. Natalie Smith, Biddeford, Maine

Seafood Medley in Pattie Shells

3 tablespoons butter or
    margarine
1 small onion, chopped
3 tablespoons flour
1 teaspoon salt
Dash pepper

1½ cups milk
2 cans frozen shrimp soup
    (10½ ounce each)
6 cups cooked fish and seafood,
    such as flounder, cod, shrimp,
    crabmeat and lobster

Melt butter in a saucepan. Add onion and brown slightly. Blend in the flour, salt and pepper. Gradually add the milk. Cook, stirring constantly, until sauce thickens. Add shrimp soup and the fish. Heat thoroughly. Add a little sherry if desired. Spoon into pattie shells. Garnish with parsley. Makes 6 to 8 generous servings.

Submitted by Mrs. John Pearse, Hope, Maine

Baked Fish Sticks

1½ pounds fresh fish sticks
2 onions, thinly sliced
3 tablespoons butter
2 tablespoons flour

½ teaspoon salt
Few grains pepper
Top milk or thin cream

Butter a baking dish and scatter the thinly sliced onions in the dish. Place the fish sticks on the onions. Sprinkle with the salt, pepper and flour. Dot with butter. Add top milk or cream to nearly cover the fish. Bake in a moderate oven, 350 degrees for 45 minutes, or until fish flakes and onions are tender.

Submitted by Mildred "Brownie" Schrumpf, Orono, Maine

Hulled corn, or hominy as it was called in the South, was a tasty staple food first learned of from the Indians. The technique of growing and harvesting Indian Maize, how to store it and use it were a great help to the early settlers. The corn was first dried and the kernels rubbed from the cob, then was slowly simmered over a wood fire. During the simmering, handfuls of the wood ash were stirred in from time to time to loosen and remove the hulls which were skimmed from the top of the kettle until all were removed. The resulting kernel had a white color and was nut-like in texture and flavor, could be stored for long periods, and was useful in a variety of ways. It might also be noted here that hulled corn was very high in food value as well as tasty.

Fish Chowder

1 quart fish	¼ cup butter
3 potatoes	Salt and pepper to taste
2 onions, sliced thin	Allspice and mace to taste
2 tablespoons of fresh pork,	3 large crackers
chopped fine	¼ gallon of milk

This recipe was taken from an 1880 cookbook and the only instructions for making the chowder are: Add enough water to cover and boil until tender. Add 3 large crackers and ¼ gallon of milk. Bring to a boil and serve hot.

Submitted by Mrs. Robina Gaddis, Calais, Maine

Fish Souffle

1 cup evaporated milk	½ pound raw haddock, ground
1 tablespoon butter or oleo	1 cup bread crumbs
Salt and pepper to taste	2 egg whites beaten until stiff
Medium-sized onion, sliced	

Saute the sliced onion in the butter until tender, add the evaporated milk and bring to the boiling point. Add the salt and pepper, bread crumbs, and haddock. Fold in the stiffly beaten egg whites, pour into an ungreased 1 quart baking dish. Bake in a pan of hot water at 350 degrees for 30 minutes, or until knife inserted in center comes out clean. This souffle does not collapse as regular ones do.

For the 1 cup (8 ounces) of evaporated milk, I use a small (6 ounce) can and fill cup with 2 ounces of water.

This souffle is good cold with a tossed salad.

Submitted by Mrs. Elsa Kigel, Warren, Maine

Easy Tuna Fish Casserole

1 can tuna, chopped fine	4 or 5 cups cooked macaroni
¾ cup canned peas	1½ cups milk
1 can cream of mushroom	1 small onion, chopped
soup	

Add to the finely chopped tuna, the mushroom soup and the milk. Mix well. Chop onion and add to the tuna mixture along with the drained peas. Drain the cooked macaroni and rinse with cold water. Stir the tuna mixture into the drained macaroni. Pour into a casserole or baking dish. Bake at 350 degrees for 45 minutes. Potato chips or cracker crumbs may be spread on top before baking.

Submitted by Mrs. Judy Spearin, Gardiner, Maine

Hot Tuna Buns

¼ pound American cheese (cubed)
3 chopped hard-cooked eggs
1 (7 oz.) can tuna, flaked
2 tablespoons minced onion
3 tablespoons chopped olives
2 tablespoons pickle relish
1 tablespoon minced green pepper
½ cup mayonnaise
6 hamburger buns

Split and butter the hamburger buns. Combine the other ingredients with the mayonnaise, and use to fill the buns. Wrap each filled bun separately in foil. These can be filled and refrigerated until ready to serve. When ready to serve, preheat the oven to 400 degrees and bake the wrapped buns for 15 minutes. Unwrap and serve hot.

Submitted by Mrs. Laurence Farrar, Millinocket, Maine

Tuna Fish Scallop

1½ cups uncooked macaroni
1 green pepper (chopped fine)
1 onion (chopped fine)
1 tablespoon flour
Dash of pepper
1 cup milk
1 teaspoon chili powder
2 tablespoons cream
1 can chicken soup
1 can tuna fish
1 slice of cheese

Cook the macaroni. Fry the onions and green pepper in a little butter. Stir the flour and pepper into the cup of milk. Dissolve the chili powder in the cream and add to the milk mixture. Place a layer of macaroni in a baking dish. Add the other ingredients in layers with the slice of cheese on top. Bake in a 350 degree oven until golden brown, about 30 minutes.

Submitted by Mrs. Lorene Hackett, Fort Kent, Maine

Fish Casserole

½ pound scallops (chopped)
¾ pound haddock (in small pieces)
1 can frozen shrimp soup
½ can evaporated milk
Buttered bread crumbs
Pepper and salt

Combine all ingredients except bread crumbs. Place in a baking dish. Top with buttered crumbs. Bake at 350 degrees for 40 minutes. Serves 6.

Submitted by Mrs. Rena Perkins, Guilford, Maine

Batter For Fish Sticks

2 eggs
1 teaspoon salt
½ teaspoon pepper
1 cup flour

¾ cup milk
1 heaping teaspoon baking powder
Squirt of lemon juice

Beat all ingredients together with mixer. Dip cut up fish in this batter and cook in deep hot fat, until golden brown from 3 to 6 minutes.

Submitted by Mrs. Francina Pelletier, Calais, Maine

Pancakes

1½ cups flour
3 teaspoons baking powder
½ teaspoon salt

1 cup milk
2 eggs
3 tablespoons melted butter

Sift flour with baking powder and salt. Beat eggs, add milk and melted butter. Combine the two mixtures. Cook on a well-greased griddle. Serve with syrup or honey.

Submitted by Mrs. Lee Pelletier, Limestone, Maine

White Flour Pancakes

2 cups white flour
2 teaspoons baking powder
1 teaspoon salt
2 tablespoons sugar

1 egg, beaten
1 small can evaporated milk
Cold water

Sift dry ingredients. Beat egg, add milk and mix with dry ingredients, stir well. Add enough cold water to make thin enough to fry.

Submitted by Mrs. Estella Farnham, Vanceboro, Maine

Mashed Potato Pancakes

1 cup fresh mashed potato
2 eggs
1¼ cups milk
2 tablespoons melted shortening

1 cup flour
2 teaspoons baking powder
½ teaspoon salt
2 tablespoons sugar

Beat egg yolks, add potato, milk and shortening. Sift baking powder, salt, and sugar with the flour. Combine the two mixtures and add the beaten egg whites last. Fry on a hot griddle.

Submitted by Mrs. R. Fred Harmon, Caribou, Maine

Molasses Johnny Cake

1 cup flour
2½ teaspoons baking powder
½ teaspoon salt
¼ teaspoon soda
½ cup corn meal
4 tablespoons sugar

1 egg yolk, beaten
4 tablespoons melted butter
¼ cup molasses
¾ cup sweet milk
1 egg white, beaten

Mix together all the dry ingredients. Add the melted butter, molasses and milk to the beaten egg yolk, and combine with the dry mixture. Fold in egg white last. Pour into an 8 x 8 pan and bake in a 425 degree oven for 15 to 20 minutes.

This is a recipe of my own making, as most of the recipes have too much corn meal. I use this when I have home baked beans. It goes over very good with my family.

Submitted by Mrs. Raymond Cota, Orono, Maine

Aunt Gertie's Johnny Cake

1 cup corn meal
1 cup flour
1½ teaspoons baking soda
2 tablespoons sugar

2 tablespoons molasses
¾ teaspoon salt
2 (scant) cups buttermilk
1 tablespoon melted shortening

Combine the dry ingredients. Mix together the milk, molasses and shortening. Add to the dry mixture. Pour into a greased 9 x 9 pan and bake at 400 degrees for 20 to 25 minutes.

Submitted by Mrs. Bea Grant, Rockland, Maine

Spider Cake

2 eggs
2 tablespoons sugar
1 cup corn meal
1 cup oatmeal

1 teaspoon soda
1 teaspoon salt
2 cups sour milk

Beat sugar and eggs thoroughly, add dry ingredients alternately with sour milk. Melt 2 tablespoons shortening in spider and pour into above mixture. Pour mixture into spider and cook for 5 minutes on top of the stove then in hot oven for 15 or 20 minutes.

Submitted by Mrs. Sylvia Poor Ellis, Wellesley, Mass.

Old-Fashioned Brown Bread
(100 Years Old)

4 slices stale bread or any
   bread
¾ cup sour milk
1/3 cup sugar
¼ cup molasses
½ cup cornmeal

3 tablespoons flour
1 teaspoon baking powder
1 teaspoon soda
½ teaspoon salt
Raisins (optional)

Soak bread in combined milk, sugar, molasses and cornmeal. Sift the flour, baking powder, soda and salt together. Combine the two mixtures and put in greased mold or coffee can (1 pound). Steam 3 hours. Add raisins to above mixture if desired.

Submitted by Melvina W. Johnson, Gorham, Maine

Brown Bread

1½ cups sifted meal
1½ cups rye flour
1½ cups white flour
1½ teaspoons salt
1 teaspoon ginger

1 cup molasses
2 cups sour milk
1 cup sweet milk
1 teaspoon soda, rounded
1 tablespoon hot water

Sift together the first five ingredients, add the molasses and stir well. Add the two milks and stir all together. Dissolve the soda in the hot water and add last. Place this mixture in a double boiler and boil four hours.

Submitted by Mrs. Gwendolyn G. Holt, Hanover, Maine

Evaporated Milk Brown Bread

1 cup molasses
1 teaspoon soda
1 cup graham flour
1½ cups cornmeal
1½ cups rolled oats

3 teaspoons baking powder,
   heaping
1 teaspoon salt
2½ cups evaporated milk
2½ cups water

Mix soda and molasses together. Mix flour, meal, oats, baking powder and salt together. Add the molasses mixture. Mix the milk and water together and add to the molasses flour mixture. Steam 3 hours and bake 1 hour.

Submitted by Clif Lufkin, Glen Cove, Maine

Angel Biscuits

5 cups unsifted all purpose
    flour
¼ cup sugar
2 teaspoons baking powder
1 teaspoon soda
1 teaspoon salt
1 cup vegetable shortening
1 envelope dry yeast or 1 cake
2 tablespoons warm water
2 cups sour milk or buttermilk

Measure flour into cup by spoonfuls. Sift together the flour with sugar, baking powder, soda and salt. Using pastry blender, blend in vegetable shortening. Dissolve yeast cake or dry yeast in warm water and let stand 5 minutes. Add this to sour or buttermilk and combine with dry ingredients. Turn onto floured board, roll to desired thickness. Cut into biscuits and dip into melted margarine. Fold over as Parker House Rolls or place flat in greased pan. Bake at 450 degrees 12 minutes. 3 dozen regular size rolls. These can be frozen unbaked.

Submitted by Mrs. Ruth Lloyd, Lincoln, Maine

Mile High Biscuits

3 cups sifted flour
4½ teaspoons baking powder
¾ teaspoon cream tartar
2½ tablespoons sugar
1 teaspoon salt
¾ cup shortening
1 egg
1 cup milk

Sift the dry ingredients. Cut in the shortening until mixture resembles corn meal. Beat egg and add milk. Mix in the dry ingredients with a fork, until dough holds together. Turn on a floured board, knead lightly and roll 1 inch thick. Cut with biscuit cutter, put on a baking sheet. Preheat oven to 450 degrees and bake biscuits 10 to 12 minutes.

Submitted by Mrs. Lucy Jackson, Rockland, Maine

Easy Biscuits

2 cups flour
2 teaspoons cream tartar
1 teaspoon soda
5 tablespoons shortening
½ teaspoon salt
2/3 cup milk

Sift together dry ingredients, and cut in the shortening. Stir in the milk. Roll out on a floured cloth or board to ½ inch thick. Will make 8 or 10 biscuits. Bake in an 8 x 8 pan for 15 minutes in a 425 degree oven.

Submitted by Mrs. Wilfred Trafton, 12 Howard Street,
Presque Isle, Maine

Nice and Light Biscuits

2 cups flour
4 teaspoons baking powder
½ teaspoon salt

White of 1 egg, beaten slightly
1 teaspoon cream tartar
1 cup milk

Sift flour, baking powder and salt, twice. Beat white of egg just enough to mix in the cream tartar and add the cup of milk. Add to the flour. Roll out on a floured board to ¾ inch thickness. Bake at 450 degrees for 15 minutes.

Submitted by Mrs. Ferne Sanborn, Bangor, Maine

Buttermilk Biscuits

2 cups flour
1 teaspoon soda
1 teaspoon baking powder
1 teaspoon cream tartar

Butter, size of a walnut
(about 2 tablespoons)
1 cup buttermilk

Sift together the dry ingredients and work in the butter. Combine with the buttermilk. Roll out on a floured board to ½ inch thickness and cut size desired. Bake on a baking sheet for 15 minutes (or until done) at 450 degrees.

Submitted by Mrs. Pauline Timberlake, Turner, Maine

Corn Fritters

1 egg
½ cup milk
2 cups canned corn
1½ cups flour

2 teaspoons baking powder
½ teaspoon salt
Dash pepper
1 teaspoon melted shortening

Beat the egg, add milk, shortening and canned corn. Add the dry ingredients sifted. Beat well. Drop by spoonfuls into hot fat. Cook until golden brown. Takes about 3 minutes to fry with frying temperature at 380 degrees. Makes about 16 fritters. Serve hot with maple syrup.

Submitted by Mrs. Mildred Adams, Clinton, Maine

Pop-Overs

1 cup flour
1 cup milk

½ teaspoon salt
3 eggs

Beat the eggs, add salt, milk and flour. Beat with a rotary beater until smooth. Pour into well greased deep muffin tin, or oven ware-cups. Bake in a hot oven 425 degrees for 45 to 50 minutes, or until golden brown.

Submitted by Marion Eagerly, Sangerville, Maine

Corn Meal Slappers or Griddle Cakes
(no soda)

1 pint corn meal
1 teaspoon butter
1 teaspoon salt
1 teaspoon sugar

2 eggs
Boiling water (or milk)
Cold milk

Mix meal, butter, salt and sugar. Pour into this mixture enough boiling water or milk to wet the meal. When cool, add the eggs well beaten, and enough cold milk to make a thin batter.

To cook griddle cakes, heat the griddle while you make the cakes. If an iron griddle be used, put a piece of salt pork, two inches square on a fork, and when griddle is hot enough for the fat to sizzle, rub it all over with the pork. Just grease it, do not leave little pools of fat on the edge to burn, and smoke the cakes. Take up a tablespoon of the mixture and pour it from the end of the spoon. The mixture should hiss or sizzle as it touches the griddle. Put one in the center and six around the outside. By the time you have put the 7th cake on, the first one will be full of bubbles and ready to turn. When the 7th is turned, the first one will have stopped puffing and be done. Wipe the griddle with a dry cloth and grease again after each cooking. Turn your griddle often, bringing each edge of it in turn over the hottest part of the stove, that the cakes may cook evenly.

This recipe was taken from an 1883 cookbook.
Submitted by Mrs. Dorothy Thompson, Robbinston, Maine

Cinnamon Rolls

2 cups prepared biscuit mix
2/3 cup milk
Soft butter to spread

¼ cup sugar
1 teaspoon cinnamon

Heat oven to 425 degrees. Grease 12 muffin cups. Stir together with a fork the biscuit mix and the milk. Beat dough vigorously 20 strokes until stiff and slightly sticky. Dust bread board or cloth lightly with flour. Roll dough around and knead gently 8 to 10 times. With lightly floured rolling pin roll dough into a rectangle about 12 x 7 inches. Spread with soft butter and sprinkle with the cinnamon sugar mixture. Beginning at the long side, tightly roll up the dough. Seal by pinching the edges. Cut into 12 slices. Place in greased muffin pan and bake 15 minutes or until brown, in a 425 degree oven.

Submitted by Rose Marie Salameda, Los Altos, Calif., 12 years old

Kernel Corn Bread
(Real nice and soft)

1 cup all-purpose flour
1 cup yellow cornmeal
4 teaspoons baking powder
1 teaspoon salt
¼ cup sugar

2 eggs, well beaten
1 cup milk
3 tablespoons melted margarine
1 cup cream style corn

Sift flour with cornmeal, baking powder, salt and sugar. In medium size bowl combine eggs, milk, melted margarine and corn. molasses, egg and salt and add to flour mixture. Pour into well greased pan. Cook at 475 degrees for 30 to 35 minutes.

Submitted by Mrs. Orrin Clark, Rockport, Maine

Coffee Ring

1 cup sugar
½ cup shortening
2 eggs
2 cups flour
1 teaspoon baking soda
1 teaspoon baking powder
½ teaspoon salt

1 teaspoon vanilla
1 cup sour milk (sweet milk
may be soured by adding 1
tablespoon vinegar)
1 cup walnut meats
½ cup brown sugar
1 tablespoon cinnamon

Cream sugar and shortening. Add eggs and beat well. Sift flour with soda, baking powder and salt. Add to the above mixture. Add vanilla and sour milk. Mix together the nut meats, brown sugar and cinnamon. In a circular ringed pan or angel tube pan, greased, alternate batter and nut mixture. Start with batter and ending with nuts. Bake in a 350 degree oven for about 45 minutes.

Submitted by Mrs. Julia Alpert, Winslow, Maine

Graham Cracker Muffins

1 cup graham cracker crumbs
1 cup milk
1 cup flour
3 teaspoons baking powder

¾ teaspoon salt
1/3 cup sugar
2 teaspoons melted shortening
1 egg

Mix crumbs with the milk. Sift the flour with baking powder, salt and sugar. Add to the milk mixture with the shortening and unbeaten egg. Mix well and pour into greased muffin pans. Bake at 425 degrees for 15 minutes.

Submitted by Mrs. Gwen "Pinky" Church, Port Clyde, Maine

Ginger Muffins

1 cup margarine
1 cup sugar
4 eggs
1 cup molasses
1 cup buttermilk
4 cups flour
2 teaspoons soda

½ teaspoon allspice
1 teaspoon cinnamon
2 teaspoons ginger
½ teaspoon salt
½ cup raisins
1 cup walnut meats

Cream margarine, add sugar, eggs, one at a time; molasses and buttermilk. Mix well. Add sifted dry ingredients, raisins and nuts. Bake in greased muffin pans at 350 degrees for 20 to 25 minutes. This batter may be kept in the refrigerator and used as needed.

Submitted by Mrs. Eva Meservey, Jefferson, Maine

French Breakfast Muffins

1/3 cup butter or margarine
½ cup white sugar
1 egg
1½ cups sifted all-purpose flour
1½ teaspoons baking powder

½ teaspoon salt
¼ teaspoon nutmeg
½ cup milk
1/3 cup melted butter or margarine
½ cup sugar
1 teaspoon cinnamon

Cream butter and sugar, add egg. Sift together flour, baking powder, salt and nutmeg. Add the flour mixture to the creamed mixture, with the milk. Spoon dough into greased muffin tins. Bake in a 350 degree oven until golden brown. Remove from pans and roll first in melted butter, then in the sugar-cinnamon mixture.

Submitted by Mrs. Thyrle Hanson, Wesley, Maine

Graham Apple Muffins

1 cup graham flour
1 cup white flour
1 egg
1 cup sweet milk
4 teaspoons baking powder

½ teaspoon salt
2 tablespoons melted shortening
1 cup finely chopped apple
2 tablespoons sugar

Sift together the white flour, baking powder, salt and sugar. Stir in the graham flour. Beat the egg lightly, add the milk and melted shortening, mixing well. Combine the flour mixture with the milk and egg. Fold in the chopped apple. Bake at 350 degrees for 30 minutes or until done.

Submitted by Miss Etta Beverage, North Haven, Maine

Blueberry Muffins

2/3 cup sugar
½ cup shortening
1 cup milk
1 egg

2 cups flour
2 teaspoons baking powder
½ teaspoon salt
1 cup blueberries

Mix together sugar, shortening, egg and milk. Add the flour, sifted with baking powder and salt. Fold in blueberries last. Bake for 20 minutes at 375 degrees.

Submitted by Mrs. Amy Russell, Fort Fairfield, Maine

Old-Fashioned Graham Rolls

3 cups bonny-clabber (sour milk)
3 teaspoons baking soda

1 tablespoon sugar (optional)
3 cups graham flour
1 tablespoon melted fat

Stir until blended. Spoon batter into greased, hot cast iron pans. (More modern muffin pans may be used.) Bake in a hot oven, 450 degrees for 15 to 20 minutes.

Submitted by Mrs. Jeanne Littlefield Hammond, Waterville, Maine

Cream Style Corn Muffins

1½ cups flour
4 teaspoons baking powder
¼ teaspoon salt
1 egg

¼ cup milk
2 tablespoons shortening
1 cup cream style canned corn

Sift together flour, baking powder, salt. Beat the egg, add milk and shortening. Combine flour and egg mixtures, stirring just enough to dampen flour. Fill greased muffin tins 2/3 full and bake at 375 degrees for 25 to 30 minutes.

Submitted by Mrs. Vida Mehuren, Searsmont, Maine

Maine Highland Cranberry Muffins

3 tablespoons butter
½ cup sugar
1½ cups highland cranberries
2 cups sifted flour
1 tablespoon baking powder

½ cup sugar
1 teaspoon salt
½ cup butter or margarine
1 egg
1 cup milk

Combine the three tablespoons of butter with the ½ cup sugar. Grease a large-cup muffin pan, 12 muffin size, and divide the sugar butter mixture into the 12 cups. Sprinkle the cranberries on top of the sugar. If cranberries are large, cut or chop coarsely.

Sift together flour, baking powder, ½ cup sugar and salt. Cut in ½ cup butter to make fine crumbs.

Combine slightly beaten egg with the milk and add to the flour mixture. Stir just enough to mix. (Batter will be slightly lumpy.) Spoon batter into muffin cups, on top of cranberries. Bake in a 400 degree oven about 25 minutes. Makes 1 dozen large muffins.

Submitted by Mrs. Aubrey Hersey, Pembroke, Maine

Mother's Bran Muffins

½ cup molasses
1 tablespoon shortening
½ cup sugar
1 egg
1 2/3 cups milk

2 cups graham or wheat flour
2 cups all bran
2 teaspoons baking powder
Pinch salt

Heat the molasses with the shortening. Mix together the sugar, egg and milk. Mix together the flour, bran, baking powder and salt. Mix all together lightly, adding the hot molasses last.

Bake in a 375 degree oven until done, about 25 minutes.

Submitted by Mrs. O. S. Allen, Ellsworth, Maine

Squash Muffins

2 cups flour
4 teaspoons baking powder
1 teaspoon salt
1 cup cooked squash

3 tablespoons sugar
2 tablespoons melted fat
1 egg
1 cup sweet milk

Sift dry ingredients. Mix squash, milk and melted butter, and combine with dry mixture. Bake in a 375 degree oven for 15 to 20 minutes.

Submitted by Mrs. Mary Bowden, Corinna, Maine

Game played an important part in the early life of the State. Rabbit, raccoon, goose, duck, moose, deer, partridge, and pheasant were targets for the hunter's skill and meat for the table. Every creature that flew, swam, crawled or walked could be turned into a tasty stew or cooked plain to fill the stomach and please the taste buds. The hides and skins of some were tanned and utilized for many things and the fat was good for cooking, tallow and making soap. Game is still important to the economy of the State. In some rural areas it is still a diet staple and of course the various hunting and fishing seasons bring in a great many out-of-state hunters with high hopes to try their luck and swell the native economy. Quite a few Maine families have a deer stashed away in the freezer for the winter too. Deer Season in November is probably the biggest of the hunting seasons and the most popular.

Ten Minute Gems

¼ cup butter or oleo
¼ cup sugar
1 egg
½ teaspoon salt

2/3 cup sweet milk
1½ cups pastry flour
3 teaspoons baking powder

Cream butter and sugar; add egg and beat well. Add milk alternately with flour, which has been sifted with baking powder and salt. Drop by spoonfuls into well greased muffin tins. Makes 12 muffins and will cook in ten minutes, at 425 degrees. A cup of blueberries may be added to this batter. If this is done, reserve ¼ cup of the flour mixture to dredge the blueberries.

Submitted by Mrs. Byrle Carter, Brooklin, Maine

Graham Buns

2 cups graham flour
2 cups white flour
1 egg
2 teaspoons soda
½ teaspoon salt

2 cups sour milk
1/3 cup molasses
¼ cup sugar
3 tablespoons melted shortening

Sift together the white flour, soda, salt and sugar. Add the graham flour unsifted. Beat the egg, add the sour milk and molasses. Mix all together and add the melted shortening last. Bake in a 350 degree oven 30 to 35 minutes.

Submitted by Mrs. Hazel Firth, Rockland, Maine

Banana Nut Bread

3 bananas, mashed
2 eggs, beaten
1 cup sugar
½ cup shortening (can be
   half butter)

2 tablespoons sour milk
2 cups sifted all-purpose flour
1 teaspoon soda
¼ teaspoon salt
½ cup nut meats

Mash bananas with a fork, add the beaten eggs. Beat well. Add the sugar, shortening and milk. Sift flour, soda and salt. Add to the banana mixture. Fold in nut meats. Bake in a well greased bread tin in a 350 degree oven for 1 hour and 15 minutes. Cool. For easier cutting this bread is better made the day before it is used. Good sliced thin and spread with cream cheese.

Submitted by Mrs. Doris Crawford, Exeter, Maine

Pineapple Pecan Loaf

3 cups biscuit mix
¼ cup sugar
½ teaspoon salt
½ teaspoon nutmeg
1 can pineapple pie filling
(1 pound 6 ounce)

1/3 cup milk
1 beaten egg
4 tablespoons melted butter
1 teaspoon vanilla
½ cup chopped pecans

Combine biscuit mix, sugar, salt and nutmeg. Stir in the pie filling, milk, egg, butter and vanilla. Mix well. Add chopped pecans. Turn batter into a greased 9 x 5 loaf pan. Bake in a 350 degree oven for 1 hour and 15 minutes. Cool in pan for 15 minutes. Remove to a rack for cooling completely.

Submitted by Mary Clark, Rockport, Maine

Grapenut Bread

½ cup grapenuts
1 cup sour milk
1 egg
½ cup sugar
½ to ¾ cup flour

2 teaspoons baking powder
½ teaspoon soda
1 teaspoon salt
1 tablespoon melted shortening
1 teaspoon vanilla

Soak grapenuts in sour milk for 10 minutes. Sift together the flour, sugar, baking powder, salt and soda. Mix the egg, vanilla, and shortening. Add the egg mixture to the sour milk. Add the sifted flour and mix well. Let rise 20 minutes before baking, in a loaf pan. Bake at 350 degrees for 45 minutes.

Submitted by Mrs. Hazel Hills, Warren, Maine

Lemon Tea Bread

1 cup sugar
6 tablespoons shortening
Grated rind 1 lemon
2 eggs
1½ cups flour

1 teaspoon baking powder
½ teaspoon salt
½ cup milk
Juice of 1 lemon
½ cup sugar

Cream together sugar, shortening, lemon rind and eggs. Sift flour with baking powder and salt. Add dry ingredients alternately with the milk to the creamed mixture. Bake 1 hour at 325 degrees. Mix the lemon juice and sugar. Pour over the bread immediately on removing from the oven. Cool in the pan.

Submitted by Mrs. Rita H. Ellis, Skowhegan, Maine

Apple-Cranberry Bread

¼ cup butter or margarine
1 cup sugar
1 egg, beaten
1½ teaspoons vanilla
2 cups sifted flour
1 teaspoon salt

1 teaspoon baking powder
1 teaspoon soda
2 cups apples, peeled
1 cup cranberries
½ cup flaked coconut or
  chopped nuts

Cream butter and sugar, add beaten egg and vanilla. Sift together, flour, salt, soda and baking powder. Better to sift twice. Finely chop the peeled apples and pack firmly in cup. The cranberries can be coarsely chopped or cut. Combine the creamed mixture with the sifted ingredients, add cranberries, apples and coconut or nuts. Mix well.

Bake in a greased loaf pan for 1 hour at 350 degrees. Cool, wrap in foil and store in a cold place.

Submitted by Mrs. Alice G. Kennedy, Bucksport, Maine

Cranberry Bread

2 cups sifted flour
½ teaspoon salt
1½ teaspoons baking powder
½ teaspoon soda
1 cup sugar
1 beaten egg

2 tablespoons melted shortening
½ cup orange juice
2 tablespoons hot water
½ cup chopped nuts
1 cup cranberries, cut in half

Sift dry ingredients together. Add shortening, orange juice, and hot water to beaten egg. Combine with dry ingredients. Add nuts and cranberries. Pour into a greased loaf pan and bake for one hour and ten minutes in a 325 degree oven. When done remove from pan and brush with butter. Wrap in wax paper and place in the refrigerator for three hours. Remove the paper and wrap in a towel. Keep in the refrigerator. We like this bread very much.

Submitted by Mrs. Wilma Newell, North Anson, Maine

Peanut Butter Bread

2 cups flour
4 tsp. baking powder
1 tsp. salt

½ cup peanut butter
1½ cups milk
1/3 cup sugar

Sift together flour, salt, baking powder. Cut the peanut butter into the flour mixture. Add the milk and sugar. Mix all together and bake in a bread tin, for about 1 hour, in a 350 degree oven.

Submitted by Mrs. Clara E. Ford, Mechanic Falls, Maine

Carrot Loaf

3 cups flour
2 teaspoons soda
2 teaspoons cinnamon
½ teaspoon salt
1 cup cooking oil

2 cups sugar
3 beaten eggs
2 cups mashed cooked carrots
1½ cups chopped nuts

Sift together the dry ingredients. Beat eggs, add sugar, oil and carrots. Gradually mix in the sifted ingredients, mixing well. Add the chopped nuts, walnuts or pecans. Pour batter into greased and floured pans. Makes 2 loaves 9 x 5 or 1 angel tube pan or 3 round loaves baked in 1 pound coffee cans (nice for holidays). Bake in a 350 degree oven for 70 minutes.

Two cups canned pumpkin may be used in place of the carrots.

Submitted by Mrs. Claire T. Garrity, Sanford, Maine

Carrot Nut Bread

2/3 cup cooking oil
1 cup granulated sugar
1½ cups flour
1 teaspoon baking powder
1 teaspoon soda
1 teaspoon cinnamon

1 teaspoon vanilla
½ teaspoon salt
2 eggs
1 cup grated carrot
½ cup chopped nuts

Dissolve the sugar in the oil. Sift together flour, soda, baking powder, salt and cinnamon. Add to the sugar-oil mixture. Add one egg at a time. Mix well. Add carrots, nuts and vanilla. Bake in a 350 degree oven for 1 hour.

Excellent for children and makes a good sandwich with cream cheese.

Submitted by Mrs. Norma Philbrook, Owls Head, Maine

Peggy's Prune Bread

1 cup cooked prunes
1 cup sugar
1 cup sour milk
2 tablespoons melted butter
1 egg

1 cup whole wheat flour
2 cups white flour
¼ teaspoon baking powder
1 teaspoon soda
1 teaspoon salt

Sift the white flour with the soda, baking powder and salt, and stir in the whole flour. Beat egg, add sugar, sour milk, melted butter and prunes, cut up. Combine the flour mixture with the egg mixture and mix well. Bake in a loaf pan 1 hour at 350 degrees.

Submitted by Mrs. Carl E. White, Jonesport, Maine

Blueberry Coffee Cake

1 cup sugar
1/3 cup butter or shortening
2 eggs
½ cup milk

2 cups flour
2 teaspoons baking powder
1½ cups Maine blueberries
(fresh or frozen)

Cream butter, sugar and eggs. Sift flour with baking powder and add alternately with the milk. Fold in blueberries last. Pour into a 9 x 12 pan and bake at 350 degrees for about 45 minutes. When taking from the oven, spread with melted butter and sprinkle with a mixture of cinnamon and sugar.

This is an old recipe to which I have added a topping.
Submitted by Mrs. Willard Waterhouse, East Millinocket, Maine

Rhubarb Coffee Cake

1½ cups brown sugar
½ cup butter
1 egg
1 cup sour milk
1 teaspoon soda

2 cups sifted flour
1 teaspoon vanilla
2 cups rhubarb, finely cut
½ cup brown sugar
1 teaspoon cinnamon

Cream butter and sugar. Add egg. Sift together flour and soda. Add flour to creamed mixture, with milk and vanilla. Fold in the 2 cups rhubarb. Spread in a 9 x 13 pan (greased). Sprinkle top with the brown sugar and cinnamon mixture. Bake at 350 degrees for 35 to 40 minutes. Can be served as is for coffee cake or as a dessert with cream or ice cream.
Submitted by Mrs. Rene Laliberty, Falmouth, Maine

Cinnamon Breakfast Cake

1 cup flour
3 teaspoons baking powder
½ cup sugar
½ teaspoon salt
1 teaspoon cinnamon

½ cup milk
1 beaten egg
4 tablespoons melted shortening
2 tablespoons sugar
¼ teaspoon cinnamon

Sift together the flour, baking powder, ½ cup sugar, salt, 1 teaspoon cinnamon. Mix together the milk, beaten egg and shortening. Add to the flour mixture. Pour into a greased and floured 9 inch round pan. Stir together the 2 tablespoons of sugar and ¼ teaspoon of cinnamon and sprinkle over the top of cake. Bake 20 minutes in 375 degree oven.
Submitted by Mrs. Elsie F. Holt, Topsham, Maine

Five Islands Tea Cake

1 cup sugar
2 eggs
½ cup shortening
3 tablespoons molasses
1 teaspoon soda
1 cup warm water

2 cups flour
2 teaspoons baking powder
½ teaspoon salt
½ teaspoon cinnamon
½ teaspoon cloves
1 teaspoon vanilla

Cream shortening, add sugar, well beaten eggs and molasses. Add vanilla. Sift together the flour, baking powder, salt, cinnamon, and cloves. Dissolve the soda in the cup of warm water and add alternately with the flour mixture to the creamed ingredients. Mix well. Bake in a 9 x 9 pan at 350 degrees for 30 minutes. Lemon flavored confectioners sugar frosting makes this cake a must for tea and delightful as a dessert.

Submitted by Mrs. Thomas Watson, Five Islands, Maine

Cape Cod Tea Bread

4 tbsp. shortening
2 cups light brown sugar
2 beaten eggs
4 cups flour
1 tsp. salt
1 tsp. soda

3 tsp. baking powder
½ cup chopped nuts
4 tbsp. hot water
1 cup orange juice
2 cups halved cranberries

After cutting cranberries in half, wash in collander in order to wash out seeds.

Cream shortening, add sugar and beat until light, add eggs and beat well. Sift the dry ingredients and add alternately to the creamed mixture with the hot water and orange juice. Stir in the cranberries and nuts. Put in 2 greased bread pans and bake for 1 hour at 350 degrees.

Submitted by Mrs. Barbara MacDonald, Kennebunk, Maine

Irish Treacle Bread

2 cups flour
1 teaspoon baking soda
¼ cup sugar
¼ teaspoon salt

3 tablespoons butter
1 tablespoon molasses
¼ cup buttermilk

Sift flour, soda, sugar and salt and cream in butter. Add molasses and buttermilk. Knead until quite smooth. Preheat oven to 350 degrees. Roll out ½ inch thick; cut with round cutter; place on a buttered, floured sheet. Bake 20 minutes in 350 degree oven or until lightly browned. Serve hot or cold.

Submitted by Carrie Libby, Palmyra, Maine

Pumpkin Bread

2 2/3 cups sugar
2/3 cup cooking oil
4 eggs
1½ cups cooked pumpkin
3 1/3 cups flour
2 teaspoons baking soda

½ teaspoon baking powder
1½ teaspoons salt
½ teaspoon cinnamon
1 cup chopped nuts
2/3 cup water

Mix sugar, oil and pumpkin, add eggs one at a time, beating after each addition. In a separate bowl sift flour, baking powder, soda and cinnamon. Combine pumpkin mixture with flour mixture. Add water and mix well. Lastly add nuts and stir again. Pour into well greased loaf pans or one pound coffee cans. This amount will fill 4 one pound cans, filling each can half full. Bake at 300 degrees for one hour. Allow bread to cool, then remove from cans. This bread freezes very well. I simply put bread back in cans (when cooled) and replace the plastic lid.

This recipe is a favorite which has been handed down in our family.

Submitted by Mrs. Mary Jane Gaudreau, Bethel, Maine

Cherry Bread

¼ cup shortening
1 cup brown sugar
1 egg, beaten
½ tsp. salt
2 cups flour
2 tsp. baking powder

2/3 cup milk
½ cup cherries, drained
   (maraschino)
1/3 cup cherry juice
½ cup chopped nuts

Cream shortening and sugar. Beat in the egg. Mix and sift flour, salt and baking powder. Add to creamed mixture, alternately, with milk and cherry juice. Chop nuts and cherries. Stir into the dough. Spoon dough into a 9 x 5 loaf pan. Let stand for 20 minutes before baking at 350 degrees for 50 minutes to 1 hour, until tests done. This is an old recipe handed down in the family.

Submitted by Mrs. Edgar G. Keenan, Owl's Head, Maine

Orange Bread

1 orange
1 cup raisins
½ cup butter
1 cup sugar
2 eggs, beaten

½ cup buttermilk
1 teaspoon soda
¼ teaspoon salt
2¼ cups flour

Put the raisins and orange, peeling and all, through the food chopper. Cream butter, sugar and eggs. Add the soda to the buttermilk then mix all ingredients in order given. Add raisin-orange mixture last. Bake in a loaf pan at 350 degrees for 1 hour or until done.

Submitted by Mrs. Francis Beaulieu, Calais, Maine

Feather Dumplings

1 cup flour
1 teaspoon salt

2 teaspoons baking powder
½ cup milk (about)

Mix all together, using milk enough to make a stiff dough. Have soup nearly done. Drop batter by spoonfuls, dipping spoon in soup each time. This amount should cover top of soup. Let cook slowly for 15 minutes uncovered, then put cover on and cook 15 minutes more. This method of cooking is the secret to light dumplings.

Submitted by Mrs. Viola Watson, Norway, Maine

All-Bran Yeast Bread

1 package dry yeast
2 cups lukewarm water
¼ cup molasses
1 egg

½ cup All-Bran
¼ cup melted shortening
1 teaspoon salt
6 cups flour

Dissolve yeast in lukewarm water. Add molasses, beaten egg, and All-Bran. Mix well. Add remaining ingredients. Mix well. Turn on floured board, knead well, let rise until double in bulk. Cut down and let rise again. Make into loaf or rolls, rise until double. Bake in 350 degree oven for 35 minutes for loaf and 400 degree oven 25 minutes for rolls or until done.

Submitted by Mary Bowden, Corinna, Maine

Golden Waffles

1¾ cups flour
2½ teaspoons baking powder
¾ teaspoon salt
2 eggs, well beaten
1½ cups milk
5 tablespoons shortening

Sift together the dry ingredients. Combine eggs and milk, add to the dry mixture and add the shortening. Mix until smooth. Bake in a hot waffle iron.

Submitted by Mrs. Arnold Bishop, Wilmington, Mass.

Delicious Raised Rolls

1 cake yeast
1 tablespoon sugar
6 cups sifted flour
6 tablespoons cooking oil
3 tablespoons sugar
1 cup lukewarm water
1 cup milk scalded and cooled
2 beaten eggs
2 teaspoons salt

Add yeast and tablespoon sugar to the lukewarm water, stir and let stand 5 to 10 minutes. Put in large mixing bowl, add milk and half the flour, beat until smooth. Add beaten eggs, shortening and rest of the flour. Knead into a medium firm dough, let rise until doubled, turn onto floured bread board and shape into rolls. Let raise in greased pan (10 x 14 x 2) until doubled in bulk. Bake in 350 degree oven for 30 minutes. EXCELLENT!!

Submitted by Viola M. Trenholm, Alfred, Maine

Overnight Refrigerator Rolls

2 packages quick-acting dry yeast
2½ cups warm water
¾ cup soft or melted shortening
¾ cup sugar
2 eggs, well beaten
8 to 8½ cups flour
2½ teaspoons salt

Soften yeast in warm water. Add shortening, sugar, eggs, 4 cups flour and salt. Stir and then beat until smooth, about 1 minute. Stir in the remaining flour. This will be a soft dough.

Cover tightly and store in the refrigerator overnight or until needed. When ready to use, punch down dough and pinch off one third. Cover remaining dough and store in the refrigerator. It will keep 2 or 3 days.

Shape into rolls and place in a greased 9 x 9 x 2 inch baking pan. Cover with a clean towel and let rise in warm place for 1 hour or until doubled in bulk. Bake in a hot oven 400 degrees for 15 or 20 minutes. Turn on wire rack. One third makes 12 rolls.

Submitted by Athelene Hilt, Union, Maine

One Hour Yeast Rolls

1¼ cups milk, scalded
2 tablespoons sugar
2 teaspoons shortening
2 yeast cakes

½ cup lukewarm water
4 cups flour
½ teaspoon salt

Scald milk and cool to lukewarm. Add sugar and shortening. Dissolve yeast in lukewarm water. Add flour and salt and mix. Let rise 15 minutes. Make into rolls. Let rise 15 minutes. Bake in 350 degree oven 25-30 minutes.

Submitted by Mrs. Homer Waters, Dexter, Maine

Parker House Rolls

1 cake yeast
1 pint milk, scalded and
  cooled
2 tablespoons sugar

4 tablespoons melted shortening
6 cups flour
1 teaspoon salt

Dissolve yeast and sugar in lukewarm milk. Add shortening and 3 cups flour, salt. Beat until perfectly smooth. Cover, let rise in warm place one hour. Add remaining flour to make a stiff dough. Knead well, place in greased bowl. Cover, let rise for about 1½ hours or until double in bulk. Roll out ¼ inch thick. Cut with 2 inch biscuit cutter, crease through center with dull edge of knife, fold over in pocket shape. Place 1 inch apart on greased pan. Rise. Bake in hot oven 400 degree oven about 20 minutes.

Submitted by Mrs. Leon C. Adams, Clinton, Maine

Buttermilk Rolls

1 cup buttermilk (warm)
¼ cup Crisco
2 eggs
¼ cup sugar

Dash of salt
½ yeast cake
¼ cup warm water
4 cups flour

Dissolve yeast in water. Stir in buttermilk, Crisco, eggs, sugar, and salt into yeast. Add flour and mix. On board, roll real thin and butter well, cut in 1½ inch strips — then stack to make three, butter between. Now cut in 1½ inch blocks the other way and put each block in your cupcake tins. Let rise ½ hour and bake as other rolls. Very good.

Submitted by Mrs. Robert C. Chamberlain, Clinton, Maine

Parker House Rolls

2 tablespoons shortening
1 teaspoon salt
¼ cup sugar
1 cake yeast

1½ cups lukewarm water
3½ cups sifted flour
1 egg, well beaten
Melted butter

Add shortening, salt, sugar and crumbled yeast to water; stir until shortening is melted. Stir in sifted flour, cover and set in a warm place, free from drafts, to rise. (Dough may be set on lower shelf of unheated oven in a pan of hot water.) When doubled in bulk, add egg. Knead lightly and let rise again until doubled in bulk. Roll out ½ inch thick on well-floured board. Cut with biscuit cutter 2 inches in diameter, crease in center with a dull knife, brush with melted butter and fold over, pinching the dough at sides to make a pocketbook. Brush tops with melted butter. Let rise and bake on a greased baking sheet in hot oven 400 degrees about 20 minutes. Makes 2 dozen rolls.

Submitted by Dorothy Quass, Presque Isle, Maine

Refrigerator Rolls

1 cup oleo
½ cup sugar
2 teaspoons salt
1 cup boiling water
2 eggs, beaten

1 cake of household yeast
(not dry yeast)
1 cup cold water
6 cups flour

Dissolve yeast in 1 cup cold water and set for 5 minutes. Pour boiling water over oleo, sugar, and salt. Blend and cool. Add beaten eggs and blend. Add dissolved yeast and mix in flour. Cover and place in refrigerator for at least 4 hours or overnight. Remove from refrigerator about 3 hours before needed. Divide dough in 3 equal parts. Roll each part to ½ inch in thickness, spread with mixed candied fruit, or sugar and cinnamon, roll up like a jelly roll and cut in ½ inch slices. Place on greased baking tin about 2 inches apart. Let rise for 2 hours at room temperature. Bake in 425 degree oven for 15 minutes or until well browned.

When cool, ice with the following icing:

1 lb. powdered sugar
1 tablespoon oleo

Juice from ½ lemon or to suit taste. Add enough hot water to spread easily.

Submitted by Mrs. Royce Chapman, Fort Fairfield, Maine

Shredded Wheat Bread

1 cup grapenuts
2 large shredded wheat biscuits
½ cup molasses
½ cup shortening
½ cup brown sugar
3 teaspoons salt
2 cups boiling water
2 cups scalded milk
2 yeast cakes
8 cups flour or more

Combine shredded wheat, shortening, molasses, grapenuts, brown sugar, and salt. Add boiling water let stand ten minutes then add milk. Stir when lukewarm. Add yeast and stir until dissolved. Add flour and turn out onto lightly floured board and knead until mixture is a firm dough. Let rise until double in bulk. Form into loaves and let rise 1 to 1½ hours. Bake in oven 350 degrees for 35 to 40 minutes.

Submitted by Carol Foster, Monticello, Maine

Oatmeal Bread

1½ cups boiling water
1 cup quick cooking oats
1/3 cup soft shortening
½ cup molasses
4 teaspoons salt
2 yeast cakes
½ cup warm water
2 eggs
5½ cups sifted flour

Combine water, oats, shortening, salt and molasses. Cool. Dissolve yeast in the ½ cup water, add to first mixture. Mix well. Blend in beaten eggs and add flour. Let rise in greased bowl. Shape into loaves and let rise again. Bake at 375 degrees for 35 minutes or until done.

Submitted by Mrs. Raymond Farrar, Sangerville, Maine

Rolled Oats Yeast Bread
No Kneading

1 cup uncooked rolled oats
2 cups milk scalded
1 tablespoon shortening
1 yeast cake
½ cup lukewarm water
½ cup molasses
2 teaspoons salt
4½ cups flour

Pour hot milk over oats and let stand until lukewarm. Dissolve yeast in lukewarm water. Add yeast, molasses, shortening, and salt. Beat in flour and allow to rise until double in bulk. Stir down and pour into 2 greased pans. Rise until double in bulk. Bake 350 degrees for 35 minutes or until done.

Submitted by Mrs. Vernon Palmer, Caribou, Maine

Oatmeal Bread

¼ cup warm water
1 teaspoon sugar
2 packages dry yeast
1 cup rolled oats
¼ cup molasses

1 tablespoon salt
1 tablespoon sugar
¼ cup shortening
2 cups boiling water
5½ cups flour

Mix first three ingredients in a cup and set aside. In a large bowl, mix rolled oats, molasses, salt, sugar, shortening and boiling water. Stir, let set until lukewarm. Add yeast mixture and sifted flour. Mix well. Put on floured board, knead and place back in bowl to rise. Mold into two loaves and place in greased tins. Let rise ½ hour. Bake 45 minutes in 400 degree oven. Very good and moist.

Submitted by Mrs. Nola Sawtelle, Corinna, Maine

Drop Feather Rolls

1 cup sweet milk, scalded
1 egg, well beaten
2 tablespoons sugar
1 teaspoon salt

2 tablespoons shortening
1 yeast cake
2¼ cups all purpose flour

Scald milk and let cool to lukewarm. Add yeast and dissolve. Add sugar, salt, egg, shortening (measured after melting), and flour. Mix well. Let rise twice its size. Drop by spoonfuls into muffin tins. Let rise a few minutes and bake in 400 degree oven for 12 to 15 minutes. You can also shape into a loaf.

Submitted by Mrs. Estella Grigg, Portland, Maine

Ice Box Rolls

1 cup boiling water
½ cup shortening
½ cup sugar
½ teaspoon salt

1 yeast cake
½ cup lukewarm water
2 eggs, beaten
4 cups flour

Combine boiling water, shortening, sugar, and salt. When cool add yeast which has been dissolved in warm water and beaten eggs. Stir in flour. Do not knead. Put in mixing bowl and grease top with melted butter. Cover with waxed paper. Chill, and use quantity as wanted by cutting in required size and putting in pan. Let rise and bake, 400 degree oven for 15 minutes.

Submitted by Mrs. Frank Violette, Caribou, Maine

Pulla — Finnish Coffee Bread

2 cups scalded milk
¼ cup butter
1 teaspoon salt
! cup sugar
2 packages dry yeast

2 eggs, beaten
¾ teaspoon ground cardamon seed
7 or 8 cups flour

Scald milk with butter, salt, sugar added; cool to lukewarm. Add yeast to lukewarm mixture. Stir until dissolved. Add beaten eggs, ¾ teaspoon ground cardamon seed, and flour. Let rise until doubled. Turn out on board and shape into braids. Place on greased pans and let double in bulk. Bake in moderate oven 350 degrees, 20 minutes or more depending on thickness of braids.

Submitted by Mrs. Lena Mustonen, Arlington, Virginia

Raised Corn Muffins

1 yeast cake
¼ cup lukewarm water
2 cups scalded milk
1 cup corn meal
1 tablespoon salt

½ cup sugar
½ cup shortening
2 eggs
4 cups flour

Soften yeast in ¼ cup water. Scald milk and pour over corn meal, sugar, and shortening. Cool until lukewarm. Beat in eggs, add softened yeast. Mix well. Add 2 cups flour, mix again well. Stir in enough flour to make stiff dough about 4 cups in all. Raise about 1 hour. Stir down. Put in greased muffins pans 2/3 full. Raise again about 1 hour. Bake in 375 degree oven 15 to 20 minutes.

Submitted by Mrs. John Workman, Prospect Harbor, Maine

Coconut Pound Cake

2 sticks oleo
2/3 cup other shortening
3 cups sugar
5 eggs
3 cups flour

1 teaspoon baking powder
1 cup milk
1 teaspoon coconut flavoring
1 (4 ounce) can flaked coconut

Cream together the oleo, shortening and sugar. Add the eggs, one at a time. Sift flour and baking powder. Add to the creamed batter with the milk. Stir in flavoring (may also use vanilla) and coconut. Bake 1½ hours in a large angel cake pan which has been greased and floured. Use a 350 degree oven.

Submitted by Mrs. Leland C. Day, Crawford, Maine

New England is famous all over the world for baked beans. In Maine, baked beans are a way of life and in every hamlet, town or city one can probably find a public supper on Saturday night featuring them in some Grange, Church or other hall. The best baked beans of all are bean-hole-beans. These go back into history quite a way and were certainly included in the early life of Maine. First, a pit is dug in the ground deep enough to hold the container with room left over and a hardwood fire is built in the bottom. After this is burned down to live coals, the prepared pot or kettle of beans is placed in the pit and the dirt that was removed is placed back on top to fill the hole. After baking for several hours the dirt is removed and the precious pot lifted out, brushed off and opened for the feast. And a very fine feast it is as all who have been fortunate enough to know will state.

Free Press White Fruit Cake

3 cups (1 pound) golden seedless raisins

2 cups (1 pound) diced citron

1 cup (½ pound) red glazed cherries, halved

1 cup (½ pound) glazed pineapple, quartered and diced

1½ cups (½ pound) slivered blanched almonds

3 cups sifted all-purpose flour

1 teaspoon salt

1 cup butter or margarine

1¼ cups sugar

5 eggs

1 teaspoon vanilla

2 teaspoons fresh grated lemon rind

1 cup undrained crushed pineapple

Line two 9⅝ x 5½ x 2¾ pans with oiled brown wrapping paper. Mix all fruits and nuts (except crushed pineapple) together in large mixing bowl.

Sift and measure flour. Resift with salt and sift over fruits and nuts. Mix until each piece is well coated with flour. Cream butter until light and fluffy. Gradually add sugar, beating until well blended. Add eggs, one at a time, beating well after each addition. Add eggs, one at a time, beating well after each addition.

Stir into creamed mixture the vanilla, lemon rind and crushed pineapple. Fold in floured fruits and nuts and mix thoroughly. Spoon into prepared pans, spreading evenly. Bake in 275 degree oven for about 2 hours or until food pick inserted in center comes out clean. If tops brown too quickly, place sheet of foil loosely on top.

Let cakes cool in pan on rack for about 20 minutes. Remove from pan and take off paper. After cakes are thoroughly cooled, wrap in foil alone or with a brandy soaked cheesecloth inner wrapping. Store in cool place. Makes two loaves.

(I do make my own little personal revisions and the results have always been most satisfactory. In place of the citron I use an equal amount of a combination of red and green glazed cherries. Sometimes I even put in extra red and green glazed cherries and pineapple. It seems to make it delicious and the extra color makes it more festive. I never have felt it necessary to wrap them in brandy soaked cheesecloth. They mellow very well in foil wrap and I put them in a plastic container in a cool place. They keep very well.)

Submitted by Geneva Cargill, California — formerly Rockland

Our Fruit Cake
(Recipe is 193 years old)

3 cups dark brown sugar
1 cup butter
1 cup dark molasses
½ cup strong black coffee
½ cup grape juice
5 eggs
5 cups flour
1 teaspoon baking soda
½ teaspoon salt

2 teaspoons cinnamon
1 teaspoon cloves
1 teaspoon allspice
3 pounds seedless raisins
2 pounds currents
½ pound citron
¼ pound orange peel
¼ pound walnut meats chopped

Sift sugar. Cream butter and sugar adding liquids in their order. Beat in eggs. Sift dry ingredients together and add to the butter and sugar mixture. Add chopped fruits. Bake in a very slow oven 275 degrees for approximately 4 hours or until it tests done. Makes four loaves. Pans should be lined with greased brown paper. Candied pineapple and candied cherries may be added to fruit by eliminating equal amounts of other fruits. White raisins may be substituted for currants. This cake will keep many months. It should be "aged" at least 6 weeks before eating. It may be frozen; and also steamed and served as a pudding.

Submitted by Ethel M. Hilton, Cape Neddick, Maine

French Fruit Cake

1/3 cup sugar
1 egg
2 tablespoons cocoa
½ cup butter
1 teaspoon vanilla
2 cups graham cracker crumbs
1 cup coconut

½ cup walnuts
2 cups confectioner's sugar
Butter size of an egg
2 tablespoons hot coffee
2 squares of chocolate
2 tablespoons butter

Combine sugar, egg, cocoa and ½ cup of butter in top of double boiler. Cook until it thickens slightly. Take from heat and add the crumbs, coconut, walnuts and vanilla. Mix well and press in a cake pan. Mix together the confectioner's sugar and butter size of an egg with hot coffee until of a spreading consistency and spread this over the cracker crumb mixture. In a small dish (over hot water) melt the chocolate and butter. Spread this as a frosting on top of the confectioner's sugar topping. Cut in squares when firm.

Submitted by Mrs. Vincent Hare, Houlton, Maine

Gumdrop Fruitcake

1 cup shortening
1¾ cups sugar
2 eggs
1½ cups apple sauce
1 teaspoon soda
1 tablespoon hot water
1 teaspoon vanilla
4 cups flour
1 teaspoon cinnamon

¼ teaspoon cloves
¼ teaspoon nutmeg
¼ teaspoon salt
1½ lbs. gumdrops (small or cut in pieces, omit black ones)
1 lb. white raisins
1 cup pecans browned in butter

Cream the shortening and sugar, add eggs one at a time. Add the apple sauce, dissolve the soda in the hot water and add. Add the vanilla. Sift together the flour with the dry ingredients. Now add ½ the flour mixture with the creamed mixture; the remaining ½ of flour mixture to the fruit and nut mixture. Combine both mixtures well. Bake at 300 degrees for 2 hours. Makes 2 loaves.

Submitted by Julia B. Parsons, Stratton, Maine

Orange Fruit Cake

1½ cups sugar
½ cup shortening
2 eggs
2/3 cup sour milk
2 cups flour

1 teaspoon soda
¼ teaspoon salt
1 orange
1 cup raisins
½ cup nuts

Squeeze orange for juice, put ½ cup sugar in it and set aside. Cream remaining sugar and shortening, add eggs and beat. Sift dry ingredients together and add to the creamed mixture alternately with the sour milk. Grind the orange, raisins and nuts with food chopper and add to the cake mixture. Cook at 325 degrees.

When done put the orange juice and sugar on hot cake. This makes a glaze topping. Leave in pan.

Submitted by Nora Stickney, Rockland, Maine

My Own Fruit Cake

1½ cup boiling water
½ cup raisins
½ cup dates
½ cup mixed nuts
¼ cup shortening
1 egg
½ cup cold water
2 cups flour

1 cup sugar
1 heaping teaspoon soda
½ teaspoon salt
½ teaspoon cloves
½ teaspoon cinnamon
½ teaspoon nutmeg
½ cup mixed candied fruit

Pour the boiling water over the raisins, dates and nuts and boil gently 15 minutes. Add the ¼ cup shortening. Cool. Beat together the egg and cold water. Sift dry ingredients. Add the egg mixture to the flour mixture, add the fruit and nut mixture and beat well. Last add the candied fruit. Pour into greased and floured 8-inch tube pan and bake at 350 degrees 45 minutes to 1 hour. Turn out on rack to cool. When cool, wrap in plastic wrap and store in cool place for four to six weeks to season. This may be served at once but is much better if stored as suggested.

Submitted by Mrs. Brooksie Hoxie, Lincoln Center, Maine

Harrison Fruit Cake

1 cup sugar
1 cup butter
3 eggs beaten
1 cup dark molasses
1 cup sweet milk
1 cup sour milk
5 cups flour
2 rounding teaspoons soda
1 teaspoon salt

1 teaspoon cinnamon
1 teaspoon allspice
½ teaspoon cloves
½ teaspoon mace
½ teaspoon nutmeg
1 pound raisins coarsely cut
½ pound currants
1 small jar citron
1 pound candied fruits

Cream sugar and butter, add beaten eggs, sweet and sour milk and the molasses. Add flour one cup at a time sifted with soda, salt and spices. Mix last 2 cups with fruits. Lastly add the floured fruits. Bake 45 minutes at 350 degrees in loaf pans. These cakes will keep for months wrapped in Saran and foil and stored in a cool place.

Submitted by Mrs. Leslie B. Johnson, East Holden, Maine

Boiled Fruit Cake

1 cup sugar
1 cup seedless raisins
1 cup water
½ cup shortening
1 teaspoon cinnamon
½ teaspoon cloves
½ teaspoon nutmeg

1 egg, beaten
1½ cups flour
1 teaspoon soda
½ teaspoon salt
1 teaspoon vanilla
Nuts (optional)

Put sugar, raisins, water, shortening, cinnamon, cloves and nutmeg in a saucepan and boil for ten minutes. Cool. Add the beaten egg. Sift together the flour, soda and salt and add to the cooled mixture. Add vanilla and nuts. Bake in loaf pan in a 350 degree oven for 1 hour.

Submitted by Mrs. Vernon Ward, Solon, Maine

Cream Cheese Fruit Cake

1 8-oz. package cream cheese
½ lb. margarine
1½ cups sugar
1½ teaspoons vanilla
4 eggs

2¼ cups flour
1½ teaspoons baking powder
1 8-oz. jar candied fruit
½ cup pecans chopped

Thoroughly blend cheese, margarine, sugar and vanilla. Add eggs one at a time. Sift 2 cups flour with the baking powder and gradually add to the creamed batter, blend well. Combine remaining ¼ cup flour with the fruit and nuts, fold into the cake mixture. Bake in greased and floured pans in 350 degree oven 1 hour or until done. Yield 2 — 9 x 5 x 3 loaf pans or 1 tube pan.

Submitted by Martha Farrington, Bryant Pond, Maine

Economical Fruit Cake

1 cup sugar
1 cup water
2 tablespoons shortening
1 teaspoon salt
1 teaspoon allspice

1 teaspoon cinnamon
1 cup raisins
2 cups flour
1 teaspoon soda

Put in a saucepan the sugar, water, shortening, salt, allspice, cinnamon and raisins and boil three minutes. When cool, sift together and add the flour and soda. Bake in a moderate 350 degree oven for 30 to 40 minutes. Coffee may be substituted for water.

Submitted by Edith R. Richards, New Vineyard, Maine

Old Town Raisin Cake

1 cup sugar
½ cup shortening
1 cup sour milk
1½ cups flour
1 teaspoon soda

¼ teaspoon cinnamon
¼ teaspoon nutmeg
¼ teaspoon cloves
1 cup chopped raisins

Cream together the sugar and shortening. Sift dry ingredients — flour, soda, cinnamon, nutmeg and cloves together; mix alternately with sour milk to the creamed mixture, beginning and ending with dry ingredients. Fold in raisins last. Bake 1 hour at 325 degrees.

Submitted by Mrs. Calla R. Shepardson, Stetson, Maine

Anna's Apple Fruit Cake

1 cup sugar
½ cup shortening
2 tablespoons molasses
2½ cups flour
1 teaspoon soda
1 teaspoon salt

1 teaspoon cinnamon
½ teaspoon cloves
1 teaspoon nutmeg
(Or vanilla instead of spices)
1 cup sour milk
1 cup chopped apples

Cream sugar, shortening and molasses together. Sift flour with soda, salt and spices and add alternately with the sour milk to the creamed mixture. Fold in the chopped apples last. Bake in a loaf pan at 350 degrees for 35 or 40 minutes or until the cake tests done.

Submitted by Etta Beverage, North Haven, Maine

Boiled Cake

1 pound raisins
2 cups sugar
3 cups water
4 tablespoons shortening
2 teaspoons cinnamon

½ teaspoon cloves
½ teaspoon allspice
4 cups flour
2 teaspoons soda
1 teaspoon salt

Boil together for 15 minutes the raisins, sugar, water, shortening, cinnamon, cloves and allspice. Let cool. Sift the flour, soda and salt together and add to the raisin mixture. Makes 2 loaves. Bake in 350 degree oven for 1 hour.

Submitted by Nellie Stetson, Bethel, Maine

Boiled Raisin Cake

2 cups white sugar
2 cups hot water
1 cup shortening
2 teaspoons cinnamon
1 teaspoon cloves
1 teaspoon salt
1 pound raisins
2 teaspoons soda
3½ cups flour

Combine in a large saucepan the sugar, hot water, shortening, cinnamon, cloves, salt and raisins and let come to a boil. Add the 2 teaspoons soda and beat hard. Let cool. Beat in the flour. For fruit cake, add cherries, mixed peels and nutmeats. Bake 1 hour in 350 degree oven. The yield is 2 bread-loaf pans.

Submitted by Mrs. D. F. London, Houlton, Maine

Raisin Cake

1 pound seeded raisins, chopped
    or cut fine
1½ teaspoons soda
1½ cups boiling water
1½ cups sugar
¾ cup shortening
2 eggs, beaten
3 cups flour
1 teaspoon salt
2 teaspoons vanilla

Chop or cut up raisins fine and put in a bowl. Sprinkle the soda over the raisins. Cover with the boiling water. Let cool. Add remaining ingredients.

At Thanksgiving time you may use this recipe for a fruit cake by adding candied fruits of all kinds to the batter. This is a very good cake recipe as the cake will keep moist for a long time.

Submitted by Marilyn M. Wiers, St. Albans, Maine

Raisin Cake

1 cup sugar
½ cup shortening, partly
    melted
½ teaspoon salt
½ teaspoon allspice
½ teaspoon nutmeg
1 cup raisins
1 cup sweet milk
1 teaspoon soda
2 cups sifted flour
2 teaspoons cream of tartar

Combine sugar, shortening, salt and seasonings and beat. Add chopped raisins, sweet milk and soda. Blend. Add sifted flour, cream of tartar and beat until smooth. Bake 35 minutes at 375 degrees.

Submitted by Mrs. Wanita Lunn, Augusta, Maine

Danish Apple Cake

3 eggs
1 cup sugar
½ cup shortening
1 teaspoon salt
1 teaspoon nutmeg

1 tablespoon lemon
1 teaspoon baking soda
2 teaspoons cream of tartar
2 cups flour
½ cup milk

Spread on large greased cookie sheet. Put sliced apples in rows on top of cake batter. Bake at 350 degrees. Five minutes before taking from oven, brush with melted butter and sprinkle with cinnamon. Take a fork and test apples. When they are soft, cake is done.

Submitted by Mrs. Philip Hansen, Westbrook, Maine

Pumpkin Cake

3 cups flour
2 teaspoons soda
2 teaspoons baking powder
2 teaspoons cinnamon

2 cups sugar
4 eggs
1½ cups cooking oil
1 can pumpkin

Sift together the flour, soda, baking powder and cinnamon. Mix in the sugar, eggs, cooking oil and pumpkin. Bake 40 to 50 minutes at 350 degrees. Bake in a 13 x 9 inch pan.

Submitted by Dorothy McIninch, Old Town, Maine

Raw Apple Cake

2 cups sugar
1 cup butter or shortening
4 eggs, beaten
3 cups flour
2 teaspoons soda
¾ teaspoon salt
2 teaspoons cinnamon

1 teaspoon nutmeg
1 teaspoon cloves
1 cup cold coffee
3 cups raw apples (sliced or grated)
1 cup raisins
1 cup nut meats (optional)

Cream butter and sugar together; add beaten eggs. Sift the dry ingredients and add to the creamed mixture alternately with the coffee. Fold in the apples, raisins and nuts last. Bake 1 hour at 350 degrees or until done. Makes 2 big loaves.

Submitted by Barbara L. Farren, Addison, Maine

Apple Sauce Cake

2½ cups flour
¼ teaspoon baking powder
1½ teaspoons salt
½ teaspoon cloves
2 cups sugar
1½ teaspoons soda
¾ teaspoon cinnamon
½ teaspoon allspice

½ cup shortening
1½ cups unsweetened apple sauce
½ cup cold water
1 large egg
½ cup nuts (chopped)
1 cup raisins (floured)

Sift together in a bowl all of the dry ingredients. Add the shortening, apple sauce, water and egg. Beat well and add nuts and raisins. Bake until done, about 1 hour, at 350 degrees.

Submitted by Mrs. Elvie Shields, Thomaston, Maine

Apple Sauce Cake

1½ cups apple sauce
½ cup butter (1 stick)
1 cup sugar
1 egg
1 teaspoon cinnamon
½ teaspoon cloves

1 teaspoon salt
1 teaspoon cocoa
½ teaspoon nutmeg
2 teaspoon soda
2 cups flour

Cream butter and sugar, add the egg and applesauce. Mix together flour, soda, salt and spices. Combine the two mixtures. Mix well. Bake at 350 degrees from 35 to 45 minutes or until it tests done.

Mrs. Mary Jane MacLauchlan, Cambridge, Maine

Molasses Apple Cake

1 cup sugar
½ cup shortening
3 scant cups flour
1 teaspoon cinnamon
1 teaspoon cloves
¼ teaspoon nutmeg

1 cup sour milk
1 tablespoon baking soda
1 cup chopped raisins
1 cup apples, diced
2 tablespoons molasses

Cook the apples with the molasses until done and set aside to cool. Cream sugar with shortening. Sift flour with cinnamon, cloves and nutmeg and add alternately to the creamed mixture with the sour milk to which the baking soda has been added. Fold into this mixture the cooled apples and the raisins. Bake at 325 degrees for approximately 1 hour.

Submitted by Mrs. T. A. Jewell, Skowhegan, Maine

Apple Loaf Cake

3 cups junked apple
1 cup molasses
½ cup melted shortening
½ cup sugar
3 cups flour
½ teaspoon cloves

½ teaspoon cinnamon
½ teaspoon nutmeg
½ teaspoon salt
1½ cups sour milk
2 rounded teaspoons soda
2/3 cup raisins

Cook the apples in the molasses until apple is soft but still in the junk. Cream the shortening and sugar. Sift together the flour, cloves, cinnamon, nutmeg and salt. Mix the sour milk and soda together; add to the creamed mixture and then add the sifted dry ingredients. Stir well. Fold in the apple molasses mixture and the raisins. Bake in a large loaf pan in a 350 degree oven for about one hour. This cake is very good for Thanksgiving and Christmas.

Submitted by Mrs. Carroll Beal, Skowhegan, Maine

Apple Sauce Cake

1 cup sugar
½ cup shortening
1 cup hot apple sauce,
  unsweetened
2 cups flour
1 teaspoon soda

½ teaspoon salt
¼ teaspoon cloves
¼ teaspoon nutmeg
¼ teaspoon cinnamon
1 egg
¾ cup raisins

Mix flour with soda, salt and spices. Mix sugar with hot apple sauce and shortening. Add the egg and beat well, then combine with the flour mixture. Add raisins. (Other fruit may be substituted for the raisins, chopped dates, chopped nuts or mixed fruit.)

Bake in either small tins to be used as gifts or an 8 x 8 tin or glass baking pan. Bake in a 340 degree oven for about 30 minutes or until done when tested. Remove from tin to cool. It may be iced with a variety of flavors. A special one, I like, is made from brown sugar with peanut butter added.

Submitted by Mrs. Emery L. Leathers, Surry, Maine

Topping for Cake

3 tablespoons butter, melted
1/3 cup brown sugar
½ cup coconut

¼ cup nuts, chopped
2 tablespoons cream

Mix well and spread on cake. Place under broiler (3 inches) until it browns or bubbles 3 to 5 minutes.

Submitted by Reta H. Ellis, Skowhegan, Maine

Dutch Apple Cake

3 or 4 cooking apples, sliced
½ cup sugar
2 cups flour
4 teaspoons baking powder
¼ teaspoon salt
4 tablespoons shortening

1 cup milk
1 egg, beaten
1 or 2 teaspoons cinnamon
 for topping
4 tablespoons sugar for
 topping

Sift dry ingredients together, cut in shortening, add egg and milk. Spread thin in pan and let stand while preparing apples. Pare and cut in wedge shaped pieces — arrange in rows on top of batter to cover the top. Mix cinnamon and sugar well and sprinkle over the apples. Bake in a quick oven 20 to 25 minutes, until a straw comes out clean. Serve warm.

Submitted by Mrs. Earl R. Gray, Blue Hill, Maine

Nobby Apple Cake

3 cups apples (diced)
1 cup sugar
¼ cup shortening
1 egg beaten
¼ cup nuts (chopped)
1 teaspoon vanilla

1 cup flour
½ teaspoon baking powder
½ teaspoon soda
½ teaspoon salt
½ teaspoon cinnamon
½ teaspoon nutmeg

Pare apples, cut into ½ inch cubes and set aside. Cream shortening with the sugar, add the beaten egg. Add apples, nuts and vanilla and sifted dry ingredients. Bake in greased 8-inch square pan 45 minutes at 350 degrees. Serve hot or cold, with or without whipped cream or ice cream. Can be cut into squares, a good substitute for brownies.

Submitted by Mrs. Willard A. Kelly, Kennebunk, Maine

Blueberry Cake

1 cup sugar
1 2/3 cups flour
1 teaspoon baking powder
½ teaspoon salt
1 unbeaten egg

¼ cup butter
1 teaspoon vanilla
1 cup milk
1 cup fresh blueberries

Cream the butter and sugar and add the egg. Sift together the flour, baking powder and salt and combine the creamed mixture with the flour and the milk. Add vanilla. Mix and beat well. Dust the blueberries with a little flour and fold into the batter. Bake in a 350 degree oven about 50 minutes.

Submitted by Mrs. Pearle Palmer, Island Falls, Maine

Blueberry Cake

2 cups sugar
1 cup shortening (half butter)
2 eggs
1 cup milk
3 cups flour
2½ teaspoons baking powder
½ teaspoon salt
2 teaspoons nutmeg (fresh grated if possible)
2 teaspoons vanilla
1 pint of blueberries

Cream sugar and shortening together. Beat in eggs, milk, flour baking powder, salt, nutmeg and vanilla. Fold in the blueberries.

This makes an 9 x 13 or 2 eight inch square cakes. We line pan with greased waxed paper. Bake at 350 degrees for 40 minutes and check — then increase temperature to 375 degrees for 10 minutes more.

Submitted by Forest O. Mavis, Orange, Conn., and Surry, Maine

Blueberry Cake

1½ cups sugar
½ cup shortening
2 eggs
2½ cups flour
1 teaspoon soda
1 teaspoon cinnamon
½ teaspoon nutmeg
½ teaspoon salt
½ cup sour milk
1½ cups blueberries (fresh or frozen)

Cream the sugar and shortening together, beat in eggs. Sift dry ingredients together and add to the creamed mixture alternately with the sour milk. Add blueberries last. Sprinkle top with 3 tablespoons sugar before baking. Bake in 375 degree oven for 45 minutes.

Submitted by Mrs. Keith Pennell, Machias, Maine

Old-Fashioned Blueberry Molasses Cake

½ cup sugar
½ cup shortening
½ cup molasses
1 egg
1¾ cups flour
½ teaspoon salt
½ teaspoon cinnamon
½ teaspoon allspice
1 teaspoon soda
¾ cup hot water
1 cup blueberries

Cream sugar and shortening together, then add the molasses and egg. Sift dry ingredients and add to the creamed mixture alternately with the hot water. Add blueberries last. Bake in 350 degree oven until done.

Submitted by Mrs. Patricia Dailey, Rockland, Maine

Wild fruits grew in abundance in the woods and meadows. The most plentiful was the wild crabapple and this hard, sour little storehouse of energy could be used in many ways. Collected after the first frost had kissed its rosy cheeks, it made a dandy apple pie or pudding and could also be dried and stored for use during the winter months ahead. You still can't beat the tangy flavor of wild Maine crabapple jelly. The wild apple was then and the cultivated apple is now a very important part of the diet and economy of the State of Maine. Cultivated orchards of all varieties can be found in just about any county but the center of the apple industry is located in the western counties along the New Hampshire border. Related industries are many — such as the making of cider, canning of pie apples and applesauce, apple jelly and of course the bottling of apple juice. From the beginning Maine has specialized in apple varieties that store well and are especially good for cooking or canning.

ANNA CROCKETT

Blueberry Pudding Cake

2 cups blueberries
1 cup flour
1 teaspoon baking powder
¼ teaspoon salt
3 tablespoons shortening
(melted)

¾ cup sugar
½ cup milk
1 cup sugar
1 tablespoon cornstarch
1 cup boiling water

Put the 2 cups blueberries in the bottom of an 8 x 8 cake tin. Mix the flour, baking powder, salt, shortening, ¾ cup sugar and milk together and spread over the berries. Now mix the 1 cup sugar and cornstarch together and sprinkle over batter in pan. Pour the cup of boiling water over this. Bake at about 350 degrees for 45 minutes.

Other fruits such as rhubarb, raspberries, or sliced apples can be deliciously substituted for the blueberries.
Submitted by Mrs. James McGrath, East Waterboro, Maine

Raspberry Upside Down Cake

½ cup sugar
3 tablespoons butter
1 egg
6 drops almond or vanilla
flavoring
1 cup all-purpose flour

1½ teaspoons baking powder
½ teaspoon salt
¼ cup milk
3 tablespoons butter
¾ cup brown sugar, packed
2½ cups raspberries

Cream together the butter, sugar and the egg; stir in the flavoring. Sift flour, baking powder and salt together and add alternately with the milk to the creamed mixture.

In a buttered 8 x 8 inch pan, melt 3 tablespoons butter, sprinkle in the ¾ cup brown sugar and allow the two to melt together. Spread the berries evenly on top of this mixture and pour the cake batter over the berries. Bake in 350 degree oven for 30 minutes. Remove from oven and turn onto a plate. Serve wih either whipped, plain cream or ice cream. This cake is best when served slightly warm but it is not to be passed up cold either.
Submitted by Mrs. Louis J. LeBretton, Orrington, Maine

Blueberry Cake

2 eggs, separated
1 cup sugar
½ cup shortening
¼ teaspoon salt
1 teaspoon vanilla

1½ cups flour
1 teaspoon baking powder
1/3 cup milk
1½ cups fresh blueberries
1 tablespoon flour

Beat egg whites until stiff. Add ¼ cup of the sugar. Cream the shortening, sugar, salt, vanilla and add the egg yolks. Beat until creamy. Add flour, sifted with baking powder, alternately with the milk. Fold in the egg whites. Sprinkle the berries with the 1 tablespoon of flour and fold into the batter. Pour into a well greased 8 x 8 pan. Sprinkle top with a little sugar. Bake in a 350 degree oven for 30 minutes.

Submitted by Mrs. Jeannette Chapman, Southwest 20, Cushing, Maine

My Strawberry Long Cake

1 quart hulled berries
½ cup sugar
2 cups flour
6 tablespoons sugar
4 teaspoons baking powder

Pinch salt
1/3 cup shortening
1 egg
2/3 cup milk

Sprinkle ½ cup sugar over berries and let set. Sift together the flour, 6 tablespoons sugar, baking powder and salt. Cut in the shortening. Beat egg with milk and add to the flour mixture. Spread dough out in greased 8 x 12 pan. Spread berries and juice over top and bake in 375 degree oven for 35 to 40 minutes. Serve with plain or whipped cream.

Submitted by Mrs. Gordon Hambrecht, Dexter, Maine

Easy Cherry Nut Cake

1 cup sugar
½ cup butter
2 eggs
2 cups flour
2½ teaspoons baking powder
½ cup milk

½ teaspoon lemon
½ teaspoon vanilla
4 tablespoons cherry juice
½ cup chopped cherries
½ cup nuts

Cream butter, sugar and egg yolks together. Sift flour and baking powder and add alternately with the milk and flavoring. Add cherries, juice and nuts. Last of all fold in egg whites. The secret is putting the egg whites in last. Frost with your favorite frosting.

Submitted by Faith Pert, Sedgwick, Maine

Lemon-Apple-Cheese Cake

1 tall can evaporated milk
1 large package lemon-
   flavored gelatin (6 ounces)
¾ cup boiling water
1 package cream cheese (8
   ounces)
½ cup sugar
2 cups apple sauce

1 teaspoon vanilla
1 cup graham cracker crumbs
   (about 10 crackers or use
   ginger snap crumbs)
2 tablespoons brown sugar
¼ cup butter or margarine
½ cup chopped nuts

Chill evaporated milk until *icy*. Add the boiling water to the gelatin and stir until dissolved, cool. Combine cream cheese and sugar and blend until creamy. Stir in the apple sauce, vanilla, and cooled gelatin mixture. Chill well.

To make the crust; melt the ¼ cup of butter in a 9 x 9 pan and mix in the crumbs, brown sugar and half of the nuts. Spread around and press firm.

Whip the cooled apple-gelatin mixture while gradually adding the chilled milk. Continue beating until about double in volume. Turn into the prepared pan and top with the rest of the nuts. Chill until set, at least 5 hours or can set overnight. Makes 12 to 16 servings.

Submitted by Mrs. Marjorie Wilder, Norridgewock, Maine

Refrigerator Cheese Cake

32 graham crackers, rolled fine
2 rounded tablespoons
   powdered sugar
¼ pound butter, melt slightly
1 package lemon flavor
   gelatin (3 ounce)

1 cup boiling water
8 ounce package cream cheese
1 cup sugar
1 large can evaporated milk
   (chilled overnight)

Mix the cracker crumbs with the powdered sugar and the butter. Line a 9 x 13 pan with the crumb mixture, reserving 1 cup for topping. Mix gelatin with boiling water until dissolved and cool.

Beat until creamy the cream cheese and the sugar. Whip until light and fluffy the evaporated milk (which has been chilled).

Mix all together, the cooled gelatin, the creamed cheese, and the whipped milk. Pour over the crumb crust. Sprinkle 1 cup crumbs over the top. Chill.

Submitted by Mrs. Anton Anzelc, Bangor, Maine

Cheese Cake

2 packages of cream cheese (8 ounce size)
1 pound cottage cheese
4 eggs
2 tablespoons lemon juice
1 teaspoon vanilla flavoring
¼ pound melted butter or margarine
1 pint sour cream
3 tablespoons flour
3 tablespoons cornstarch
1½ cups sugar

Have all ingredients at room temperature. Put cream cheese and cottage cheese through a sieve and add the slightly beaten eggs, also 1 cup of the sugar. Mix well and add lemon juice and vanilla. Stir in the melted butter, mixing well. Sift flour, cornstarch and ½ cup of sugar, adding to the creamed mixture. Then add the sour cream.

Grease well a spring form or tube cake pan and pour in cake batter.

Bake in a 325 degree oven for one hour or longer. When done, shut off the oven and leave cake in oven until cold. (Cake rises while baking and then deflates slightly.) When cool, refrigerate.

Submitted by Mrs. C. W. Schmidt, Westfield, Maine

Grated Apple Cake

3 medium sized apples
1 cup flour
1 level teaspoon soda
1 teaspoon cinnamon
1 teaspoon nutmeg
½ teaspoon salt
1 egg
¼ cup cooking oil
1 cup sugar
1 cup raisins
¼ teaspoon grated orange rind

Using a large grater, grate the apples on the side of the grater with the medium round holes. This makes slivers.

Sift together the flour, soda, cinnamon, nutmeg and salt 3 times. Beat up the egg with the oil and the sugar. Alternate the egg mixture with the flour mixture then add the grated apples, the raisins and the orange rind mixed in a little flour. Pour into an 8 x 8 inch cake pan and bake in a moderate oven about 350 degrees about 35 minutes.

Submitted by Llewellyn Farnham, Scarboro, Maine

Margaret's Date Cake

1 cup sugar
¼ cup shortening
1 egg
1 cup hot water
1 cup chopped dates

½ cup chopped nuts
1 1/3 cups flour
1 teaspoon soda
½ teaspoon salt

Chop dates. Sprinkle soda over dates, add hot water and let stand until cool. Cream shortening and sugar, add egg and beat well. Add date mixture, flour and salt. Add nuts. Bake in an 8 x 8 pan at 375 degrees for 25 to 30 minutes. Cool and frost with creamy frosting as follows:

½ cup shortening (part butter)
2 tablespoons flour
¼ teaspoon salt

½ cup milk
3 cups confectioner's sugar
1 teaspoon vanilla

Melt shortening in a saucepan, blend in flour, salt and slowly stir in the milk. Bring to a boil stirring constantly. Boil 1 minute. Remove from heat, place saucepan in a pan of ice water and stir in confectioner's sugar and the vanilla. Stir until thick enough to spread.

Submitted by Mrs. Robert Wright, Hope, Maine

Aunt Lizzie's Date Cake

½ pound dates
1 cup boiling water
1 teaspoon soda
2 tablespoons butter
1 cup white sugar
1 large egg

1¾ cups flour
½ teaspoon salt
1 teaspoon vanilla
½ cup chopped nuts
   (walnuts preferred)

Cut dates in quarters and pour hot water in which soda has been dissolved, over them. Let stand while mixing other ingredients. Cream sugar and butter well, add beaten egg. Sift flour, salt and add to the creamed mixture alternately with the dates. Mix thoroughly. Add nuts which have been tossed with a teaspoon of flour. Bake at 350 degrees for about 40 minutes. Ice with a coffee or plain butter frosting.

Aunt Lizzie came from Deer Isle, Maine, and this was her favorite cake for church fairs, lodge suppers, or even when the minister came to call.

Submitted by Mrs. Doris B. Jordan, Portland, Maine

Golden Date Cake

2 cups plus 2 tablespoons
flour
1½ cups sugar
1 teaspoon salt
3 teaspoons baking powder
½ cup shortening

1 cup milk
1½ teaspoons vanilla
2 medium eggs
1 cup dates, cut fine
½ cup chopped nuts

Sift the flour with the sugar, salt, and baking powder. Add the shortening, milk and vanilla. Beat vigorously with a spoon for 2 minutes or on medium speed of electric mixer for 2 minutes. Add the eggs and dates, continue beating 2 more minutes. Fold in the nuts. This will make 2 round 8-inch layers or an oblong 13 x 9. Grease and flour pans. Bake in a 375 degree oven for 30 to 35 minutes.

Submitted by Donna Smith, Corinna, Maine

Rhubarb Upside Down Cake

3 cups rhubarb (diced)
¾ cup sugar
¾ cup miniature marshmal-
lows
¼ cup butter
1 cup sugar

1 egg
2 cups flour
2 teaspoons baking powder
¼ teaspoon salt
¾ cup milk
½ teaspoon vanilla

In an iron skillet, mix the rhubarb, sugar and marshmallows. Cream together butter, sugar and egg. Sift dry ingredients and add alternately with milk to the creamed mixture. Add vanilla and pour batter on top of rhubarb in the skillet. Bake at 350 degrees for 40 minutes or until done.

Submitted by Mrs. Ralph Ranger, Fairfield, Maine

Nut Cake

2 cups flour
1 1/3 cups sugar
2½ teaspoons baking powder
¾ teaspoon salt
½ cup shortening

2/3 cup milk
1½ teaspoons vanilla
2 unbeaten eggs
¼ cup milk
½ cup chopped nuts

Sift flour with sugar, baking powder and salt. Add shortening and 2/3 cup of milk with the vanilla. Beat all together for 2 minutes. Add the 2 unbeaten eggs and ¼ cup of milk and beat 2 more minutes. Add nuts. Bake in a 9 x 9 pan for 25 minutes at 350 degrees.

Submitted by Mrs. Myra D. White, Fort Fairfield, Maine

Sauerkraut Cake

2/3 cup butter or margarine
1½ cups white sugar
3 eggs
2¼ cups flour
1 teaspoon soda
1 teaspoon baking powder

1 teaspoon salt
½ cup cocoa
1 cup cold water
2/3 cup drained and rinsed
    sauerkraut (chopped)

Cream butter and sugar together, add eggs, one at a time and beat well. Sift flour, soda, baking powder, salt and cocoa together and add to the creamed mixture alternately with the cold water. Fold in sauerkraut last. Cook at 350 degrees 30 minutes or until done.

Submitted by Mrs. Annie Rogers, Thomaston, Maine

Spud and Spice Cake

1¾ cups sugar
1 cup cold mashed potato
¾ cup soft shortening
3 unbeaten eggs
2 cups sifted flour
1 teaspoon cinnamon

½ teaspoon nutmeg
½ teaspoon salt
1 teaspoon soda
1 cup buttermilk or sour milk
¾ cup walnuts, chopped

Cream together the sugar, potato and shortening, add eggs one at a time. Sift together the flour, cinnamon, nutmeg and salt. Add the soda to the milk and add alternately to the creamed mixture with the flour mixture. Mix in walnuts last. Cook in a 350 degree oven approximately 40 minutes or until done. Frost with the following frosting.

FROSTING

¼ cup butter
¾ cup packed brown sugar

3 tablespoons milk
Powdered sugar

Melt the butter in saucepan, stir in the brown sugar and cook over low heat 2 minutes. Add the milk and bring to a full boil; cool to lukewarm. Mix with enough powdered sugar to spread easily on cake.

Submitted by Mrs. Pauline Timberlake, Turner, Maine

Carrot Cake

4 eggs
2 cups sugar
1½ cups cooking oil
2 cups grated raw carrots
2 cups flour

1 teaspoon cinnamon
1 teaspoon soda
1 teaspoon baking powder
½ teaspoon salt

Beat the four eggs, then beat in the 2 cups sugar, 1½ cups cooking oil. Stir in the 2 cups grated raw carrots. Sift dry ingredients together and stir in above mixture. Bake in two 9-inch round pans. Bake at 375 degrees for about 25 minutes or until done.

FILLING AND FROSTING

½ cup oleo
1 pound (scant) confectioner's sugar
1 8-ounce package cream cheese

1 teaspoon vanilla
¾ cup nuts

Cream the first three ingredients, add vanilla and put between layers and on top of cake, spreading nuts over the top.
Submitted by Mrs. Mahlon Salsbury, Ellsworth Falls, Maine

Christmas Nut Loaf

1½ cups flour
1½ cups sugar
1 teaspoon baking powder
1 teaspoon salt
2 pounds pitted dates or
1 pound dates and
1 pound candied fruit
2 cups Brazil nuts

4 cups walnuts
2 cups pecans
1 8-ounce bottle red maraschino cherries
1 8-ounce bottle green maraschino cherries
5 large eggs
1 teaspoon vanilla

Sift together in large bowl the flour, sugar, baking powder and salt. Add — do not chop — the dates, fruit and nuts, drain the cherries and add. Stir with flour mixture to coat nuts and fruits. Beat the eggs with the vanilla and mix in with flour and nut mixture with large spoon or hands, being careful not to break cherries and nuts. Put into pans or molds and bake in a 275 degree oven for 1½ hours.
Submitted by Mrs. Stacy A. Meister, Washburn, Maine

Plantation Cake

½ cup sugar
½ cup shortening
½ teaspoon soda
1 teaspoon grated lemon rind
½ cup molasses
2 cups sifted flour

1 teaspoon salt
1 teaspoon baking powder or
1½ teaspoons cream of tartar
1½ teaspoons cinnamon
2 eggs
2/3 cup milk

Cream together the sugar, shortening, soda and lemon rind. Add molasses. Sift flour, salt, baking powder and cinnamon together. Stir ½ cup of the flour mixture into the creamed mixture, beat in eggs. Add milk alternately with remaining flour mixture. Beat about ½ minute. Bake in two greased layer pans, lightly floured, in a 350 degree oven about 25 minutes or until well done.

Submitted by Mrs. Joseph Couture, Jr., Oakland, Maine

Grandma Joy's Jelly Cake

½ cup butter
1 cup sugar
Yolks of 2 eggs
½ cup milk
1½ cups flour

1 teaspoon cream of tartar
½ teaspoon soda
Pinch of salt
2 egg whites

Combine first 4 ingredients, beating until smooth. Add sifted dry ingredients and beat well. Add whites of eggs stiffly beaten and 1 teaspoon vanilla. Bake in 350 degree oven in two layer tins. When cool, put layers of cake together, using apple jelly or raspberry jam. Dust top and sides with sifted confectioner's sugar.

Submitted by Inga F. Chase, Glen Cove, Maine

Crumb Cake

½ cup shortening
1 cup sugar
2 cups flour
1 teaspoon nutmeg
1 teaspoon cloves
1 teaspoon cinnamon

1 egg
2 tablespoons molasses
1 cup sour milk
1 teaspoon soda
½ teaspoon salt

Make a crumb mixture with the shortening, sugar, flour and spices. Set aside 1 cup of this crumb for topping. To the rest of the mixture add the egg, molasses, sour milk with the soda added, and the salt. Pour into a 9 x 13 pan and cover the top with the cup of crumb mixture. Bake for 30 minutes at 350 degrees.

Submitted by Ada E. Shaw, Frye, Maine

Spice Cake and Frosting

½ cup shortening
½ teaspoon salt
¾ teaspoon ginger
1 teaspoon cinnamon
½ teaspoon cloves
½ teaspoon allspice
1 teaspoon vanilla

1 cup brown sugar
1 unbeaten egg
2½ cups sifted flour
½ teaspoon soda
2 teaspoons baking powder
1 cup thick sour milk

Blend shortening, salt, spices and vanilla; add sugar gradually and beat well. Add egg and beat. Sift the flour with the soda and baking powder; add flour to creamed mixture, alternating with the milk, mixing after each addition until the batter is smooth. Bake in a 10 x 10 inch pan in a slow oven, 325 degrees, for 45 to 50 minutes or until the cake tests done. Top with the following frosting.

FROSTING

1 cup brown sugar
3 tablespoons cocoa
3 tablespoons butter
½ teaspoon salt

¼ cup milk
1½ cups sifted confectioner's
sugar
1 teaspoon vanilla

Combine sugar, cocoa, shortening, salt and milk in a saucepan and bring to a boil, stirring three minutes. Boil slowly three more minutes. Cool until lukewarm, add powdered sugar and vanilla and beat until thick enough to spread.

Submitted by Mrs. Clarence W. Spiller, Bridgton, Maine

Golden Sponge Cake

5 eggs, separated
1 cup sugar
¼ teaspoon salt
¼ teaspoon cream of tartar

Juice and rind from 1 orange
or lemon
1 cup sifted flour

Beat the 5 egg whites, salt and cream of tartar until foamy. Continue beating at medium speed until the mixture is stiff enough to hold up in peaks, but not dry. Add ½ cup of the sugar, beating rapidly.

In another bowl, beat until thick and light the 5 egg yolks, the remaining ½ cup of sugar, 1½ teaspoons of orange or lemon rind, grated, and 4 tablespoons of the juice. Add the flour and stir until blended. Fold the yolk mixture into the whites and blend well. Bake in an ungreased tube pan in a 325 degree oven for 1 hour or until it tests done.

Submitted by Mrs. Lloyd E. Fernald, Franklin, Maine

Brother pig was very important in the cooking native to Maine. Not much could be made without good old sowbelly. There was almost always a brine barrel in the cellar or shed. Eaten by itself, fried to a crusty brown, swimming in its own gravy, it is quite a tasty dish but its biggest role is in enhancing the natural flavors of other foods. No real chowder or stew could be made without it. Of course, salt pork is the main flavoring ingredient in baked beans. Pork, both fresh and cured, was and is a good robust dish but it was the fat of the pig, salted and plain that was the indispensable ingredient in the bulk of our native dishes. Salt pork is especially good when stewed with wild greens such as the common dandelion. This dish is considered quite a delicacy by most folks in Maine.

Josie Barker's Sponge Cake

4 eggs
1 teaspoon vinegar

1 cup sugar
1 cup flour

Beat the egg yolks, add the vinegar and sugar. Beat the egg whites to a stiff froth and add to the yolks. Add the flour. Bake in a 350 degree oven about 35 minutes.

Josie Barker lived a long life. She was 94 when she died. Her friends were numberless. She always said, "Never did anyone have as good friends as I have." She loved to do good things for her friends and she often came bringing a cake. In fact, this cake might well be called, "Josie's Friendship Cake." It is delicious and easy to make.

Submitted by Esther E. Wood, Gorham, Maine

Hot Milk Sponge Cake

2 eggs
1 cup sugar
½ teaspoon vanilla
1 cup flour

1 teaspoon baking powder
¼ teaspoon salt
½ cup milk
Dab of butter

Beat eggs until very thick and light, gradually add sugar and vanilla beating constantly. Add sifted flour, baking powder and salt. Bring milk and butter to a boil. Add to cake batter and stir quickly. Bake in 9 x 5 x 2 inch pan at 325 degrees for about 45 minutes.

Submitted by Mrs. Etta I. Jones, Auburn, Maine

Ellen's Molasses Sponge Cake

½ cup shortening
½ cup sugar
1 egg
1 cup molasses
Dessert spoon of soda (2 scant teaspoons)

2½ cups flour
1 teaspoon salt
1 teaspoon cloves
1 teaspoon cinnamon
1 teaspoon nutmeg
1 cup boiling water

Cream shortening and sugar. Add egg and molasses. Sift dry ingredients together. Add to first mixture and beat thoroughly and then add boiling water. Beat again. Bake in moderate oven, 350-375 degrees.

Submitted by Evelyne Ware, Skowhegan, Maine

Oatmeal Mocha Cake

2 tablespoons instant coffee
1½ cups boiling water
1 cup rolled oats
¾ cup soft shortening
1 cup white sugar
1 cup brown sugar

2 eggs
1½ teaspoons vanilla
2 cups sifted all-purpose flour
1¼ teaspoons soda
¾ teaspoon salt
3 tablespoons cocoa

ICING

1½ tablespoons butter
1 cup confectioner's sugar
Dash of salt

½ teaspoon vanilla
1½ tablespoons liquid coffee

Stir together the 2 tablespoons of instant coffee, the rolled oats and the 1½ cups of boiling water. Cook for 5 minutes and let cool.

Cream together the shortening, sugars, eggs and vanilla. Sift the flour with the soda, salt, and cocoa. Combine all mixtures and pour into a well greased 9 x 13 pan and bake at 350 degrees 50 to 55 minutes.

Combine ingredients for the icing and beat well. Drizzle over the cake.

Submitted by Mrs. Allan Wood, Woodland, Maine

Brown Sugar Cupcakes

1/3 cup butter or other
    shortening
1 cup brown sugar
1 egg, separated
½ cup sour milk

1 teaspoon soda
1½ cups flour
½ teaspoon salt
½ cup nuts
1 teaspoon vanilla

Cream together the sugar, butter and egg yolk. Sift flour with salt and soda. Add alternately to the creamed mixture with the sour milk. Add nuts, cut fine and vanilla. Last fold in the stiffly beaten egg white. Bake at 350 degrees for 25 minutes.

NEVER FAIL FROSTING

½ cup brown sugar
2 tablespoons butter
¼ cup water

1 square chocolate
1 teaspoon vanilla
Powdered sugar

Boil brown sugar, butter, water, chocolate and vanilla altogether for 3 minutes. Cool awhile and mix enough powdered sugar to make a smooth spread.

Submitted by Ann Condon, Thomaston, Maine

Orange Fruit Cake

1½ cups sugar
½ cup lard
1 cup sour milk
2 cups flour
1 teaspoon soda

Pinch of salt
1 teaspoon vanilla
1 orange
1 cup raisins

Take ½ orange and squeeze 2 tablespoons juice for frosting. Grind rest of orange with the cup of raisins, set this aside. Cream 1 cup sugar and lard together; sift dry ingredients and add alternately to the creamed mixture with the sour milk. Mix in the raisin mixture and bake in a 350 degree oven for approximately 40 minutes or until it tests done. Mix orange juice with ½ cup of sugar, spread on hot cake and put back in oven and let glaze.
Submitted by Mrs. Elizabeth Collins, West Forke, Maine

Mincemeat Cake

1¾ cups sugar
2 cups water
1 9-ounce package mince-
meat
¾ cup cooking oil

3¼ cups sifted flour
2 teaspoons soda
1 teaspoon salt
½ cup walnut meats

Put sugar, water, mincemeat and oil in saucepan and boil 5 minutes. Stir often. Remove from stove and cool. Sift the flour, salt and soda together and add to the mincemeat mixture. Mix well and add walnuts. Bake in 325 degree oven 40 minutes.
Submitted by Mildred L. Hooper, Shapleigh, Maine

Golden Spice Cake

½ cup cooking oil
1 cup sugar
2 eggs
1 tablespoon molasses
1 cup sour milk
2 cups flour

½ teaspoon salt
¼ teaspoon nutmeg
½ teaspoon cinnamon
½ teaspoon cloves
1 teaspoon soda

Put cooking oil into bowl, add sugar and mix. Add eggs and beat well. Mix in molasses. Sift dry ingredients and add alternately to sugar mixture with the sour milk. Beat well. Bake in greased pan 350 degrees 45 to 50 minutes. When cool, frost with butter frosting. About ¼ teaspoon instant coffee added to frosting makes it delicious.
Submitted by Mrs. Ida Mercier, Skowhegan, Maine

Ribbon Cake

Part 1

2 cups sugar
3 eggs
2/3 cup butter
1 cup sweet milk

3 cups flour
2 teaspoons cream of tartar
1 teaspoon soda

PART 2

1 tablespoon molasses
1 cup raisins

Allspice and nutmeg to taste
1 tablespoon flour

Combine ingredients of Part 1 by creaming sugar, eggs and butter together. Sift dry ingredients together and add to the creamed mixture alternately with the milk. Flavor with lemon. Pour two-thirds of this batter into 2 8-inch layer cake pans. Add the ingredients of Part 2 to the remainder and pour into a third 8-inch pan. Bake at 375 degrees. Put the three layers together with jelly.

Submitted by Mrs. Edith Chester, Waterville, Maine

Forty Day Cake

2 cups sugar
2 cups sour milk or buttermilk
2 rounded teaspoons soda
1 lb. seedless raisins (ground)

1 cup melted lard
1 teaspoon salt
1 teaspoon cinnamon
1 teaspoon cloves
4½ cups sifted flour

Mix together sugar and milk with soda dissolved in milk. Add salt and spices, lard and ground raisins. If raisins are sticky mix with lard to separate them before adding to other mixture. Mix in flour a little at a time. Pour into greased bread tins for three small cakes or a large angel cake pan. Bake in a 325 degree oven for 1½ hours. A large jar of candied fruit and one cup of chopped nuts may be added if desired.

This is a very old favorite used in wood camps when I used to cook there. It will keep for weeks. I also used to send it over seas to my sons during World War II. If every thing else in the box was spoiled this was always good.

Submitted by Mrs. John Porter, Lowell, Maine

3 Minute Spice Cake

1 1/3 cups sugar
2 eggs
2 cups sifted cake flour or all purpose
1 teaspoon baking soda
½ teaspoon salt
¾ teaspoon cinnamon
¼ teaspoon cloves
1 teaspoon allspice
½ teaspoon nutmeg
¼ cup vinegar
½ cup milk
1 teaspoon vanilla
½ cup shortening

Beat together the sugar and eggs for 1 minute. Sift together the flour, baking soda, salt, cinnamon, cloves, allspice and nutmeg and add to the sugar and eggs mixture. Combine the vinegar, milk and vanilla. Add ½ of the liquid and all the shortening to the sugar and flour mixture and beat vigorously 1 minute. Add remaining liquid and beat one minute. Bake at 375 degrees 25 to 30 minutes. Makes 2 8-inch layers.

Submitted by Ruth Russell, Rockland, Maine

Raisin Shortcake

1 cup flour
1 cup sugar
2 teaspoons baking powder
¼ teaspoon salt
1 scant cup seedless raisins
½ cup milk
1 cup brown sugar
2 tablespoons butter
2 cups boiling water

Sift together the flour, sugar, baking powder and salt. Add the raisins and milk and stir into the flour mixture. Put the brown sugar, butter and boiling water into an 8 x 8 baking dish and bring to a boil. Pour the above batter into this mixture and bake at 350 degrees for 30-40 minutes. Serve with cream or ice cream.

Submitted by Mrs. Roy Barteaux, Brewer, Maine

Cheap Chocolate Cake

2 squares chocolate
1 tablespoon butter
1 cup sugar
1 egg yolk
1 1/3 cups flour
1 teaspoon salt
1 cup sweet milk
½ teaspoon soda, dissolved in 1 tablespoon hot water

Melt chocolate and butter together over hot water. Take from stove and add sugar and egg yolk, beat well. Sift flour with salt and add to chocolate mixture alternately with milk. Add soda last. Bake in 350 degree oven until done — approximately 35 minutes.

Submitted by Mrs. John Ackley, East Machias, Maine

Throw Together Chocolate Cake

1 egg
½ cup cocoa
½ cup melted shortening
1½ cups sifted flour
1 cup sugar

1 teaspoon soda
½ teaspoon salt
1 teaspoon vanilla
½ cup sour milk
½ cup boiling water

No matter what order you use in putting this cake together, it always comes out good. Bake in a 350 degree oven about 45 minutes.

Submitted by Mrs. Ina Firth, Rockland, Maine

Chocolate Cake

1 cup sugar
⅛ pound butter or oleo
2 eggs
½ cup cold water
1 cup flour

1 teaspoon cream of tartar
½ teaspoon soda
¼ teaspoon salt
2 squares melted chocolate
1 teaspoon vanilla

Beat whites of 2 eggs and set aside. Cream sugar and butter together, add the yolks of the 2 eggs mixed with the cold water. Sift together the flour, cream of tartar, soda and salt, and mix alternately with the creamed mixture. Add melted chocolate and vanilla. Fold in the whites of eggs last and bake in a 400 degree oven for about 30 to 35 minutes.

Submitted by Mrs. Birdene Shackleton, Boothbay, Maine

Chocolate Potato Cake

½ pound butter
2 cups sugar
4 eggs beaten
3 ounces melted chocolate
1 teaspoon cinnamon
¼ teaspoon nutmeg

1 cup cold mashed potatoes
2 cups sifted flour
1 teaspoon baking soda
1 cup sour milk
1 cup coarsely chopped nuts

Cream the butter, add sugar gradually beating until light and fluffy. Add eggs and beat well; add the chocolate, potatoes, cinnamon and nutmeg. Sift flour with baking soda and add to the creamed mixture alternately with the sour milk. Fold in nuts last. Pour in deep buttered baking pan. Bake in a 350 degree oven 45 minutes. This makes a large cake.

Submitted by Mrs. Eula H. Foss, Solon, Maine

Fudge Cake

1 cup sugar
½ cup shortening
1 egg
½ cup sour milk
1 teaspoon soda

1½ cups sifted flour
2 tablespoons cocoa
1 teaspoon vanilla
¼ cup boiling water

Cream sugar and shortening together, beat in egg. Add soda to sour milk and set aside. Sift flour with cocoa and add to the creamed mixture alternately with the sour milk. Add vanilla and boiling water last. Pour in layer cake pans and bake for 35 minutes in 350 degree oven. When cool, use following filling:

FILLING

1 cup water
2/3 cup sugar
1 tablespoon cocoa

1 tablespoon butter
2 tablespoons cornstarch

Boil until thick and add vanilla to flavor.

Submitted by Mrs. Marian Calligan, Grand Lake Stream, Maine

Fudge Cake

1 cup shortening (soft)
2 cups sugar
2 eggs
1 cup sour milk
2 teaspoons vanilla

2¼ cups flour
½ cup cocoa
2 teaspoons soda
¼ teaspoon salt
1 cup boiling water

Place shortening, sugar, eggs, sour milk and vanilla in bowl and stir well. Sift together 3 times the cocoa, salt, flour and soda. Add to first mixture and beat thoroughly. Add the boiling water and mix until smooth. Bake in 3 well-greased 8-inch pans at 350 degrees, 25 to 30 minutes. (Remember that over-cooking impairs the flavor of chocolate.) This is a dark and moist cake.

Submitted by Mrs. Marie Boucher, East Lebanon, Maine

Salad Dressing Cake

2 cups flour
1 cup sugar
4 heaping tablespoons cocoa
2 level teaspoons soda

Little salt
1 cup salad dressing
1 cup cold water
1 teaspoon vanilla

Sift dry ingredients together three times. Mix in the salad dressing, water and vanilla and beat well.

Submitted by Mrs. Stella Hollister, Hartland, Maine

Chocolate Cake Deluxe

2/3 cup soft shortening
1 2/3 cups sugar
3 eggs
2¼ cups sifted flour
2/3 cup cocoa
¼ teaspoon baking powder

1¼ teaspoons soda
1 teaspoon salt
1 1/3 cups water
1 teaspoon instant coffee
1½ teaspoons vanilla

Cream shortening with sugar, add eggs and beat well. Sift flour with cocoa, baking powder, soda and salt. Mix water with coffee. Mix flour mixture alternately with water to the creamed mixture, add vanilla. Bake in oblong or layer pans in a 350 degree oven for 30 minutes.

Submitted by Mrs. Clytie Fall, Berwick, Maine

Molasses Chocolate Cake

1 cup sugar
½ cup shortening
2 eggs well beaten
½ cup molasses
1 cup boiling water

1 teaspoon soda
1¾ cups sifted flour
3 tablespoons cocoa
½ teaspoon salt
1 teaspoon vanilla

Cream together the sugar and shortening, add the eggs and beat well. Add molasses and the soda which has been dissolved in the boiling water. Sift dry ingredients together and add to above mixture. Add vanilla. Bake in 2 well greased layer cake pans in moderate oven 350 degrees about 30 minutes. Cake remains moist a long time.

Submitted by Mrs. Olive Speed, Carmel, Maine

Never Fail Chocolate Cake

1 cup sugar
1 egg
¼ cup melted shortening
4 tablespoons cocoa
¼ cup hot water

1 teaspoon baking soda
¾ cup sour milk
1¼ cups flour
½ teaspoon salt
1 teaspoon vanilla

Beat egg and sugar, add melted shortening. Dissolve cocoa in hot water and add to first mixture. Dissolve soda in sour milk and add. Sift flour and salt into all and beat well. Add vanilla last. Bake at 375 degrees for 25 to 30 minutes or until done.

Submitted by Mrs. Mabelle S. Miller, Bangor, Maine

Spanish Chocolate Cake

1 cup sugar
3 ounces melted chocolate
1 egg yolk
1 cup milk
Vanilla
1 cup sugar
½ cup butter

2 eggs
2½ cups flour
½ cup sweet milk
1 teaspoon soda dissolved in
   hot water (just enough to
   dissolve soda)

Melt the chocolate over hot water, stir in the sugar, yolk of egg and one cup milk. Cook until thick, flavor with vanilla. While chocolate mixture is cooling, cream 1 cup sugar with the butter, beat in eggs. Add flour to the creamed mixture alternately with the milk. Add dissolved soda. Combine the two mixtures and bake in layer tins in a 350 degree oven approximately 30 minutes. Frost on top and between layers with fudge or white icing.

Submitted by Roger E. Hanscom, Newry, Maine

Wowie Cake

1 cup sugar
1½ cups flour
½ teaspoon salt
¼ cup cocoa
1 teaspoon soda

1 tablespoon vinegar
1/3 cup cooking oil
1 teaspoon vanilla
1 cup cold water

Sift into ungreased 8 x 8 inch pan the sugar, flour, salt, cocoa and soda. Add the vinegar, cooking oil, vanilla and water. Mix until smooth and well blended. Scrape sides if necessary. Bake in a 350 degree oven 35 minutes.

Submitted by Olena V. Taylor, Anson, Maine

Chocolate Cake

1½ cups sugar
1/3 cup shortening
1 cup sour milk
2 cups flour
1/3 cup cocoa

1 teaspoon soda
1 teaspoon salt
½ cup boiling water
1 teaspoon vanilla

Cream sugar and shortening; add sour milk and vanilla. Stir in flour sifted with the cocoa, soda and salt. Beat in last the ½ cup of boiling water. Bake in a 350 degree oven about 40 minutes.

Submitted by Mrs. John A. Mann, Surry, Maine

Peanut Butter Cake

1 cup sugar
¼ cup shortening
¼ cup peanut butter
1 egg
1 cup sour milk

1 teaspoon soda
1½ cups flour
½ teaspoon salt
1 teaspoon vanilla

Cream the sugar, shortening and peanut butter together; then add the egg and continue to beat until nice and light. Add the soda to the sour milk and add to the creamed mixture. Sift the dry ingredients together and add to the above creamed mixture. Flavor with the vanilla. Grease and flour an 8 x 8 pan. Bake in a 375 degree oven for 35 minutes.

FROSTING

1 large teaspoon butter
1 tablespoon peanut butter

Little hot water
Confectioner's sugar

Cream butter, peanut butter and water together, add enough confectioner's sugar to make a spreading consistency.

Submitted by Eaino Heikkenine, South Paris, Maine

Chocolate Date Cake

1 cup chopped dates
1 cup hot water
1 teaspoon soda
2/3 cup shortening
1 cup sugar
2 eggs, unbeaten
1¾ cups sifted flour

1 tablespoon cocoa
½ teaspoon salt
1 teaspoon vanilla
1 cup semi-sweet chocolate
  pieces
½ cup chopped walnuts

Combine dates, hot water and soda, set aside while mixing the rest of the cake. Blend shortening with sugar and eggs, until very light and fluffy. Add the date mixture alternately with the flour which has been sifted with the cocoa and salt. Stir in the vanilla. Add ½ of the chocolate bits and the nuts. Pour into a greased 9 x 13 baking pan and sprinkle remaining ½ cup of bits over top of batter. Bake in a 350 degree oven about 40 minutes.

This cake makes its own frosting, travels well and will keep for days.

Submitted by Mrs. Fern Cummings, Edinburg, Maine

Aaron's Bundles

½ cup white sugar
½ cup brown sugar
¾ cup shortening
1 egg beaten
3 tablespoons molasses
2¼ cups all-purpose flour
1 teaspoon soda
1 teaspoon salt

1 teaspoon cinnamon
½ teaspoon nutmeg
¼ teaspoon cloves
1 cup buttermilk
1 cup seedless raisins
(softened in boiling water
and drained)

Cream shortening, sugars, molasses and beaten egg. Sift dry ingredients together and add alternately with buttermilk, reserving ¼ cup flour to mix with drained raisins. Beat well and add raisins. Fill cupcake tins ½ full, sprinkle tops with chopped nuts (or frost with butter frosting when cool). Bake in 350 degree oven for 20 minutes.

Submitted by Mrs. Reita Holden, Thomaston, Maine

Golden Butter Cake

½ pound oleo
1 2/3 cups sugar
5 eggs

1½ cups flour
1 teaspoon vanilla or lemon
flavoring

Melt the oleo and add the sugar. Beat in the eggs, one at a time. Add flour and flavoring. Beat two minutes. Put in a greased, glass 9 x 5 loaf pan. Cook 1 hour at 350 degrees. After removing cake from pan, sprinkle with confectioner's sugar.

This recipe makes a good "camp cake" because it stays moist, does not crumble and keeps well.

Submitted by Mrs. Mabel Batty, South Thomaston, Maine

Crumb Cake (Dark)

1 cup brown sugar (light)
2 cups flour
1 teaspoon cinnamon
1 teaspoon cloves
½ cup butter

1 cup sour milk
1 teaspoon soda
1 egg
1 cup raisins

In a mixing bowl, mix the sugar, flour, spices and butter together to make a crumb texture. Take out 1 cup for topping. To the remainder, add the sour milk with the soda dissolved in it, the egg and the raisins. Pour into a greased 9 x 9 pan. Sprinkle with the cup of crumb topping. Bake at 350 degrees for 35 minutes.

Submitted by Mrs. Wallace Saunders, Bethel, Maine

Easy Fruit Cocktail Cake

2 cups flour
1 cup sugar
½ teaspoon salt
2 teaspoons soda
2 eggs

Juice from No. 303 can of
    fruit cocktail
½ cup brown sugar
½ cup chopped nuts

Put all dry ingredients into mixing bowl. Break the eggs into the dry ingredients and add the fruit juice. Beat until smooth. Fold in the fruit cocktail. Pour into greased 10 x 10 x 2 inch pan or similar sized oblong pan. Sprinkle ½ cup brown sugar and the chopped nuts over top. Bake in 350 degree oven for 40 minutes. Cover with following icing.

ICING

2/3 cup sugar
1 cup canned milk

½ stick butter or margarine

Boil ten minutes. Pour over hot cake. Leave in pan. Very tasty without icing.

Submitted by Mrs. John Person, Bangor, Maine

Butterscotch Sundae Cake

2¼ cups sifted flour
3 teaspoons baking powder
1 teaspoon salt
1¾ cups brown sugar (packed)

½ cup soft shortening
1 cup milk
1 teaspoon vanilla
½ to 2/3 cup unbeaten eggs

Sift flour, baking powder and salt into a bowl. Add brown sugar, shortening, milk and vanilla and beat 2 minutes at medium speed on electric mixer or 300 strokes by hand, scraping sides and bottom of bowl constantly to guide batter into beater; add eggs, beating 2 more minutes. Bake in a 350 degree oven 35 to 45 minutes. Frost with fluffy, white, cooked icing and dribble with Butterscotch Sundae Glaze.

BUTTERSCOTCH SUNDAE GLAZE

¼ cup brown sugar (packed)
3 tablespoons butter

2 tablespoons water

Bring all ingredients to a rolling boil in a saucepan and boil hard for 1½ minutes, without stirring. Do not overcook. Take from heat and dribble over iced cake.

Submitted by Mrs. Mary E. Hanson, Washburn, Maine

Hungry Cake

2 cups brown sugar
½ cup butter (or margarine)
2 egg yolks
2½ cups flour

1 teaspoon soda
½ teaspoon cloves
1 cup sour milk

Cream brown sugar with butter, add egg yolks and beat. Sift dry ingredients together and add to creamed mixture alternately with the sour milk. Bake in layers in 350 degree oven. Put together with following filling:

FILLING

1 cup sugar
½ cup water

2 egg whites
1 cup chopped raisins

Boil sugar and water together until it threads. Pour into beaten egg whites, add one cup chopped raisins. Beat until thick.

Submitted by Mrs. Charles R. Monteith, Rockland, Maine

Almond Cake

¾ cup butter
1 cup sugar
3 eggs
2 cups flour
2 teaspoons baking powder

½ cup sweet milk
1 lb. almonds, blanched and sliced
Vanilla

Cream butter, sugar and yolks of eggs together. Sift flour with the baking powder and add alternately to the creamed mixture with the milk. Add vanilla. Beat whites of eggs and fold in last. Stir in almonds. Save whole almonds for the top of your favorite icing. Bake in 350 degree oven.

Submitted by Mrs. Elwood S. Round, Orono, Maine

Grandmother's Sour Cream Cake

½ cup butter
1½ cups sugar
1 cup sour cream
2 cups flour

1 teaspoon soda
¼ teaspoon salt
1 tablespoon lemon flavoring
3 eggs

Cream butter and sugar. Add soda and salt to sour cream and beat into creamed mixture alternately with the flour. Beat in the eggs, one at a time. Add lemon. Bake in a greased loaf pan as for pound cake. Use a 325 degree oven and cook about an hour, or until done.

Submitted by Mrs. Alexander Stewart, Waldoboro, Maine

Pork Cake

1 lb. salt pork, ground fine	1 lb. walnuts, cut fine
1 pint boiling water	½ lb. citron, cut fine
2 cups sugar	4 cups flour
1 cup molasses	1 teaspoon cloves
2 teaspoons soda	2 teaspoons cinnamon
1 lb. raisins	1 teaspoon ginger
1 lb. currants	1 teaspoon nutmeg

Pour boiling water over the ground pork. Let cool, then add remaining ingredients. Bake very slow for two hours.

To this my mother sometimes added fruit mix, and used the cake for a fruit cake. It keeps well.

Submitted by Gladys MacIlroy, Bridgewater, Maine

Martha Washington Cake

1 cup shortening	3 cups flour
2 cups sugar	2 teaspoons baking powder
4 eggs	½ teaspoon salt
1 cup milk	2 teaspoons vanilla

Mix the shortening, sugar and egg yolks until smooth. Sift the flour, baking powder and salt together and add to the above mixture, alternately with the milk. Add vanilla. Last of all, beat the egg whites until stiff and add to the mixture, stirring only long enough to blend.

Submitted by Mrs. Wilbur Wiley, Houlton, Maine

Hardtack or Townmeeting Gingerbread

2 eggs	¼ teaspoon salt
2 cups molasses	1 teaspoon ginger
2/3 cup lard, melted	Flour to handle — 4½ cups
2/3 cup cold water	or more
1 teaspoon soda	

Dissolve soda in the cold water. Mix all ingredients and put enough flour in to handle the dough. Take 1 heaping tablespoon of dough, roll in flour, and roll between palms of hands until about 6 inches long. Place on cookie sheet and flatten with creasing pin. Bake in moderate oven. This is delicious with a glass of cold milk.

Submitted by Mrs. Theodora Hall, Waterboro, Maine

Sugar Gingerbread

1 cup sugar
¾ cup shortening
1 egg
1 teaspoon ginger
1 teaspoon salt
½ teaspoon soda
½ cup milk
2 cups flour

Mix all ingredients, spread in pan, sprinkle with sugar. Bake for 35 minutes at 350 degrees. When done, cool and cut in squares.

Submitted by Mrs. Herbert Dunham, Bryant Pond, Maine

Lasses Gingerbread

Iron fry pan or spider, used to bake the gingerbread in
1 teaspoon lard or vegetable shortening
½ cup brown sugar or maple sugar
1 tablespoon butter
½ cup molasses
1 level teaspoon soda
½ cup thick sour milk
2 cups flour
1 teaspoon ginger
Little ground cloves and salt
1 well beaten egg

Place 1 teaspoon shortening to melt in iron fry pan while you mix the batter. Dissolve soda in sour milk. Mix all ingredients together, beating well. Turn the batter into the iron pan and bake in 350 degree oven until done. The bottom will be as brown as the top.

This is a very old recipe, probably 150 years old.

Submitted by Mrs. Lillian Clarkson, Weld, Maine

Spiced Gingerbread

(This was a favorite of Lafayette's, taken from an old cookbook.)

½ cup fresh butter
½ cup brown sugar
1 cup molasses
½ cup warm milk
2 tablespoons ginger
1 teaspoon cinnamon
1 teaspoon mace
1 teaspoon nutmeg
1 wine glass of brandy (coffee may be used)
3 eggs, beaten very light
3 cups flour
Juice and rind of orange
1 teaspoon soda
Warm water
1 cup raisins

Cut the butter and sugar into a pan and beat to a cream. Add molasses and warm milk, spices and brandy or coffee. Add flour and eggs alternately to the batter. Mix in the juice and rind of orange. Dissolve soda in a little warm wtaer and add to mixture. Beat until very light. Last add raisins. Bake in a moderate oven.

Submitted by Mrs. Dorothy Edwards, Skowhegan, Maine

Gingerbread

1 cup white sugar
½ cup shortening
1 egg
½ cup molasses
1 teaspoon soda
2 cups flour
½ teaspoon cloves
½ teaspoon ginger
½ teaspoon salt
1 cup boiling water
Raisins, dates, or citron, if
    desired
2 tablespoons sugar
1 teaspoon cinnamon

Stir ingredients together and then add boiling water. If you desire, add raisins, dates or citron. Sprinkle with 2 tablespoons sugar before baking. Bake in 350 degree oven until done.

Submitted by Mrs. D. F. London, Houlton, Maine

Old-Fashioned Hard Gingerbread

2 cups flour
1½ teaspoons soda
1 teaspoon ginger or cinnamon
4 tablespoons melted shortening
3 tablespoons hot water
Molasses

In a cup put 3 tablespoons of melted shortening, 3 tablespoons hot water and fill cup with molasses. Put dry ingredients in bowl along with 1 tablespoon melted shortening. Mix. Add more flour to knead if necessary. Roll out about 8 x 10 inches. Divide dough in three sections. Bake like cookies. Cut in bars or squares while still warm.

Submitted by Mrs. John Whitaker, Gouldsboro, Maine

Grandma's Cake

1 cup molasses
1 cup sugar
1 cup sour milk (if lacking sour milk, 1 tablespoon vinegar may be added to sweet milk)
3 cups flour
½ cup butter or vegetable shortening
1 pound raisins
1 teaspoon soda
½ teaspoon cinnamon
Dash of cloves
Salt

Beat sugar and butter together, then add molasses and spices, then the sour milk in which the soda is dissolved. Add flour and last add the raisins. Bake in a 9 x 9 inch pan or in loaves, in a 350 degree oven.

Submitted by Lucille Moore, Gorham, Maine

Wild berries of all varieties were plentiful in the meadows, thickets and marshes. Cranberries, blackberries, raspberries, huckleberries, blueberries and most delicious of all, the wild strawberry, could be found just about anywhere in season. These were gathered and used in many ways, in sauces, jams, jellies, and pies. There were also a variety of spirits that enterprising souls could make from the fruit of the vine if so inclined. Cultivated berries of all varieties are common in Maine but the blueberry barrens are probably the most productive and provide the basic ingredient for the numerous blueberry recipes to be found in our cookbooks. Each summer there are blueberry festivals during the harvest where one can fill up on muffins, pancakes, cakes, pies, tarts and other dishes made from this tasty little berry. The main part of the crop are wild lowbush berries which have an excellent texture, flavor and color. When passing an apparently wild field or meadow which is all lined off with stakes and string, you can be sure that it is a Maine blueberry field ready for harvest.

Old-Fashioned Gingerbread

1½ teaspoons soda
2 cups flour
½ teaspoon salt
1 teaspoon ginger
1 teaspoon cinnamon
½ teaspoon cloves
½ cup sugar
½ cup shortening
1 egg
1 cup molasses
1 cup hot water

Cream shortening and sugar. Add egg. Measure and sift dry ingredients. Mix hot water and molasses together and then add alternately with dry ingredients. Bake at 375 degrees.

Submitted by Emily Sadler, West Jonesport, Maine

Nellie's Gingerbread

½ cup sugar
½ cup shortening
1 egg, beaten
1 cup molasses
2½ cups flour, sifted with
1½ teaspoons soda
1 teaspoon lemon extract
½ teaspoon ginger
Salt
1 cup hot coffee

Mix in order given. Add the coffee last.

Submitted by Eleanor M. Curtis, Enfield, Maine

Bride's Gingerbread

1 egg
¼ cup sugar
¼ cup molasses
¼ cup liquid shortening
¼ cup sour milk
1 cup flour
1 teaspoon baking soda
1 teaspoon ginger

Mix in order listed and pour mixture into greased 8-inch square pan. Bake for 20-25 minutes in 350 degree oven.

Submitted by Joan Henley, Bryant Pond, Maine

Great-great-grandmother's Muster Gingerbread

1½ cups molasses
2/3 cup shortening
1 heaping teaspoon of soda
1 cup hot water
1 tablespoon of vinegar
Ginger to taste
Enough flour to make a soft dough

Dissolve soda in the cup of hot water. Mix with rest of ingredients. Knead as little as possible and roll out in thin sheets. Bake in a 350 degree oven.

Submitted by Mrs. John F. Wood, Gorham, Maine

Never Fail Frosting

½ stick margarine
1 square chocolate
1 cup sugar

¼ cup milk
1 teaspoon vanilla

Melt margarine and chocolate in saucepan, add sugar and milk. Bring to a rolling boil and boil slowly for 2 minutes. Take from heat and add vanilla. Cool and beat. Spread quickly when it shows signs of thickening.
Submitted by Mrs. Birdene Shackleton, Boothbay, Maine

Decorator's Icing

2 cups confectioner's sugar
½ cup vegetable shortening
¼ teaspoon glycerine

½ teaspoon vanilla
1½ to 2 tablespoons milk
¼ teaspoon salt

Beat all together until the frosting stands in stiff peaks.
Submitted by Mrs. R. Fred Harmon, Caribou, Maine

Pineapple Topping for Angel Food Cake

1 small can crushed pineapple, drained
1 package instant vanilla pudding

Small jar cherries
½ to 1 cup nuts, chopped
½ pint cream

Drain pineapple well and add the instant pudding mix. Mix well. Add cherries and nuts. Whip the cream and fold into the pineapple pudding mix. This is a very good topping. Use more cherries if you prefer.
Submitted by Mrs. Raymond Doughty, Howland, Maine

Apple Pie Crumb Topping

½ cup margarine
½ cup brown sugar

1 cup flour

Mix together to crumb stage, pat on top of apple pie and bake.
Submitted by Donna Smith, Corinna, Maine

7 Minute Fluffy White Frosting

¾ cup sugar
2 tablespoons cold water
1 egg white, unbeaten
⅛ teaspoon salt
1 teaspoon white corn syrup

⅛ teaspoon cream of tartar
½ teaspoon vanilla
Nuts or grated coconut
(optional)

Place in double boiler over boiling water, the sugar, cold water, egg white, salt, syrup and cream of tartar. Beat constantly with rotary or electric beater until mixture holds peaks. Remove from heat and blend in the vanilla. Cool before spreading. Sprinkle coconut or nuts over top, if desired.

Submitted by Mrs. John Ackley, East Machias, Maine

Whipped Frosting

½ cup margarine
½ cup shortening
1 cup granulated sugar

1 teaspoon vanilla
4 teaspoons flour
1 cup milk

Blend margarine and shortening about 4 minutes in mixer. Add sugar and blend some more, then add vanilla. Add flour to milk and cook until it thickens, stirring so it won't become lumpy. Cool and then add to creamed mixture. Beat for about 4 minutes more.

Submitted by Mrs. Francina Pelletier, Calais, Maine

Butterscotch Frosting

½ cup brown sugar
6 tablespoons margarine
1/3 cup milk

¼ teaspoon salt
1½ cups confectioner's sugar
½ teaspoon vanilla

Melt margarine and brown sugar slowly, add milk and boil for 2 minutes. Chill thoroughly — add confectioner's sugar and salt. Beat at high speed on electric mixer until thick enough to spread. Add vanilla.

Submitted by Ruth Russell, Rockland, Maine

Coffee Icing

1½ cups powdered sugar
2 heaping tablespoons vegetable
shortening

¼ teaspoon salt
Hot instant coffee

Combine first three ingredients with just enough instant coffee to mix.

Submitted by Mrs. Louise Fleming, Howland, Maine

Michigan Fudge Frosting

½ cup brown sugar
¼ cup water
1 square chocolate
⅛ teaspoon salt

2 tablespoons butter
Powdered sugar
1 teaspoon vanilla
½ cup nuts, chopped

Mix first 5 ingredients together in a saucepan and bring to a boil. Boil for 3 minutes, stirring constantly to prevent sticking. Cool slightly. Add enough powdered sugar to spread. Add vanilla and nuts.

Submitted by Mrs. Philip Hansen, Westbrook, Maine

Quick Caramel Frosting

4 tablespoons butter
¾ cup brown sugar
6 tablespoons cream

1 cup powdered sugar
(approximately)
½ teaspoon vanilla

Melt butter in saucepan, add brown sugar, melt again. Add cream and bring to a vigorous boil, boil 1 minute. Remove and let cool a few minutes then add powdered sugar slowly, beating constantly. Add vanilla and more powdered sugar if necessary until frosting is of spreading consistency.

Submitted by Mrs. Amy S. Russell, Fort Fairfield, Maine

Frosting

1 cup raisins, chopped fine
1 cup sugar

½ cup water
1 egg

Combine sugar and water and bring to a boil. Beat egg to a stiff fluff and add to the raisins. Pour into the boiling sugar solution slowly and cook until it "begins to hair." Spread on cake.

This is excellent on a plain white cake.

Submitted by Mrs. Norris H. Moore, Burlington, Maine

Light Fudge

3 cups white sugar
¼ pound oleo
1 (6 ounce) can of milk
2/3 cup peanut butter

2 heaping tablespoons marshmallow fluff
1 teaspoon vanilla
½ cup nut meats

Mix sugar, milk and oleo; bring to a boil and boil for 5 minutes. Remove from heat and add the peanut butter, marshmallow, vanilla and nuts. Beat until well mixed. Pour into a greased 8 x 8 pan. Cut when cool.

Submitted by Mrs. Carl Braley, Newport, Maine

Caramels

3 cups granulated sugar
4½ cups heavy cream
1 bottle red label Karo syrup

1 tablespoon vanilla
1½ cups nut meats

In a heavy kettle combine the sugar, syrup and 1½ cups of the cream. Mix and cook to 232 degrees on your candy thermometer. Remove the kettle from the heat, remove the thermometer and stir in another 1½ cups of cream and again cook to 232 degrees; then add the last 1½ cups cream and cook to 242 degrees. This candy requires constant stirring to prevent sticking. Add the vanilla during the last cooking. Remove from heat and add the nut meats. Pour into a buttered pan 8 x 18 x 1. Cool. Turn from the pan onto a board and cut in squares with a heavy knife. Wrap in wax paper. Yield 3½ pounds of candy.

Submitted by Mildred B. Schrumpf, Orono, Maine

Walnut Clusters

¼ cup soft butter
1 egg, unbeaten
1½ squares unsweetened
  melted chocolate
½ teaspoon salt
½ cup white sugar

¼ teaspoon baking powder
1¼ teaspoons vanilla
½ cup sifted flour
2 cups` coarsely broken
  walnuts

Cream butter and sugar until fluffy; add egg, well beaten. Add vanilla. Stir in melted chocolate, then flour, baking powder and salt. Add walnuts. Drop by teaspoon on a greased sheet. Bake in 350 degree oven for 10 minutes. Cool on rack.

Submitted by Katherine F. Crockett, Machias, Maine

Brown Sugar Fudge

1 pound brown sugar
½ cup milk
¼ pound margarine

¾ cup peanut butter
1 teaspoon vanilla
1 pound powdered sugar

Boil brown sugar, milk and margarine two minutes. Remove from heat and add the peanut butter and vanilla. Mix well. Now add the powdered sugar and beat until smooth. This will harden fast so one must work fast. Spread in pan and cool. Makes a large amount.

Submitted by Donna Smith, Corinna, Maine

Chocolate Fudge

4½ cups sugar
½ pound butter
1 large can evaporated milk
1 giant size sweet chocolate candy bar
1 giant size bag chocolate chips
1 jar marshmallow fluff
1 cup nuts
Vanilla

Combine sugar, butter and milk. Cook for 20 minutes or until it forms a soft ball when tried in cold water, stirring constantly. Remove from heat and add the sweet chocolate bar, chips, marshmallow, nuts and vanilla. Beat until smooth. Pour into a well buttered 13⅛ x 9½ x 2-inch pan. Yields over 6 pounds of candy. This keeps very well wrapped up and put in freezer.

Submitted by Eva Meservey, Jefferson, Maine

Chocolate Fudge Supreme

2 cups sugar
3 teaspoons butter
¼ cup corn syrup
½ cup cream
½ cup milk
½ cup walnuts, chopped
2 squares baking chocolate, melted
1 teaspoon vanilla

Boil all ingredients together except nuts, chocolate and vanilla. Cook to soft ball stage, 238 to 240 degrees. Stir occasionally to keep from burning. Pour half in one dish, add nuts and ½ teaspoon vanilla. Add the melted chocolate and ½ teaspoon vanilla to the other half. Beat each half with wooden spoon until creamy. Pour the contents of one bowl into a buttered pan and top with the other. When cool cut into squares.

Submitted by Mrs. T. A. Jewell, Skowhegan, Maine

Easy Never Fail Chocolate Fudge

1 stick margarine
2 packages 4-ounce chocolate pudding mix
½ cup milk
1 pound confectioner's sugar
2 teaspoons vanilla
½ cup nuts, chopped

In a saucepan, melt the margarine, stir in the pudding mix and the milk. Heat to boiling and boil one minute, stirring constantly. Remove from heat and beat in the confectioner's sugar, vanilla and nuts. Pour into a 10 x 6 x 1½-inch baking pan. Chill before cutting into squares. Makes 24 pieces.

Submitted by Mrs. Ruth King, Lincoln, Maine

Foolproof Fudge

½ pound marshmallows
¼ cup water
2½ cups sugar
¼ pound butter or margarine

1 6-ounce can evaporated milk
¼ teaspoon salt
1½ cups semi-sweet chocolate bits

In top of double boiler, combine marshmallows and water. Cook over boiling water until marshmallows are melted. Stir occasionally. In a heavy saucepan combine sugar, butter or margarine, milk and salt. Mix thoroughly. Bring to a rolling boil over medium heat, stirring constantly to prevent sticking.

Remove from heat and stir in melted marshmallows and chocolate bits. Mix until thoroughly blended and the chocolate bits are melted. Pour into buttered 8 x 12-inch pan. Cool and cut into squares.

Variations: Add 1 cup chopped nuts or shredded coconut to fudge before pouring into pan to cool.

Submitted by Katherine F. Crockett, Machias, Maine

Chocolate Caramels

2 cups brown sugar
2 cups white sugar
1 cup white corn syrup
8 ounces chocolate

½ can condensed milk plus enough milk to make 2 cups
1 tablespoon butter
1 teaspoon vanilla
1 cup walnuts

Combine the two sugars, corn syrup, chocolate and milk. Boil until hard ball is formed in cold water (about 238 degrees). Add the butter, vanilla and walnuts. Do not stir except to mix. Pour into slightly buttered pan. When cold, cut and wrap in wax paper.

Submitted by Huldah Monfette, Ashland, Maine

Pineapple Candy

3 cups sugar
1 small can crushed pineapple
2 tablespoons light corn syrup

12 marshmallows
2 tablespoons butter
1 teaspoon vanilla
½ cup nuts, chopped

Cook sugar, pineapple, syrup and marshmallows like fudge (325 degrees). Remove from heat and add butter. Cool, then beat until creamy. Add vanilla and nuts just before pouring into pan.

Submitted by Edith Knox, Fryeburg, Maine

Peanut Butter Fudge

2 cups white sugar
2¼ cups brown sugar
¼ teaspoon salt
¾ cup milk
1 12-ounce jar peanut butter
1 7½-ounce jar marshmallow creme
1 cup nuts, chopped
1 teaspoon vanilla

Combine the two sugars, salt and milk in a good size pan and bring to a boil. Boil 5 minutes. Remove from heat and add the peanut butter, marshmallow, nuts and vanilla. Mix quickly and put into 2 well greased 8 x 8-inch pans. Allow to set. Cut in squares.

Submitted by Mrs. Kenneth L. Hodgdon, Sr., Dennysville, Maine

Peanut Butter Fudge

2 cups sugar
½ cup milk
2 tablespoons white corn syrup
Pinch salt
1 cup peanut butter
1 cup marshmallow fluff

Mix sugar, milk, syrup and salt together, cook to soft ball stage, stirring constantly. Add peanut butter and fluff. Pour into buttered pan, cool slightly and cut. Cool completely.

Submitted by Naomi Powell, Mechanic Falls, Maine

Southern Pralines

1 cup brown sugar
1 cup confectioner's sugar
1 tablespoon butter
5 tablespoons boiling water
½ teaspoon vanilla
1 cup pecan meats

Combine brown sugar and confectioner's sugar with the butter and boiling water. Boil just one minute. Remove from heat and add vanilla and pecans. Beat until it begins to thicken, slightly. Pour quickly by teaspoonfuls onto waxed paper or aluminum foil. Cool. Makes 20 pralines.

Submitted by Margaret F. Stevens, Old Town, Maine

Old-Fashioned Molasses Candy

½ cup molasses
6 tablespoons water
½ cup sugar
¼ teaspoon salt
¼ pound margarine

Combine all ingredients and cook in saucepan until it forms a hard ball. Pour onto cookie sheet and let set. Then crack.

Submitted by Mrs. Roger Murphy, Houlton, Maine

Divinity Fudge

3 cups granulated sugar
½ cup light corn syrup
½ cup cold water
2 egg whites

⅛ teaspoon salt
1 teaspoon vanilla
½ cup walnuts

This is a never fail recipe and a candy thermometer is a must. Place sugar, syrup and water in a saucepan over low heat. Stir until sugar is dissolved. Cook to 234 degrees F. Beat the egg whites (which have been kept at room temperature beforehand) stiffly, and pour one-half of the cooked syrup mixture slowly into them, beating continually as you pour. Cook the remaining syrup to 280 degrees F. Add this syrup slowly to egg mixture, beating constantly. Add vanilla and salt. Add the walnuts, cut up. Continue beating until mixture is thick enough to drop from spoon and when dropped on a piece of waxed paper will not lose shape. Pour immediately into a buttered 9 x 9 pan. As soon as it sets, cut into squares.

Dropped by spoonfuls onto waxed paper, makes dainty bites. A bit of food coloring added to some of the mixture while beating will give a variety for the candy dish.

Submitted by Mrs. Ruth Wiggin, Rockland, Maine

Three-Minute Fudge

2 cups brown sugar
1 cup white sugar
3 tablespoons cornstarch
2 tablespoons butter

½ cup sweet milk
¼ teaspoon vanilla
½ cup (or more) chopped
walnuts

Boil together sugars, cornstarch, butter and milk; boil hard for exactly 3 minutes. Add vanilla and walnuts. Beat until thick. Pour into greased pan. Cut when cool.

Submitted by Mrs. Mertie Grover, Thomaston, Maine

Needhams

1 medium-sized potato
1 pound confectioner's sugar
(or more)

1 teaspoon vanilla
½ cup coconut

Cook the potato and while it is still warm, stir in the sugar and vanilla. (Use enough sugar to make a firm texture.) Add coconut; mix well; press into a well-greased pan. Cool and cut in squares. Dip in melted chocolate and place on waxed paper to set.

Submitted by Mrs. Ann Day, Thomaston, Maine

Wheat-Flour Applesauce Doughnuts

4½ cups unsifted
½ cup wheat flour
4 teaspoons baking powder
1 teaspoon soda
2 teaspoons salt
1 teaspoon cinnamon
1 teaspoon nutmeg
¼ teaspoon mace
1 cup sugar
¼ cup shortening
3 eggs
1 teaspoon vanilla
1 cup applesauce
½ cup buttermilk

Measure flour and wheat flour, baking powder, soda, salt and spices onto wax paper. Stir well to blend. Cream shortening, sugar, eggs and vanilla thoroughly. Stir in applesauce and buttermilk, mixing well. Add blended dry ingredients, one cup at a time beating until smooth after each addition. Refrigerate dough for 2 hours. Preheat lard to 375 degrees.

Turn dough out onto a well floured board with additional flour for handling. Cut with floured 2½-inch doughnut cutter. Remove centers. Fry doughnuts a few at a time about 1 minute on each side. Drain on paper toweling. Sprinkle with sugar. Makes 4 to 4½ dozen.

Submitted by Marion Hunter, Lincoln, Maine

Maine Potato Donuts

1 cup sugar
2 eggs
¾ cup milk
¾ cup cold mashed potato
3¾ cups flour
¼ cup melted shortening
1 teaspoon vanilla
4 teaspoons baking powder
¾ teaspoon ginger

Mix sugar and eggs, add milk and potato. Add shortening and vanilla. Sift dry ingredients, add and mix well. Chill 1 hour before frying. Roll, cut out and fry in deep fat at 375 degrees.

Submitted by Mrs. Margaret Bedard, Hollis Center, Maine

Chocolate Doughnuts

2 eggs
1½ cups sugar
1 cup buttermilk
3 oz. chocolate
1 rounded teaspoon soda
Pinch ginger
Salt and vanilla
About 3 cups flour

Fry in deep fat.

Submitted by Grace Irvin, Warren, Maine

Buttermilk Donuts

2 eggs, beaten
1 heaping cup sugar
2 teaspoons margarine, melted
½ teaspoon nutmeg
½ teaspoon ginger
½ teaspoon vanilla extract

1 full cup buttermilk
3 cups sifted flour, more or less — depends on flour
2 level teaspoons soda
3 level teaspoons baking powder
1 level teaspoon salt

Beat eggs and add sugar, margarine, nutmeg, ginger, vanilla, and buttermilk. Mix in order given. Add dry ingredients sifted together. Fry in hot fat. May be sugared or left plain.

Submitted by Mrs. R. W. McMannus, Smyrna Mills, Maine

Sugar Doughnuts

2 eggs, well beaten
1 teaspoon salt
1 cup sugar
¼ cup sour cream or 2 teaspoon butter or oleo
½ teaspoon nutmeg

1 teaspoon ginger
1 cup sour milk
1 teaspoon soda
4 cups flour or enough to roll
2 teaspoons baking powder

Mix together the eggs, salt, sugar, cream, nutmeg and ginger. Add the soda to milk. Add to first mixture. Add flour, to which the baking powder has been added. Fry in very hot fat.

Submitted by Ruth J. Prior, Friendship, Maine

Never Fail Doughnuts

3 eggs (slightly beaten)
1 cup sugar
¼ cup melted butter
1 cup sour milk
2 teaspoons soda

2 teaspoons of cream of tartar
Dash of nutmeg
¼ teaspoon ginger
½ teaspoon salt
3 cups flour (approximately)

Combine the eggs, sugar, butter and sour milk. Sift and add 2 cups of flour with soda, cream of tartar, salt and spices. Add enough flour to make a soft dough. Fry in deep fat.

Submitted by Mrs. Nellie F. Cummings, Bethel, Maine

Sugarless Doughnuts
(Wartime Recipe)

2 eggs
14 oz. can of condensed milk
¾ cup buttermilk
1 teaspoon vanilla

4 cups flour
1½ teaspoons soda
1 teaspoon salt
i teaspoon nutmeg

Break eggs into mixing bowl, beat well. Add condensed milk, buttermilk, vanilla and stir well. Add flour, soda, salt, and nutmeg that have been sifted together. Add to milk mixture, blending well. Cut and fry as all other donuts. These are good.

Submitted by Mrs. Raymond H. Rice, Stonington, Maine

Plain Doughnuts

1 cup sugar
2 eggs
1 teaspoon nutmeg
1 cup buttermilk
3 cups flour

2 tablespoons Crisco, level
1 teaspoon baking powder
1 teaspoon soda
2 teaspoons vanilla

Cream sugar and shortening, both eggs, then vanilla and buttermilk. Last add dry ingredients. Chill overnight. Roll out and fry in hot fat.

Submitted by Mrs. Louise Fleming, Howland, Maine

Squash Donuts

2 eggs, beaten
2 tablespoons shortening
1¼ cups sugar
½ cup sour milk
About 1½ cups squash cooked
1½ teaspoons soda
1 teaspoon cream tartar

1 heaping teaspoon baking powder
½ teaspoon salt
1 teaspoon nutmeg
½ teaspoon ginger
Flour to roll

Mix these as usual.

Submitted by Mrs. Vincent Hare, Houlton, Maine

Brown Sugar Doughnuts

2 eggs, beaten
1½ cups brown sugar
1 cup sour milk
2 teaspoons soda
2 teaspoons cream of tartar

2 tablespoons melted butter
1 teaspoon ginger
1 teaspoon nutmeg
1 teaspoon salt
Flour to roll

Fry in 375 degree fat.

Submitted by Mrs. Leroy Dewitt, Howland, Maine

Chocolate Doughnuts

2 tablespoons pure lard, softened
1 cup sugar
2 eggs
1/3 cup dark cocoa
1½ teaspoons vanilla
1 cup sour milk or buttermilk
3¾ cups flour
1 teaspoon soda
½ teaspoon salt
½ teaspoon cream tartar

Cream shortening and sugar. Add eggs and beat well. Add cocoa and vanilla, beat well. Add sifted dry ingredients alternately with sour milk and mix until smooth. Chill for a few hours or overnight, then fry in deep fat. Doughnuts may be sugared while still warm or left plain.

Submitted by Mrs. Ida Mercier, Skowhegan, Maine

Molasses Doughnuts

2 eggs, well beaten
½ cup sugar
¼ teaspoon salt
¼ teaspoon nutmeg
1 teaspoon cinnamon
1 teaspoon ginger
2 tablespoons fat
1 cup molasses
1 heaping teaspoon soda
1 cup sour milk
5 cups flour

Beat the eggs well, add sugar, salt, nutmeg, cinnamon, ginger, and melted fat, mix well. Add molasses, beat all together. Add soda to milk and dissolve, add to first mixture. Add flour and mix well. Refrigerate overnight. This is a soft dough. Roll out and fry in hot fat.

Submitted by Rena Perkins, Guilford, Maine

Raised Doughnuts

1 cup milk
½ cup Spry
1 teaspoon salt
¾ cup sugar
2 yeast cakes
2 eggs beaten
4 cups flour sifted

Scald milk, Spry, salt and sugar. Stir until dissolved. Cool to lukewarm. Add yeast, beaten eggs and flour and knead to smooth dough. Roll out and cut. Raise until doubled. Fry in deep fat putting raised side in first.

Submitted by Mrs. Kermit K. Bailey, Caribou, Maine

Asparagus — Ham Bake

Water
1 6 oz. can (2/3) cup
  evaporated milk
2 cups cubed cooked ham or
  spam
2 cups cooked rice
½ cup shredded cheese
1 can condensed cream of
  mushroom soup

3 tablespoon finely chopped
  onion
1 10 oz. package frozen
  asparagus spears
½ cup corn flake crumbs
3 tablespoons butter or
  maragine, melted

Add water to evaporated milk to make ¾ cup. Combine
with ham, rice, cheese, soup and onion. Pour boiling water over
asparagus spears to separate them. Drain.

Spoon half of ham mixture into 10 x 6 x 1½ inch baking
dish, top with asparagus spears, then with remaining ham mixture.
Combine corn flake crumbs and butter. Sprinkle over top. Bake
at 375 degrees for 25 or 30 minutes, or until heated through
and top is lightly browned.

Submitted by Mrs. Barbara MacDonald, Kennebunk, Maine

Ham Slices With Cranberry

1 slice ham (1 to 2 inches
  thick)
Whole cloves

1½ cups cranberries
¾ cup strained honey

Trim ham and insert cloves into fat. Wash cranberries, dry and
mix with honey. Pour over ham and bake in moderate oven 350
degrees, 1¼ hours or until ham is cooked. Baste occasionally with
liquid in pan. One center slice will serve 6.

Submitted by Mrs. Dorothy E. Preble, Stillwater, Maine

Easy Chicken Casserole

1 can chicken rice soup
1 can cream of mushroom soup
1 can Chinese noodles

1 small can evaporated milk
1 can chicken or 2 chicken
  breasts, cooked

Stir all together. Place in baking dish and cover with crushed
potato chips. Bake in a 350 degree oven until bubbling, about
25 minutes.

Submitted by Mrs. A. Jasper Willey, Scarboro, Maine

Domesticated fowl, especially chicken, were a welcome addition to the bill of fare of our pioneer families. Most families raised a few for eggs and for the table. Served roasted and stuffed, in a stew with dumplings or as a basis for a pie it was a welcome change from the sometimes seasonally limited diet. The fat is very tasty and made a very light and flavorful cake or bisquit. The feathers, though sometimes a little prickly, could be used to stuff a mattress and were probably less prickly than the spruce or fir tips sometimes used for such purposes. Modern poultry processing plants bring chicken to the kitchen all ready to cook. The poultry industry in Maine is thriving and growing and produces a good many economical meals for today's cook with relatively little preparation.

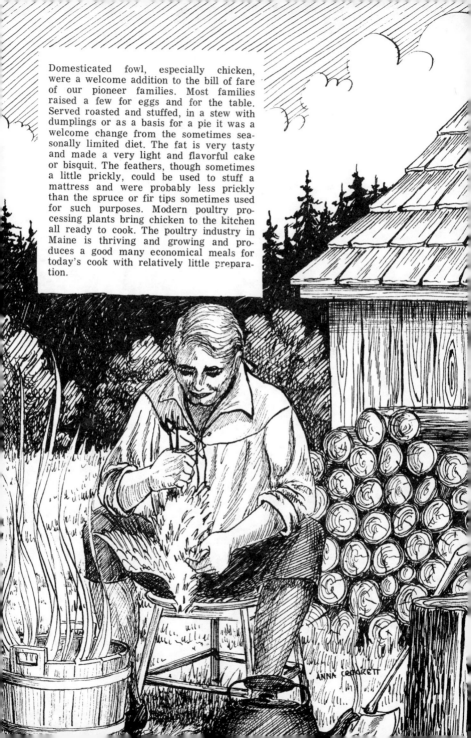

Chicken Casserole

1 cup green peppers, chopped fine
½ cup celery, chopped fine
2 small onions, chopped fine
1 tablespoon oil
2 cans boned chicken (5 ounce size)
1 can mushroom soup
½ cup milk
½ cup chopped almonds
1 package frozen peas
1 can chow mein noodles (3 ounce size)

Cook the peppers, celery and onions in oil until tender. Add the chicken, soup, milk, almonds and peas to the green pepper mixture. Place half of the noodles in an ungreased casserole and pour the chicken mixture over the noodles. Sprinkle the rest of the noodles on top of chicken mixture. Bake in a 350 degree oven for 45 minutes. Very delicious.

Submitted by Mrs. Nellie Lawton, Rockport, Maine

Chicken Casserole

2 cups leftover chicken, cut in small pieces
4 cups of vegetables, cut in small pieces (not too fine)
2 tablespoons butter
Leftover gravy
Water

Turnips, carrots, onions and potatoes are a good combination for this casserole. Put vegetables in a 1½ quart casserole, dot with the butter, add salt and pepper. Add the chicken and cover with leftover gravy and water. Bake with cover on until vegetables are done and liquid is cooked down so it will be quite thick.

Submitted by Mrs. Byrle Carter, Brooklin, Maine

Rice Scallop

1 cup boiled rice
¾ cup sharp cheese
2 eggs
1½ cups milk
½ teaspoon salt
Dash of pepper
1 small can pimiento

Beat the eggs, add the milk. Stir in rice, cheese broken in pieces, salt and pepper. Cut up the pimientos and stir all through the mixture. Pour into a buttered casserole dish which has been placed in a shallow pan of water and bake slowly in a 350 degree oven until a knife comes out clear when inserted. Serves 6.

Submitted by Mrs. Edith B. Pomeroy, Bangor, Maine

Chicken A-Go-Go

2½ pound broiler-fryer (cut up)
1 cup bread crumbs
¼ cup grated Parmesan cheese
¼ cup chopped blanched almonds
2 tablespoons minced parsley
1 teaspoon salt
½ cup butter, melted
1 teaspoon minced onion

Combine bread crumbs, cheese, almonds, parsley and salt. Stir together melted butter and onion. Dip pieces of chicken in the onion-butter, then in the crumb mixture. Place in a shallow baking pan and bake uncovered in a 400 degree oven approximately one hour. Do not turn chicken. Serves 4.

This recipe won first prize in the Junior Division of a National Poultry Cooking Contest for:

Miss Jane M. Callaghan, Bangor, Maine

Barbecued Chicken With Mushrooms

1 chicken, 3 pound, or size desired
¼ cup salad oil
2 cups water
1 teaspoon salt
½ teaspoon pepper
¾ teaspoon chili powder
1 cup catsup
¼ cup vinegar
1 can mushrooms (save juice)

Brown chicken slowly in the salad oil. Transfer to a roasting pan. Combine the water with the salt, pepper, chili powder, catsup, vinegar, mushrooms and juice. Bring to a boil and pour over the chicken in roasting pan. Bake in a 325 degree oven for 1½ hours or until chicken is done. Makes 4 generous servings.

Submitted by Mrs. Fern Sanborn, Bangor, Maine

Busy Day Casserole

3 pounds cut-up chicken
1 onion, chopped
1 can cream of chicken soup
¼ pound spaghetti, cooked
Salt and seasoning to suit taste.

Wash chicken until water runs clear. Do not wipe. Place a layer of chicken in bottom of casserole dish, then a layer of spaghetti and a little onion. Add the rest of the chicken, spaghetti and onion. Cover all with the soup undiluted. Bake until chicken is done, in a 350 degree oven for about 1 hour.

This is a good dish for church suppers or for meals that have to wait.

Submitted by Mrs. Bertis Davenport, Westfield, Maine

Chicken Casserole

1 cooked stewing hen
½ cup oleo or butter
½ cup flour
1 quart chicken stock
½ teaspoon salt
3 eggs
½ pound butter or oleo

1 medium onion
1 small loaf stale bread
1 tablespoon poultry seasoning
½ teaspoon salt
Dash pepper
1 cup celery chopped

Remove meat from bones and cut in bite size pieces. Make sauce by combining ½ cup oleo, ½ cup flour, chicken stock and salt. Cook until thick. Cool. Beat the 3 eggs until light, and pour over the sauce. Chill thoroughly overnight preferably.

Make dressing with ½ pound butter, medium onion and cook until onion is soft. Add the bread crumbled, salt, pepper, poultry seasoning and chopped celery. Mix well.

In a large casserole put a layer of dressing, a layer of sauce and one of chicken. Repeat, using up dressing, sauce and chicken. Cover with bread crumbs. Bake ½ hour at 350 degrees.

Good for a large picnic.

Submitted by Mrs. Charles Everett, Presque Isle, Maine

Pennsylvania Dutch Turkey Stuffing

5 pounds white potatoes
1½ pounds sausage meat
1½ packages frozen chopped
  onions
1 bunch celery (chopped in
  small pieces)

1½ large packages commer-
  cial stuffing mix
1 pound butter
Milk for mashed potatoes
Butter for mashed potatoes

Cook potatoes and mash with butter and milk. Fry sausage in large frying pan and discard drippings. Mix sausage with potato. In the same frying pan fry onions and celery in ½ pound of butter, only until onions are transparent, then add to the potato-sausage mixture. Warm the stuffing mix in the remaining ½ pound of butter and add to the potato mixture. Stir well and cool completely before stuffing turkey. This recipe is for a 15 pound bird.

Submitted by Mrs. Doris Wallis, Jefferson, Maine

Chicken Casserole

2 cups diced chicken (cooked with celery, onion, carrot)
1 can cream of chicken soup
2 teaspoons minced onion
1 cup diced celery
½ teaspoon salt
¼ teaspoon pepper
1 teaspoon lemon juice
¾ cup mayonnaise
2 hard-cooked eggs, sliced

Mix all together. Place in a casserole and top with crushed potato chips (about 2 cups). Bake in a 350 degree oven for 30 minutes.

Submitted by Mrs. H. Earl Graves, Oakland, Maine

Chicken Casserole

1 cut-up chicken
½ cup chopped onion
Salt to season
½ cup chopped celery
½ cup chopped green pepper
½ cup chopped cashew nuts
1 can chow mein noodles
2 cans mushroom soup
1 can chicken stock

Cook the chicken with the onion and salt. Reserve the stock to use in mixing. Cut chicken into chunks. Add all of the other ingredients. Mix well. Reserve a few noodles for topping. Pour into a casserole. Bake at 350 degrees for 45 minutes.

Submitted by Mrs. Ralph Porter, Houlton, Maine

Baked Sesame Chicken

1-3 pound broiler-fryer, cut-up
1 egg, slightly beaten
½ cup evaporated milk
½ cup flour
¼ teaspoon baking powder
1 teaspoon salt
¼ teaspoon pepper
4 teaspoons paprika
3 teaspoons sesame seed
¼ cup chopped nuts (optional)
½ cup butter

Combine beaten egg with evaporated milk. Mix dry ingredients. Dip pieces of chicken into egg mixture, then into dry mixture to coat both sides. Melt the ½ cup of butter in a shallow pan, in the oven. (Preheat oven to 400 degrees.) Remove pan from oven and place the coated pieces of chicken, skin side down in a single layer, in the melted butter. Bake uncovered for 25 minutes. Turn and bake 25 to 35 minutes more, or until done at 400 degrees.

Submitted by Mrs. Clyde A. Sherwood, Orono, Maine

Roast Beef — Lamb or Chicken

4 lb. roast
1 envelope of onion soup

1 can undiluted mushroom
soup

Place roast in baking pan, cover with onion soup (no liquid added) and cover that with a can of undiluted mushroom soup. Cover and bake 4 hours at 350 degrees. The gravy is all made and the roast will be perfectly seasoned.

TO COOK LAMB OR CHICKEN add cream of chicken soup and reduce baking time.

Submitted by Lela Rice, Stonington, Maine

Honey Baked Chicken

8 pieces of chicken (breasts
or legs)
2 eggs
¼ cup real fine bread crumbs

1 teaspoon salt
1/3 cup honey
2 tablespoons cold water

Dry chicken thoroughly. Beat the eggs, with the 2 tablespoons of cold water. Add bread crumbs and salt. Mixture should be thick like gravy. With a small pastry brush cover the chicken pieces on both sides with honey. Then dip in the egg mixture coating well. Arrange on a shallow baking dish and bake at 325 degrees for about an hour or until tender.

Submitted by Mrs. Arnold Bishop, Wilmington, Mass.

Chicken Apple Scallop

2 cups cooked chicken
1 tablespoon prepared mustard
2 cups sliced cooked apples
1 tablespoon lemon juice
½ teaspoon salt
1 can cream of mushroom
soup

1/3 cup light cream
½ cup fine bread crumbs
2 tablespoons margarine,
melted

Combine the chicken and the mustard. Spread in a 1 quart baking dish. Top with the apples. Sprinkle with lemon juice and salt. Combine the soup and the cream. Pour over all.

Mix crumbs with the margarine. Sprinkle on top of mixture and bake at 350 degrees for 20 minutes.

Submitted by Mrs. John Pearse, Hope, Maine

Chicken That's Different

1 frying chicken, cut-up
¾ cup commercially soured cream
½ teaspoon tarragon
½ teaspoon oregano
½ teaspoon rosemary
½ teaspoon paprika
½ teaspoon salt
½ teaspoon pepper
½ teaspoon Accent
1½ cups finely crushed corn flakes
¼ cup butter or chicken fat
2 cups milk

Rinse chicken pieces in cold water and dry. Combine and blend together sour cream and seasonings. Dip chicken in sour cream mixture and then in crushed corn flakes. Place butter in baking pan and melt in a 400 degree oven. Remove pan from oven and arrange chicken in a single layer, skin side down. Add 1 cup of milk and bake in a 400 degree oven for 25 minutes. Turn chicken, add the remaining cup of milk and bake another 15 minutes or until tender. Arrange on a hot platter, sprinkle with chopped parsley and chives. Serve with your favorite vegetable and potato. And don't forget the hot biscuits!

Submitted by Arthur J. Cummings, Bethel, Maine

Colonial Chicken

3 to 3½ pounds cut-up frying chicken
¼ cup flour
1 teaspoon salt
¼ teaspoon pepper
½ cup shortening, for frying
1½ cups sifted flour
1½ teaspoons baking powder
1 teaspoon salt
4 eggs
1½ cups milk
3 tablespoons melted oleo

Mix together the ¼ cup flour, 1 teaspoon salt and ¼ teaspoon pepper. Roll pieces of chicken in this flour mixture. Melt the ½ cup shortening in frying pan and brown the chicken on all sides. Remove from the pan and drain. In a medium sized bowl sift the flour, baking powder and salt. In another bowl beat the 4 eggs with a rotary beater until very light. Stir in the milk and melted oleo. Slowly blend the dry ingredients into the egg and milk mixture. Beat until just smooth. Pour batter into a large greased baking dish and arrange the pieces of chicken on top. Bake 1 hour at 350 degrees.

Leftover chicken or turkey, about 4 cups, may be substituted, and poured on the batter.

Submitted by Mrs. Winfield L. Chatto, Rockland, Maine

Pineapple Chicken — Chinese

1 pound uncooked chicken meat
2 tablespoons cold water
1 tablespoon cornstarch
1 teaspoon salt
1 tablespoon soy sauce
4 tablespoons cooking oil
10 water chestnuts, sliced
   lengthwise

1½ cups onions, sliced
   lengthwise
4 large slices canned pineapple,
   cut in wedges
4 tablespoons pineapple juice
1 cup celery, cut diagonally

Cut the chicken meat in 1 inch pieces, dredge with a mixture of cornstarch, salt, water and soy sauce. Saute the onions in 1 tablespoon of oil for 2 minutes. Remove. Saute water chestnuts and celery for 2 minutes (or less) in 1 tablespoon of oil and remove from pan. Saute the chicken in 2 tablespoons of oil until brown.*

Add the vegetables, pineapple and finally the pineapple juice to the chicken and simmer until thoroughly heated. Serve hot with rice.

*May be made in advance to this point and refrigerated until ready to put together.

Note: The vegetables should be crisp and not cooked soft. Beef or pork may be substituted for the chicken.

Submitted by Terry Niedermann, Northeast 9, Cushing, Maine

Chicken Rice Casserole

1 cup chicken broth
1 can sliced mushrooms (using
   the juice)
1 tablespoon flour
¼ teaspoon garlic salt
½ teaspoon pepper

¼ cup cream or top milk
½ cup grated cheese
2 cups cooked cut-up chicken
2 cups cooked rice
¼ cup peas

Heat together the broth and mushrooms. Blend the flour, garlic salt, pepper and cream. Stir into the broth and cook until thickened. Remove from the heat and stir in the grated cheese.

Mix together the cut-up chicken, cooked rice and the peas. Pour into a buttered casserole. Top with 2 strips of crumbled bacon, ¼ cup cracker crumbs and ¼ teaspoon poultry seasoning. Bake 15 minutes at 450 degrees.

Submitted by Mrs. Eleanor Clark, Thomaston, Maine

Pork Chops With Apple Stuffing

4 pork chops
¾ teaspoon salt
¼ cup raisins
2 tablespoons sugar

1½ cups chopped apples
1 quart bread cubes
Onion if desired

Brown chops on both sides 7 to 10 minutes. Add onion, salt, sugar, raisins, apples, and water to the bread cubes. Place mixture in shallow casserole. Put chops on top. Bake covered in 350 degree oven about 1 hour. Remove cover from casserole the last 10 minutes of baking time to finish browning the chops.

Submitted by Hazel Hills, Warren, Maine

Tourtiere a la viande
(Pork Pie)

3 cups mashed potatoes
3 lbs. lean pork (ground)
1 cup water
¼ teaspoon nutmeg

¼ teaspoon allspice
1 tablespoon salt
¼ teaspoon pepper
½ cup chopped onion

Put meat in saucepan and add water, nutmeg, allspice, salt, pepper, onion. Cook for 30 minutes over moderate heat, stirring often to prevent sticking. Remove from heat and add 3 cups mashed potatoes. Mix well and cool. Line a pie plate with pie crust, add filling and top with second crust. Make incision in top of crust for vent. Bake in hot oven 450 degrees about 30 minutes or until well browned. Serve hot or cold as preferred. Makes enough for two 9 inch pies.

Submitted by Mrs. Rosario C. Tardiff, West Bowdoin, Maine

Apple 'N Pork Pie

8 apples
½ cup finely diced fat salt
pork (rinse with boiling water,
then drain)
¾ cup molasses
¾ cup sugar

12 soda crackers, rolled fine
½ teaspoon cinnamon
½ teaspoon allspice
¼ teaspoon clove
Pie crust

Line 8 inch square cake tin with pie crust. Make layers of apples and other ingredients. Cover with top crust. Bake in 400 degree oven for 2 hours. Cover with foil the last hour.

Submitted by Mrs. Grace M. Downs, Harmony, Maine

Pork Chop Gumbo-French Style

6 pork chops
2 onions, medium size or 4 small
4 16 oz. cans yellow wax string beans
4 cans tomatoes, 16 oz. cans
6 potatoes, whole

3 beef bouillon cubes
1 tablespoon parsley flakes
1 tablespoon salt
½ tablespoon pepper
2½ cups water

In a hot frying pan brown pork chops. Add ½ cup water and drain into large pot. Keep adding ½ cup water and draining juice into large pot about four more times. Remove chops and put in large pot. Add a little water to frying pan to remove the last bit of juice and put in pot. Add 3 bouillon cubes to juice and salt and pepper. Add whole onions, tomatoes, and sprinkle parsley flakes over it. Add string beans, salt and pepper again. Cover, let simmer ½ hour. Add potatoes (whole) and simmer 1 hour. Serves 6 people. However, if more, add another pork chop and another potato.

Submitted by Mrs. Jean McLean, Millinocket, Maine

Sweet 'N Sour Pork

2 cups diced lean pork
1 chicken bouillon cube
1 cup boiling water
1/3 cup sugar
1½ teaspoons salt
¼ teaspoon pepper

2 tablespoons vinegar
2 teaspoons soy sauce
2 cups green pepper strips
1 can pineapple chunks
2/3 cup pineapple syrup
2 teaspoons cornstarch

Brown pork in hot fat. Pour off excess fat. Dissolve bouillon cube in boiling water. Add to pork along with seasonings, green pepper and pineapple. Cover and simmer about 20 minutes. Mix pineapple syrup and cornstarch. Stir into mixture in pan. Cook and stir until mixture thickens and boils. Serve over rice.

Submitted by Mrs. Beulah Gerald, South China, Maine

Chuck Wagon Special

2 large stewing chickens
½ cup minced onions
3 tablespoons vegetable flakes

2 teaspoons salt
½ teaspoon pepper
1 package wide noodles

Place chicken, onions, and vegetable flakes in a large kettle. Stew until meat falls from the bones. Remove the bones. Add noodles to the broth, and cook until noodles are tender.

Submitted by Mrs. Nora Wortman, Thorndike, Maine

Hamburg Stroganoff

½ cup minced onion
1 clove garlic, minced
¼ cup butter
1 lb. ground beef
2 tablespoons flour
2 teaspoons salt

¼ teaspoon pepper
1 lb. fresh mushrooms or 1
  8 oz. can (optional)
1 can cream of chicken soup
1 cup commercial sour cream

Saute onion and garlic in butter over medium heat. Add meat and brown. Add flour, salt, pepper and mushrooms. Cook 5 minutes. Add soup. Simmer uncovered for 10 minutes. Stir in sour cream. Heat through. Serve with noodles or rice. 4-6 servings.
Submitted by Mrs. Harold White, Ellsworth, Maine

Beef Stroganoff

2 pounds of ground beef
2 tablespoons oil
2 quarts of water
2 teaspoons of salt
2 packages Noodles Romanoff
¼ cup butter

2 cups cream of mushroom
  soup
2 tablespoons of minced onion
2 tablespoons chopped pimiento
2 cups milk

Brown the ground beef in oil. Cook noodles as directed, drain but do not rinse. Blend together the sauce mix (included with the noodles) butter and milk, and blend with the noodles. Add the browned meat, soup, onion and pimiento. Mix well. Bake in an uncovered casserole, in a 350 degree oven for 25 minutes.
Submitted by Mrs. Beverly Hussey, Old Town, Maine

Cedric's Casserole

1 medium onion
3 tablespoons oleo
½ pound hamburg
¾ teaspoon salt
⅛ teaspoon pepper

6 cups coarsely shredded
  cabbage
1 can tomato soup, (10½
  ounce)

Fry the onion in the oleo. Add the hamburg, salt and pepper. Heat through but do not brown. Spread 3 cups of the cabbage in a greased casserole, cover with the meat mixture, and place the rest of the cabbage on top. Pour the can of tomato soup over all. Bake covered in a 350 degree oven about 1 hour.
Submitted by Mrs. Harold Flint, Monson, Maine

Meat Balls Deluxe

2 lbs. ground beef
1 cup applesauce
1 cup bread crumbs
2 eggs
Salt and pepper to taste
2 tablespoons flour

2 tablespoons lard
2 cups tomato juice
1 carrot
1 green pepper
1 small onion
1 stalk celery

Combine ground beef, applesauce, eggs and bread crumbs. Season with salt and pepper. Make into small balls and roll in flour. Brown in hot lard and when nicely browned put in pan or large casserole. Finely slice onion, carrot, celery and pepper and place over meat balls. Add tomato juice and bake in 350 degree oven one hour. Remove meat balls and thicken gravy if desired. Serves 6 to 8.

Submitted by Sarah Graham, Belfast, Maine

Grandmother's Sage Stuffing

1½ quarts of firmly packed biscuit or bread crumbs or crackers, or can use all three.
2 teaspoons sage
2 teaspoons dry minced onion

or
2 tablespoons of fresh minced onion
½ teaspoon salt
3 eggs (not beaten)
About 2½ cups milk

Stir all ingredients together, mixing well. I use this recipe for stuffing fowl or turkeys, also with meats. My family is very fond of stuffing with roast pork and baked chicken breasts.

For cooking, it can be steamed for 3 hours in a tightly covered greased container as one would steam a brownbread. This makes a very moist product and may be placed in the oven a short time after steaming to dry.

It is a bit drier if baked in a greased bread tin wrapped in at least 2 thicknesses of heavy foil, at 325 degrees for about 3 hours. Open foil for the last 45 minutes of baking.

A few years ago I tried several new stuffing recipes. None appealed to my husband. He said he liked my "junkless stuffing" better. You may not care for this recipe but perhaps you will enjoy his name for it.

Submitted by Mrs. Donald C. Varney, Bethel, Maine

Ham and Cheese Strata with Broccoli

12 slices white bread*
¾ lb. sharp process American cheese, sliced
1 10 oz. package frozen chopped broccoli
2 cups diced ham, cooked or canned
6 slightly beaten eggs
3½ cups milk
2 tablespoons instant minced onion
½ teaspoon salt
¼ teaspoon dry mustard

Cut 12 doughnuts and holes from bread. Set aside. Fit the scraps of bread in bottom of 9 x 13 x 2 inch baking dish. Place cheese in a layer over bread, add a layer of broccoli, then ham. Arrange bread doughnuts and holes on top. Combine remaining ingredients, pour over bread and all. Cover and refrigerate at least 6 hours or overnight.

Bake uncovered in slow oven 325 degrees, 55 minutes. For a pretty finish, sprinkle with shredded cheese 5 minutes before end of baking time. Before cutting in squares let stand out 10 minutes to firm. Makes 12 servings.

*Nicer edges if you freeze bread then cut doughnuts while frozen.

Submitted by Mrs. Albert Levenseler, Rockland, Maine

Caracus

1 No. 2½ can tomatoes
1 medium size onion, minced
1 pound process cheese, diced or grated
1 package (4 or 5 ounces) chipped beef shredded — broken into small pieces
2 eggs, well beaten

Put tomatoes, onion and cheese in saucepan over low heat, be sure they do not boil. Heat until cheese melts and onions cook. Add chipped beef and heat. Just before serving, add the beaten eggs. Serve over saltine crackers.

*If one is on a restricted salt diet, the beef can be put into a strainer after it has been shredded, and let warm water wash some of salt out. "Unsalted Tops" crackers can be used for the same reason.

Submitted by Margaret F. Stevens, Old Town, Maine

Corn and Cheese Casserole

3 eggs, well beaten
2 cups milk
3 tablespoons sugar
½ teaspoon salt
½ teaspoon paprika
1 can of creamed corn (or drained whole kernel corn)
3 tablespoons melted butter or margarine
½ teaspoon dry mustard
1 tablespoon Worcestershire Sauce
¼ cup finely cut green pepper
1½ cups herb-seasoned stuffing
½ cup cubed cheese
Crumbs for top

Beat the eggs in a large mixing bowl and add the ingredients in the order given. Pour into a buttered casserole and sprinkle corn flake crumbs or buttered bread crumbs over the top. Bake in a 350 degree oven for about 45 minutes. When done, it will be custard-like.

Submitted by Ruby E. Johnson, Lubec, Maine

Potato-Egg Casserole

4 cups diced cooked potatoes
6 hard-cooked eggs, sliced
1 can cream of chicken soup
1 cup milk
½ teaspoon salt
⅛ teaspoon pepper
1 cup shredded cheese

Place potatoes and eggs in layers in a 2 quart casserole which has been well greased. Blend the soup with the milk and seasonings. Pour over layers and top with the shredded cheese. Bake 30 minutes at 375 degrees.

Submitted by Harold Bonney, West Paris, Maine

My Spaghetti Sauce

1 large onion
1 green pepper
2 pounds ground beef
Garlic salt
Salt
Pepper
1 teaspoon cayenne pepper
1 large can tomatoes
4 large cans tomato sauce
2 cans mushroom steak sauce
¼ bottle ketchup
3 to 4 tablespoons sugar

Saute the onion and green pepper for 5 minutes, stirring constantly. Add the beef and scramble, mixing until cooked. Add garlic salt, salt and pepper to taste, cayenne pepper, tomatoes, tomato sauce, muchroom sauce, ketchup and sugar. Cook all day. This is also good for a hurry-up meal. Very good on mashed potatoes or bread, as well as spaghetti.

Submitted by Carol E. Grover, St. George, Maine

Hamburger Meat Loaf

2 lbs. hamburg
2 cups cracker crumbs
1 cup milk
2 eggs, beaten

2 grated onions
2 medium cooked potatoes, mashed
2 cooked carrots, mashed
Salt and pepper to taste

Mix all ingredients together, pack into bread tins. Bake 40 minutes in 350 degree oven. Serves 6 to 8.

Submitted by Leola M. McAtee, Plymouth, Maine

Spaghetti and Meat Balls

1 pound ground beef
¼ cup bread crumbs
1 egg, slightly beaten
3 large garlic cloves,
   minced
½ teaspoon salt

4 slices bacon
1 medium bay leaf
1 teaspoon oregano
2 cans tomato soup
1 cup water

Combine crumbs, beef, egg and salt. Shape into 16 meat balls. In a large fry pan cook the bacon until crisp, remove and crumble. Pour off all but 2 tablespoons of fat. Place meat balls in the fry pan and brown with the garlic, bay leaf and oregano. Add the soup and water. Simmer for 30 minutes. Stir now and then. Remove the bay leaf. Add crumbled bacon. Serve over hot spaghetti. Can top with grated cheese.

Submitted by Mrs. Gordon Hemphill, Dover-Foxcroft, Maine

Swedish Meat Balls

1 lb. ground beef
Onions to suit taste
¾ cup fine dry bread crumbs
1 teaspoon Worcestershire
   Sauce

1 tablespoon minced parsley
1½ teaspoons salt
⅛ teaspoon pepper
1 egg
½ cup milk

Mix well and shape in balls size of walnuts. Brown in ¼ cup hot fat or salad oil. Remove meat balls and stir in fat the following:

¼ cup flour
1 teaspoon paprika
½ teaspoon salt

⅛ teaspoon pepper
2 cups boiling water
¾ cup sweet milk

Mix well and return meat balls to gravy and simmer 15 to 20 minutes. Serve on mashed potatoes.

Submitted by Rose Marie Cox, Fort Fairfield, Maine

Southern Hamburg

1 medium onion, chopped
1 medium green pepper
2 tablespoons cooking oil
1 pound hamburg

3 tablespoons catsup
3 tablespoons prepared mustard
1 can chicken gumbo soup
Season to taste

Cook the onions and green pepper in the oil, until onions are light yellow. Add the hamburg and cook until light brown. Add catsup, mustard and soup undiluted. Season to taste. Simmer for ½ hour. Serve on hamburg rolls.

Submitted by Mrs. Claude Hemphill, Presque Isle, Maine

Bean-Pot Hamburg

2 lbs. lean hamburg
1 teaspoon salt
1 tablespoon sugar
¾ teaspoon poultry seasoning

1 large onion, chopped fine
1 can (10½ oz.) consomme soup.
Fill soup can with cold water

Mix all ingredients well. Place in bean pot and stir over medium heat constantly until meat loses all color, and is not lumpy. Cover, place in moderate slow oven 250 degrees to 300 degrees for 1½ to 2 hours. Stir occasionally. When cooked, may be thickened or not, as desired.

I find this equally good cooked in an electric casserole, also I vary the soup for a choice of flavors such as tomato, mushroom, celery, cheese, etc.

Submitted by Mrs. Mary C. Sprowl, Liberty, Maine

Burlington Barbecue Beef

1 lb. stew beef
3 large onions
1 green pepper
½ cup catsup
2 tablespoons vinegar
1 cup fruit syrup (from canned fruit)

2 tablespoons Worcestershire Sauce
2 teaspoons salt
2 tablespoons brown sugar
¼ teaspoon oregano

Brown stew beef slowly with onions and pepper. Add catsup, vinegar, fruit syrup, Worcestershire sauce, salt, brown sugar, and oregano. Simmer 2-3 hours (covered) until done or tender. Thicken gravy with flour. Serve on rice or noodles.

Submitted by Mrs. Albert W. Blasenak, Sr., Littleton, N. H.

Swedish Meat Balls

1 lb. chopped beef
1 chopped, gently fried onion
½ teaspoon garlic salt
4 or 5 slices of bread soaked in milk

2 whole eggs
Salt and pepper
½ teaspoon dry mustard
2 teaspoons chopped parsley
Pinch nutmeg

Mix with hands very thoroughly. Make tiny balls the size of walnuts. Fry quickly and put in sauce.

SAUCE

1 bottle chili sauce
1 can whole cranberry sauce

Mix in sauce pan and simmer. Drop meatballs in and simmer. Serve in chafing dish.

Submitted by Mrs. Kenneth M. Curtis, Blaine House
Augusta, Maine

Upside Down Pie

½ lb. hamburg
½ teaspoon salt
¼ cup chopped onion
1 can tomato soup
2 tablespoons shortening
1½ cups flour
3 teaspoons baking powder

½ teaspoon salt
3 tablespoons shortening
1 teaspoon paprika
1 teaspoon celery salt or seeds
¾ cup milk

In heavy fry pan, fry onion in 2 tablespoons of shortening until soft. Add hamburg and soup. Bring to boil.

Mix as for biscuits, flour, baking powder, salt, shortening, paprika, celery salt, and milk. Use grated cheese if desired. Spoon on top of hamburg mixture in heavy fry pan. Bake 475 degrees, 20 minutes. Turn upside down when done.

Submitted by Mrs. Crystal Farrar, Sangerville, Maine

Bean Pot Stew

1 lb. stew beef
1 whole onion
1 can tomato soup
¼ can water (rinse out soup can)

1 small jar green olives (juice and all)

Cook in bean pot (covered) until meat is done, 325 degree oven about 3 hours. I serve this over cooked noodles.

Submitted by Mrs. Shirley Jones, Orrington, Maine

Barbecued Frankfurters

2 lbs. frankfurters, cut
   diagonally in 1 inch pieces
¾ chopped onion
2 tablespoons vinegar
2 tablespoons brown sugar
¼ cup lemon juice

1 cup catsup
3 tablespoons Worcestershire
   sauce
¾ cup water
⅛ teaspoon cayenne pepper
   if desired

Combine all ingredients except frankfurters. Simmer 20 minutes. Add frankfurters and cook slowly 10 minutes, stirring occasionally. Recipe makes 8 servings.

Submitted by Mrs. Diane Spack, Guilford, Maine

Hamburg Pie

Bisquick or regular biscuit
   dough
1½ lbs. hamburg
1 onion
2 tablespoons flour

Salt and pepper
2 eggs, beaten
1 cup cheese
Paprika

Mix Bisquick or regular biscuit dough, knead lightly and fit into a 9 inch pie tin. Saute hamburg and onion, diced, add flour, salt and pepper. Spread in dough-lined pan. Beat eggs and blend in cheese. Pour over meat and sprinkle with paprika and bake 30 minutes. Serve cut in wedges with baked potato and green salad. Makes a nice meal. Serves 6 amply.

Submitted by Mrs. Alvah Graves, Santa Cruz, California

Becky's Meat Loaf

1½ lbs. ground beef
¾ cup oatmeal
1½ teaspoons salt
1 teaspoon onion salt

1 teaspoon celery salt
1 can tomato paste
1 egg, beaten

Combine all ingredients thoroughly. Pack firmly into an ungreased 8½ x 4½ x 2½ inch loaf pan. Bake in a preheated moderate oven (350 degrees) 1 hour and 15 minutes. Let stand 5 minutes before slicing. Makes 8 servings.

TO VARY THIS USE ¾ cup bread crumbs and ¾ cup of grated carrot. Very good.

Submitted by Becky Wiers, St. Albans, Maine

Baked Beef Heart

1 beef heart or 2 veal hearts
2 cups stock or diluted tomato juice
4 slices bacon or salt pork
2 tablespoons butter
1 tablespoon minced onion
1 cup bread (cubed)
½ teaspoon salt
¼ teaspoon poultry seasoning
¼ -½ cup water or milk

Wash heart well, remove veins, arteries and blood. Tie heart with string and place on rack in baking dish. Add stock or tomato juice. Sprinkle the meat with salt and pepper and seasoning and lay bacon or pork over the meat. Cover and bake in a slow oven 325 degrees until tender. A beef heart may take 4 to 5 hours, veal about 2 hours. Remove the heart, cool slightly. Untie and fill the cavity with stuffing made with the butter, onion, cubed bread, salt, and seasoning, mixed with the milk or water. Retie the heart, return to oven and cook about 30 minutes or until stuffing is thoroughly heated. Thicken gravy in the pan.

Submitted by Mrs. Ruth King, Lincoln, Maine

Dutch Meat Loaf

1½ lbs. ground beef
½ can condensed tomato soup
1 cup rolled oats, uncooked
¼ teaspoon pepper
1½ teaspoons salt
1 medium onion, finely chopped
1 egg, beaten

SAUCE

2 tablespoons prepared mustard
½ can of condensed tomato soup
¼ cup vinegar
¼ cup brown sugar, packed
1 cup water

In a bowl combine meat, soup, rolled oats, salt, pepper and onion. Mix well, then mix in the beaten egg. Spoon the mixture lightly into a greased bread tin. Bake in a moderate oven 350 degrees for about 1½ hours. After the meat oaf has gone into the oven, prepare a sauce with which to baste the meat as it bakes.

Combine prepared mustard, tomato soup, vinegar, brown sugar, and water. Baste the meat as it cooks.

Submitted by Mrs. Fred McIntire, Washburn, Maine

Spring brought on addition to the winter-ravished pantry. Fish by the millions began their spawning runs up the rivers along the coastline from Kittery to Calais. Smelts, alewives, herring and salmon crowded the streams and could literally be scooped out by the handful. The salmon, being larger, were, of course netted, speared or caught with a hook and line. Herring came inshore in schools and could be caught in nets and weirs. Smelts fried in a spider, alewives baked to a crusty brown, laced through with salt pork, salmon boiled in the good old Maine way and herring pickled in vinegar were all fit beginnings for a spring feast. They went pretty well with a mess of greens and salt pork too.

Barbecued Hamburg

1 pound of ground meat
1 teaspoon butter
1 medium onion, cut-up
1 cup celery, cut in small
  pieces
½ teaspoon salt
Dash of pepper

½ cup ketchup
½ teaspoon Worcestershire Sauce
1 tablespoon vinegar
1 tablespoon prepared mustard
2 teaspoons sugar
3 teaspoons chili sauce

Combine all ingredients and mix well. Simmer in the teaspoon of butter for 15 minutes or until done to your taste. Serve in hot dog rolls or hamburg buns. Good for people in trailers or campers.

Submitted by Mae Perry, Rockland, Maine

French Fried Onion Rings

1 cup flour
½ cup oil
1 egg, beaten

1½ cups milk
Onions

Slice onions and pull apart into rings. Soak onions in the milk for 1 hour, then drain, saving the milk. Mix flour and oil together thoroughly, then add the beaten egg and the milk. Dip the onion rings in the batter and fry in hot fat, until golden brosn.

Submitted by Mrs. Donna Bond, Jefferson, Maine

Scalloped Corn

1¼ cups crushed crackers-
  saltines
1 can cream style corn

1 egg, beaten
1 cup milk
1 onion, diced

Combine the beaten egg with the milk and corn. Mix well. Add crushed crackers and diced onion. Pour into a greased casserole. Bake at 350 degrees for ½ hour.

Submitted by Mrs. Thomas Watson, Five Islands, Maine

Creamy Lamb Stew

1½ pounds lamb
3 tablespoons flour
2 teaspoons salt
¼ teaspoon pepper
3 tablespoons salad oil
4 medium potatoes
2 large onions
4 carrots
½ cup water
½ cup frozen peas
½ cup commercial sour cream
1 tablespoon flour
½ teaspoon salt
Snipped parsley

Combine flour, salt and pepper. Coat lamb with the flour. Heat the salad oil in pressure saucepan and brown lamb on all sides. Add the ½ cup of water and cook lamb at 10 pounds pressure for 25 minutes. Reduce heat and add the potatoes, pared and quartered; the onions cut in thick slices; and carrots cut in large pieces. Return to heat and cook under pressure for 3 minutes. Reduce heat, remove cover, push vegetables to one side and add the frozen peas. Cook in the broth for 2 minutes, uncovered. Stir the flour and salt into the sour cream and stir into the stew until thickened. Garnish with parsley. Serve hot with hot biscuits.

Submitted by Mrs. Gertrude Hupper, Tenants Harbor, Maine

Veal Parmesan

4 frozen veal patties
Salt and pepper
Flour
1 egg
1 tablespoon water
Fine bread crumbs
1 tablespoon butter
1 tablespoon oil
1 8 oz. can tomato sauce
¼ teaspoon oregano
½ lb. Mozzarella cheese
Grated Parmesan cheese
Paprika

Season veal and dust with flour. Beat egg and water. Dip veal in egg mix then in crumbs, coating well. Place in single layer on platter and chill. Brown meat in oil and butter quickly. Place meat in single layer in greased pan. In the meantime combine the sauce and oregano and let simmer. Arrange the thinly sliced Mozzarella cheese on the meat to almost cover each piece, spoon over some of the sauce, and sprinkle on a layer of Parmesan cheese. Spoon about a teaspoon pan drippings over each piece. Sprinkle lightly with paprika and bake in a 325 degree oven for 30 minutes.

Submitted by Mrs. Esther Graves, Rockland, Maine

Quick and Easy Lasagne

½ lb. Lasagne noodles
2 cans tomato soup
1 large can tomato sauce
1 6 oz. can sliced mushrooms
½ cup olive oil

2 tablespoons minced onions
½ teaspoon oregano
Grated cheese and some
  extra sharp cheese
1 lb. cooked hamburg

Cook noodles in boiling salted water. Put a little olive oil in water to prevent noodles from sticking. Drain, combine tomato sauce, mushrooms with their liquid, onions, oil and oregano and 1 lb. of cooked hamburg. Put a little sauce in bottom of pie plate, — layer lasagne — more sauce — cheese and so on until dish is full. Bake in 350 degree oven until cheese is melted.

Submitted by Helen Waller, Winslow, Maine

Liverwurst

Pig liver
Pig heart
1 pound fresh pork fat
  (or salt pork)

1 pound onions (scant)
Salt
Pepper
Poultry seasoning

Boil together the liver, heart and salt pork for 1 hour. Grind, except the rind, first a piece of pork, then one of liver, then onions. Add salt, pepper and seasoning to taste. Add enough of the water the meat was cooked in, to mix as thick as graham muffins. Cook about 20 minutes, long enough to cook the onions. Press into a loaf pan. Cool. Keep refrigerated.

Submitted by Mrs. Lloyd Ingham, Winthrop, Maine

Liver Loaf

1½ lb. liver (cooked)
½ cup of celery
1½ cups of bread crumbs
Salt and pepper to taste

2 eggs, beaten
½ cup tomatoes
1 cup liquid (can be broth)
2 tablespoons butter

Cook liver and put it through the meat grinder. Add celery, bread crumbs, salt and pepper, eggs, beaten, tomatoes and broth, you can use some tomato juice if you don't have enough broth to make the 1 cup of liquid. Mix well and put in pan. Put butter on top of loaf before putting in oven. If desired you may put bacon on top of loaf in place of butter. Bake in 350 degree oven for about 1 hour.

Submitted by Marilyn M. Wiers, St. Albans, Maine

Liver and Bacon Loaf

1½ lb. liver, cooked
1 lb. beef, cooked
4 cups bread crumbs
8 tablespoons tomato catsup
2 tablespoons onion juice

2 eggs, well beaten
Juice of lemon
Salt and pepper to taste
Bacon strips

Put liver and beef through meat grinder. Mix bread crumbs, catsup, onion juice, eggs, juice of lemon, salt and pepper to taste. Line pan with bacon strips. Put ingredients in pan, and place bacon strips on top, pressing them firmly on. Bake in moderate oven, 350 degrees, about 1 hour.

Submitted by Elizabeth Shyne, Rockland, Maine

Chicken Liver Stroganoff

1 medium onion, sliced
2 tablespoons butter
1 pound frozen chicken livers
2/3 cup sliced mushrooms
2 teaspoons paprika

½ teaspoon salt
Dash pepper
1 tablespoon flour
1 cup dairy sour cream
3 cups cooked long grain rice

Cook onion in butter until tender. Halve the livers and add to the onion with the undrained mushrooms. Stir in the paprika, salt and pepper. Cover and cook over low heat about 10 minutes until livers are tender.

Stir the flour into the sour cream and add to the above mixture. Heat through but do not boil. Serve over the hot cooked rice. Makes 6 servings.

Submitted by Mrs. M. Richard Audet, Poland Spring, Maine

Dutch Casserole

2 lbs. beef from round
1 grated onion
1 cup peas
¾ cup soft bread crumbs
1 slice salt pork chopped
1 carrot, chopped

½ cup tomatoes
2 cups water
2 tablespoons minute tapioca
Salt
Pepper
3 cloves

Cut beef into inch cubes, mix with other ingredients and cook in casserole 3 or 4 hours. This is an old recipe.

Submitted by Mrs. Ernest Bliss, West Baldwin, Maine

Bertha's Baked Beans

2 pounds of dry beans
¼ cup sugar
½ cup molasses (scant)
¼ teaspoon salt
½ teaspoon dry mustard
Dash pepper
1 pound salt pork

Place beans in a pan of warm water and set aside for 4 or 5 hours. Drain. Mix together sugar, molasses, salt, mustard and pepper. Stir into the drained beans. Put into bean pot with pork on top. Add enough water to cover and bake at 300 to 325 degrees for several hours until done. Add more water when necessary. When cooking overnight, I add a lot of water the first time.

Submitted by Mrs. Bertha Lovejoy, Thomaston, Maine

Boston Baked Beans

1 pound of yellow or pea beans
¼ pound brown sugar
½ pound salt pork
1 small onion
½ teaspoon salt
½ teaspoon pepper
½ teaspoon dry mustard
1/3 cup molasses
5 cups hot water

Add sugar, onion, salt, pepper, dry mustard, molasses to beans. Place pork on top of beans, fill pot with water and bake in oven (325 degrees) for about 7-8 hours. Add remaining water from time to time.

Submitted by Olive Terrio, Howland, Maine

Baked Beans With Maple Syrup

2 pounds soldier beans (I always use these)
1 cup maple syrup
½ cup sugar
¼ cup molasses
2 teaspoons dry mustard
1 teaspoon ginger
2 teaspoons salt
Salt pork and onion, if desired

Soak beans overnight. Add ingredients in morning and bake as usual, adding only water as needed.

Submitted by Mrs. Louise Dick, Morrisville, Vt.

Fried Asparagus

1 can asparagus spears
1 egg
½ cup flour
2 tablespoons water (or milk)
2 tablespoons butter (or margarine)
Salt and pepper to taste
Dash garlic salt (optional)

Beat the egg, add water (or milk), salt, pepper and garlic salt. Drain liquid from asparagus and dip the spears in the egg mixture. Roll in flour. Heat butter in frying pan and fry spears until golden brown and crisp.

These are delicious and my family is very fond of them. I have never seen this recipe in any cookbook.

Submitted by Mrs. Phyllis Briggs, Madison, Maine

Zucchini Casserole

2 or 3 small zucchini squash
3 tablespoons onion soup mix
1 cup grated cheese
1 cup bread crumbs
1 can celery soup (10½ ounce)
Grated Parmesan cheese

In a buttered 1½ quart casserole, put a layer of zucchini, which has been cut in cubes. (Do not peel or remove seeds. Slice crosswise about ½ inch thick, then cut in cubes.) On this layer, sprinkle half of the soup mix, part of the grated cheese and bread crumbs. Make another layer of squash, the rest of the soup mix, cheese and bread crumbs. Pour the can of celery soup over all. Sprinkle generously with grated Parmesan cheese. Cover and bake in a 350 degree oven for 1½ hours, or until squash is tender. Uncover and brown the crumbs.

Submitted by Mrs. Elford H. Morison, Wilton, Maine

Tomato Casserole

2 cups whole tomatoes (canned)
½ cup cracker crumbs
2 tablespoons minced onions
½ teaspoon salt
Dash pepper
4 tablespoons butter
½ cup grated cheese
1 egg

Reserve 2 tablespoons of crumbs and grated cheese for the top. Combine the ingredients in the order given. Put in a well greased baking dish and top with crumbs and cheese. Bake for 1 hour in a 350 degree oven. Serves 4.

Submitted by Mrs. Lloyd E. Fernald, Franklin, Maine

New Flavor Scalloped Potatoes

4 cups thinly sliced potatoes
1 teaspoon salt
1/8 teaspoon pepper
1 tablespoon flour
1 tablespoon butter or oleo

1 can condensed cream of
    chicken soup
Milk to make 2 cups liquid,
    with the soup

In a greased, 1½ quart casserole, put ½ of the potatoes. Mix together the flour, salt and pepper. Sprinkle part of the flour mixture over the layer of potatoes in casserole. Dot with half of the butter. Make another layer with the rest of the potatoes, flour and butter. Measure the soup and add enough milk to make 2 cups of liquid. Pour over the potatoes. Cover and bake at 350 degrees for 1 hour. Remove cover and continue baking for 45 minutes at 400 degrees, until done. Potatoes vary in cooking time at different times of the year.

Submitted by Mrs. Eula Goodwin, Anson, Maine

Green Bean Casserole

1 package frozen (French
    style) beans
1 can French fried onion
    rings

1 can cream of mushroom
    soup
½ cup water

Cook beans until tender. Drain. Mix mushroom soup with water. Put a layer of beans, one of onion rings and soup. Top with onions. Bake in a 350 degree oven until light brown on top.

Submitted by Mrs. Hester McGown, Carmel, Maine

Onion and Apple Casserole

3 large onions
4 large apples
2 cups of beef or chicken
    bouillon

Salt and pepper to taste
1 cup bread crumbs (plain or
    seasoned)
1 tablespoon butter

Place the apples, onions, bread crumbs and seasonings in a greased casserole in layers. Dot with butter and pour on the bouillon. Bake for 1 hour at 350 degrees. Serve with Yorkshire pudding and roast pork.

Submitted by Mrs. Arnold Bishop, Wilmington, Mass.

Spinach Pie

1 pound chopped spinach
(may be frozen)
2 eggs, beaten
2 tablespoons butter, softened
Grated cheese (2 ounces)
¼ pound boiled ham

1 teaspoon baking powder
½ cup bread crumbs
Salt, pepper, paprika to taste
2 tablespoons milk
Butter and grated cheese to
garnish top

Boil spinach in a small amount of water for 5 minutes. Drain and let cool for 5 minutes. Mix spinach and eggs with the butter. Add the 2 ounces of grated cheese and the ham, cut into little pieces. Add baking powder and bread crumbs. Add seasonings and milk. Mix well together and put into an 8 x 8 baking pan. Add small pieces of butter to top of pie and sprinkle grated cheese on top. Bake for 15 minutes in a 450 degree oven so that it is a golden brown on top.

Submitted by Mrs. John Migueis, Bangor, Maine

Eggplant — Farmer's Style

2 medium eggplants
1 pound chopped meat
1 large onion, sliced

2 eggs
1 cup bread crumbs
Salt and pepper to taste

Boil the eggplant until soft, split open and remove the meat. Put in a flat pan and mash. Set aside. Fry onion in butter until soft. Add the chopped meat and cook 5 minutes; add to the eggplant with the bread crumbs, salt and pepper. Add the eggs and mix well. Put in a buttered casserole and sprinkle the top with grated cheese. Bake for 35 to 40 minutes at 400 degrees. Serves 6.

Submitted by Mrs. Sara M. Baxter, Gray, Maine

Cabbage Scramble

4 cups shredded cabbage
1½ cups canned tomatoes
1 large onion, cut fine
½ teaspoon salt
½ teaspoon sugar

Dash of pepper
2 tablespoons butter
Buttered bread crumbs
Grated cheese

Cook cabbage, tomatoes and onions in a small amount of boiling water about 10 minutes. Add seasonings and butter. Garnish with buttered bread crumbs and grated cheese. Bake in a 350 degree oven for 20 minutes.

Submitted by Mrs. Claribel Andrews, Tenants Harbor, Maine

Stuffed Green Peppers

3 large green peppers
1 pound ground beef (good grade)
1 large onion
½ cup crushed pineapple
1 cup thawed frozen corn
½ cup leftover mashed potato
Seasonings to taste
1 can tomato soup
¾ cup water
½ cup Russian dressing

Halve the peppers and remove stem and seed portions. Place in boiling salted water for 5 minutes. Remove and drain well.

Slice the onion and saute lightly in a little oleo. Place in a large bowl, beef, sauteed onion, pineapple, corn, mashed potatoes and seasonings. (Seasoned salt, Accent, pepper and onion salt may be used.) Mix together well and generously fill the pepper halves. Place in a glass baking dish, stuffing side up. Mix together the tomato soup, water and Russian dressing. Pour over the stuffed peppers. Bake in a preheated oven at 350 degrees for 45 minutes.

Submitted by Terry Niedermann, Northeast 9, Cushing, Maine

Fried Tomatoes

4 large tomatoes
Butter, drippings or olive oil for frying
Salt and pepper to taste
½ cup of cream

Cut the tomatoes in thick slices and fry in butter, (drippings or olive oil) until they are brown, turn and brown other side. Do not overcook, just brown. Lift to a hot flat dish and dust with salt and pepper. Into the gravy in the spider, pour the cream, stir quickly and pour over the tomatoes. Serve hot.

Submitted by Mrs. Leola Peaslee, No. Edgecomb, Maine

Potato Puff

2 teaspoons butter
1 cup hot milk
2 cups mashed potato
1 egg, beaten
2 tablespoons grated cheese
Salt and pepper to taste

Melt the butter in the hot milk. Add the mashed potato, beat until light. Add the beaten egg, cheese, salt and pepper to taste. Beat again. Pour into a well greased casserole and bake at 350 degrees until nice and brown. Serve hot.

Submitted by Mrs. Joseph Couture, Jr., Oakland, Maine

Sandwich Spread

1 can chopped meat
1 small onion, chopped
¼ cup chopped green pepper
¼ cup chopped celery

½ cup chopped lettuce
2 teaspoons prepared mustard
3 to 4 tablespoons mayonnaise

Mix all ingredients together. Refrigerate until ready to use. I call this my "Little Bit of Everything Sandwich Spread."

Submitted by Mrs. Marilyn R. Grant, Temple, Maine

Meat Sauce

1 pound ground beef
1 chopped onion
3 slices chopped cooked bacon
¼ cup salad oil

1 large can tomatoes
2 tablespoons tomato paste
2 teaspoons salt
½ teaspoon pepper

Heat oil in a saucepan, mix beef and onion, add to the oil with the bacon. Cook, stirring constantly. Strain the tomatoes and add to the meat, with the tomato paste and seasonings. Simmer for 1 hour. Good on spaghetti.

Submitted by Mrs. Gordon Hambrecht, Dexter, Maine

Horseradish Sauce

3 tablespoons grated horseradish root
1 tablespoon lemon juice
¼ teaspoon salt

Few grains cayenne
8 tablespoons heavy cream
(½ cup)

Mix together the horseradish, lemon juice, salt and cayenne and stir into the stiffly beaten cream. Good with cold meats. Keep refrigerated.

Submitted by Mrs. Dorothy Robbins, Ellsworth, Maine·

Brown Sugar Syrup for Pancakes

1 cup white sugar
2 cups brown sugar

1 cup boiling water
1 teaspoon vanilla

Boil sugars and water together for 5 minutes. Let cool. Add vanilla.

Submitted by Mrs. Athelene Hilt, Union, Maine

100 Years Pie Crust

2½ cups flour
1 teaspoon salt
¼ cup sugar (scant)

1 cup shortening
½ cup milk

Sift flour, salt and sugar. Cut in shortening. Add milk and mix lightly but thoroughly. Roll out to fit pie plate.

Submitted by Mrs. Harold White, Ellsworth, Maine

Pie Crust Mix

Cold milk
6 cups flour
1 lb. lard

3 tablespoons sugar
1 teaspoon salt

Mix the flour, lard, sugar and salt together. Store in refrigerator in covered container — like empty Crisco can. When needed, take 2 cups from can and mix with cold milk. This is very good to have on hand to make a quick pie!

Submitted by Carrie C. Libby, Newport, Maine

Pie Crust

2½ cups flour
1 cup lard
½ cup milk

1 tablespoon vinegar
1 teaspoon salt

Cut lard into flour until fine. Add the ½ cup milk with the 1 tablespoon vinegar mixed in, directly. If not enough, add more milk to make a soft dough. This is enough for 2 9-inch pies.

Submitted by Della M. Wiers, Newport, Maine

Pie Crust

6 cups flour (sifted and
  measured)
1 pound lard

2 teaspoons salt
1 beaten egg
Cold water

Mix together the flour, salt, and lard. Put the beaten egg in a measuring cup and fill with cold water. Pour over first mixture. Mix. Makes 4 or 5 pies. May be refrigerated 2 to 3 weeks before using.

Submitted by Adelia Baker, Presque Isle, Maine

Pie Crust

5 cups flour
¼ cup sugar
1 tablespoon salt

1 pound lard
1 egg yolk, beaten
Cold water

Sift flour with sugar and salt; cut or work in the lard. Beat egg yolk, pour in a cup and fill with cold water. Mix well. This will keep in refrigerator for 3 weeks, well wrapped. When ready to use, remove from refrigerator and let stand at room temperature for ½ hour before rolling out. Omit the sugar when making crust for meat pies.

Submitted by Evelyn Osborne, Guilford, Maine

Lemon Meringue Pie

3½ tablespoons cornstarch
1¼ cups sugar
¼ teaspoon salt
¼ cup lemon juice
1 tablespoon grated lemon rind
3 eggs, separated
1½ cups boiling water

1 tablespoon butter
6 tablespoons sugar
1 teaspoon lemon juice
2 tablespoons cold water
1 tablespoon cornstarch
½ cup boiling water
1 baked pie shell (9 inch)

In a saucepan, combine the 3½ tablespoons cornstarch, 1¼ cups sugar, salt, ¼ cup lemon juice and the lemon rind. Beat the egg yolks and add to cornstarch mixture, mix well. Gradually add the 1½ cups boiling water. Heat to boiling over direct heat, then boil gently for 4 minutes, stirring constantly. When the mixture has thickened (it may take more than 4 minutes) stir in the butter. Pour the filling into the baked pie shell. In a small saucepan combine the 1 tablespoon of cornstarch and the 2 tablespoons of cold water. Stir in the ½ cup of boiling water and cook for 2 minutes or until thickened. Cool to room temperature. While this is cooling, add the 1 teaspoon of lemon juice to the egg whites which are at room temperature, and beat until soft peaks form. Gradually add the 6 tablespoons of sugar, beating all the while until firm peaks form. Beat in the cornstarch mixture. Spread meringue over pie filling, being sure to touch the crust all around, and bake at 350 degrees for 12 minutes, or until a light brown. Cool.

Submitted by Mildred Brown Schrumpf, Orono, Maine

The first attempt to can corn was by Isaac Winslow in 1839 near Portland. After trying many methods and failing he finally achieved success with the open boiler method of processing the cans. Although successful with his method by 1844, he failed to obtain a patent and it was left to his son, Nathan Winslow, to begin the first commercial canning in a factory in Riverton, Maine in 1852. He was joined by his nephew, J. Winslow Jones, in the business in 1853 and the venture was off to a successful start. From this beginning the canning of corn has become a very important part of the economy of Maine.

Frozen Lemon Pie

½ cup fine graham crackers crumbs
3 eggs, separated
½ cup sugar
3 teaspoons grated lemon peel
¼-½ cup lemon juice
1 cup cream, whipped stiff

Sprinkle a well-greased 9-inch pie pan with ¼ cup fine graham cracker crumbs, and chill. Be sure to grease pie pan with butter or margarine first.

Beat egg whites until frothy and add gradually ½ cup sugar and beat stiff. Beat egg yolks until thick and lemon colored. Then add 3 teaspoons grated lemon peel and lemon juice to egg yolks. Fold in the egg whites. Have ready the whipped cream beaten stiff and fold into the egg mixture. Pour into graham cracker lined pie pan and sprinkle with ¼ cup of graham cracker crumbs. Freeze and serve frozen, as it melts quickly.

Submitted by Mrs. Arthur Briggs, Monticello, Maine

Lemon Rhubarb Pie

3 cups diced rhubarb
1 cup sugar
1 tablespoon flour
½ cup water
1 beaten egg
¾ teaspoon grated lemon rind
1 tablespoon lemon juice

Put diced rhubarb into pastry lined plate. Combine flour and sugar. Stir in egg, rind and juice, and water. Cook in double boiler until thickened. Pour over rhubarb. Top with lattice crust. Bake in 450 degree oven for 10 minutes. Reduce heat to 350 degrees and cook for 20-30 minutes.

Submitted by Mrs. Hilda A. DeBisschop, Sedgwick, Maine

Lemon Icebox Pie

1 can Carnation milk, chilled
¾ to 1 cup sugar (depending on desired sweetness)
1 package of lemon Jello
1 cup boiling water
Juice of 1 lemon, unstrained except for seeds
Graham cracker pie shell

Mix Jello with 1 cup boiling water and cool to jelly stage. Beat milk until thickened. Add sugar, continue to beat, add Jello and beat, add lemon juice and beat. When thoroughly mixed, put into graham cracker pie shell and refrigerate until ready to serve.

Submitted by Ida Fox Briggs, Hartland, Maine

Lemon Sponge Pie

¼ cup soft butter or margarine
1 cup granulated sugar
3 eggs, separated (yolks from whites)
3 tablespoons flour
¼ teaspoon salt
6 tablespoons lemon juice
1 teaspoon grated lemon rind
2 cups milk
Pastry for a 10-inch pie plate

Line a 10-inch pie plate with your favorite pie crust recipe. Separate eggs and beat the whites until they hold up in peaks. Add about ¼ cup of the sugar to these so that they will hold up. Cream butter, add salt and remaining sugar. Add 2 unbeaten egg yolks, beat well, add the flour, lemon juice and lemon rind. Add milk, then fold in the beaten whites.

Pour into the unbaked pastry pie shell. Bake at 425 degrees for 15 minutes, reduce heat to 325 degrees and continue to bake for 25 minutes. Place pie on rack to cool. Serves 6.

Submitted by Mrs. Francis J. Cyr, Old Town, Maine

Southern Pecan Pie

4 eggs, beaten
1 cup white sugar
1 cup dark Karo syrup
1 tablespoon flour
3 tablespoons butter
2 teaspoons vanilla
1 cup pecan meats, chopped

Combine all ingredients in order given. Pour into unbaked pie shell. Bake 400 degrees about 20 minutes. Reset oven to 350 degrees and bake pie about 40 minutes until a knife can be inserted and comes out almost clean.

Submitted by Mrs. Francis Beaulieu, Calais, Maine

Blueberry Pie

3 cups blueberries, fresh or frozen
2 tablespoons flour
½ cup granulated sugar
¼ cup brown sugar
⅛ teaspoon salt
Grated rind of ½ orange

Prepare blueberries, add flour, both brown and white sugar, salt and orange rind. Mix thoroughly. Line a 9-inch pie plate with pastry. Fill with the berries. Dot with 1 tablespoon butter. Put on the top crust, prick well and bake in a 425-450 degree oven for 35-40 minutes.

Submitted by Mrs. Thelma Cunningham, West Minot, Maine

Squash Pie

2 cups mashed squash
2 eggs
½ cup sugar
½ cup milk
Dash of ginger

Beat the eggs, blend in squash, sugar, milk and ginger. Line an 8-inch pie plate with pie crust and crimp the edges. This will help retain the filling. Bake at 425 degrees for the first 15 minutes and at 350 degrees until firm.

This is an old-time family recipe.

Submitted by Mrs. Winnie Thomas, Camden, Maine

New England Squash Pie

1¾ cups strained mashed
  cooked squash
1 teaspoon salt
1½ cups milk
3 eggs
½ cup molasses
½ cup white sugar
1 teaspoon cinnamon
1 teaspoon vanilla

Beat all ingredients together with rotary beater. Pour into 9-inch pastry-lined pie pan. Bake until a silver knife inserted 1" from side of filling comes out clean. The center may still look soft, but will set later. Bake 45 to 55 minutes in a 425 degree oven.

Submitted by Marilyn M. Wiers

Squash Pie (without eggs)

1 cup squash
1½ cups hot milk
1/3 cup sugar
Salt, nutmeg and cassia to
  taste
1 Boston brown baked cracker
rolled fine or same amount
of any crackers (about ¼ cup
crumbs)

If you want to make a pumpkin pie, add to the above recipe 1 tablespoon molasses and some ginger.

This *can* be made with 2 eggs in place of crackers.

Submitted by Harriet M. H. True, Yarmouth, Maine

Green Tomato Pie

1¼ cups white sugar
1 tablespoon flour
3 cups thinly sliced green
tomatoes

⅛ teaspoon nutmeg
½ teaspoon cinnamon
¼ teaspoon salt

Line pie plate with pie crust. Mix and sift the white sugar and flour. Sprinkle half of the mixture over the crust. Add the sliced green tomatoes, and sprinkle the remainder of the sugar and flour mixture over them. Sprinkle with the nutmeg, cinnamon, and salt. Dot with butter and put on top crust. Bake 40 minutes in a 350 degree oven until the tomatoes are done and the crust is a light brown.

Submitted by Mrs. Forrest A. Stowell, Paris, Maine

Cranberry-Raisin Pie

2¼ cups cranberries
1 cup raisins
4 small crackers

1 cup sugar
½ teaspoon vanilla
½ cup water

Chop cranberries and raisins and crackers. Add sugar, vanilla and water. Mix well and bake in double crust in 9-inch pie plate for 30 minutes in 400 degree oven.

Submitted by Mrs. Thelma Cunningham, West Minot, Maine

Cranberry Pie

1 cup cranberries — put
through food chopper
1½ cups sugar

½ cup water
2 tablespoons flour
1 teaspoon vanilla

Put cranberries through food chopper. Mix the sugar, water, flour and vanilla in with the cranberries. Let stand overnight. Put in cooked crust and bake.

(This filling may be kept for months in refrigerator.)

Submitted by Huldah Monfette, Ashland, Maine

Muskmelon Pie

2 cups of muskmelon (yellow meated, and stewed)
½ cup sugar
2 tablespoons cornstarch
¼ teaspoon nutmeg

1 tablespoon butter
2 egg yolks, well beaten
2 egg whites
¼ teaspoon cream of tartar
¼ cup sugar

Cook and mash the muskmelon, add ½ cup sugar, cornstarch, nutmeg, butter, and well beaten egg yolks. Cook over low heat until thick. Add filling to baked pie crust, in 8-inch pie plate. Beat egg whites and cream of tartar until frothy. Gradually beat in sugar, a little at a time. Continue beating until stiff and glossy. Cover filling with meringue and bake 8 to 10 minutes in 400 degree oven.

Submitted by Mrs. Jannie Wiers, St. Albans, Maine

Custard Pie

4 slightly beaten eggs
½ cup sugar
¼ teaspoon salt

2½ cups scalded milk
1 teaspoon vanilla
1 9-inch unbaked pie shell

Thoroughly mix eggs, sugar, salt and vanilla. Stir in hot milk. Pour at once into unbaked pastry shell. Dash top with nutmeg. Bake in hot oven 475 degrees for 5 minutes, reduce heat to 425 degrees. Bake 10 minutes longer or until a knife put in pie, halfway between center and edge, comes out clean. Cool on rack.

Submitted by Mrs. Charles Buxton, Bangor Road, Houlton, Maine

Beautiful Custard Pie

1 egg white, beaten stiff
½ cup sugar
¼ teaspoon salt
1 teaspoon vanilla

2 eggs and 1 egg yolk
2½ cups warmed milk
Nutmeg

Beat egg white stiff, add sugar, salt and vanilla, beat these into the egg white. Beat the egg yolk and 2 large eggs slightly. Add to the beaten white. Add the warmed milk.

Pour into unbaked 9-inch pastry shell, sprinkle with nutmeg and place in a 450 degree oven. Reset control to 425 degrees and bake 30 minutes.

Submitted by Mrs. Edwin B. Leach, Perry, Maine

Strawberry Cheese Pie

¾ lb. Philadelphia cream
   cheese
½ cup granulated sugar
1 teaspoon vanilla
⅛ teaspoon almond flavoring
3 eggs, separated
1 pint frozen strawberries
Graham cracker crust (9-inch
   pie plate)

TOPPING
1 cup sour cream (commercial)
2 tablespoons sugar
½ teaspoon vanilla
1/6 teaspoon almond
   flavoring

Blend cheese and sugar. Beat egg yolks until thick (5 minutes). Add yolks and flavorings to cheese and mix well. Pour into a chilled 9-inch graham cracker crust, not baked. Bake at 325 degrees for 40 minutes. Spread on topping and bake exactly 10 minutes (no longer). Cool and refrigerate. Serve topped with the thawed strawberries.

Submitted by Mrs. Gail Snell, Brewer, Maine

Grandmother's Buttermilk Pie

1 cup sugar
1 teaspoon flour
Pinch salt
2 eggs

½ teaspoon lemon extract
2 cups or so of buttermilk
   (to fill an average sized pie
   tin)

Mix all ingredients together and pour into unbaked pie shell. Cook as you would for custard pie.

Submitted by Mrs. Lloyd Torrey, Surry, Maine

Butter Pie

3 eggs, well beaten
¾ cup sugar
2 tablespoons flour
Little salt

1 teaspoon vanilla
1 pint milk
2 tablespoons butter

Put butter in milk and heat until butter melts. Add sugar and flour. Mix well, add beaten eggs, vanilla. Cook in unbaked pie shell as for custard pie.

Submitted by Nora Stickney, Rockland, Maine

Coffee Toffee Pie

PASTRY SHELL

1 tablespoon water
½ package pie crust mix
¼ cup light brown sugar
¾ cup finely chopped walnuts

1 square unsweetened chocolate (grated)
1 teaspoon vanilla

FILLING

½ cup soft butter or margarine
2/3 cup white sugar
2 teaspoons instant coffee

1 square unsweetened chocolate (melted and cooled)
2 eggs

TOPPING

1 cup of whipped cream
Sugar and vanilla to taste

Preheat oven to 375 degrees. Make pastry shell. In medium bowl combine pie crust with brown sugar, walnuts and grated chocolate. Add 1 tablespoon water and the vanilla. NOTE: Do not use amount of water as shown on pie crust box. Using fork, mix well until blended. Turn into well greased 9-inch pie plate, press firmly against bottom and sides of pie plate. Bake for 15 minutes. Cool pastry shell in pie plate on wire rack. Meanwhile, make filling.

In a small bowl, with electric mixer at medium speed, beat butter and granulated sugar until light. Blend in cooled melted chocolate and the instant coffee. Add 1 egg, beat for 5 minutes; add remaining egg, beat 5 minutes longer. Turn filling into cooled, baked pie shell, refrigerate uncovered overnight. When ready to serve, whip cream and put on top of pie. May garnish with chocolate curls. Eight servings.

Submitted by Joy W. Stewart, Dexter, Maine

Raisin Pie With Meringue

¾ cup milk
1 heaping teaspoon flour
¾ cup sugar
1 cup chopped raisins (seedless)

½ teaspoon salt
2 eggs, separated
1 tablespoon butter
1 teaspoon vanilla
2 tablespoons sugar

Mix flour with sugar. Add salt and egg yolk, beaten together, to the milk. Then add chopped raisins and butter to the above mixture and cook over low heat until thickened. When thickened, take off stove and add vanilla. Place in baked pie shell, and cover with meringue made from egg whites. Brown in oven.

Submitted by Mrs. Emma Knox, Fryeburg, Maine

Pumpkin Pie

CRUST:

1 cup flour	½ teaspoon salt
2 tablespoons sugar	¾ cup water
1 teaspoon baking powder	2/3 cup Crisco

Blend well at low speed; beat 2 minutes at medium speed Spread batter in 9 or 10-inch deep pie pan.

FILLING:

1 scant quart uncooked pump-kin, cut in very small pieces	½ teaspoon nutmeg
	4 tablespoons water
2/3 cup honey	½ teaspoon vanilla
½ cup sugar	Pinch salt
1 teaspoon cinnamon	

Mix all together and spoon carefully on top pie crust. Cover with foil and bake at 425 degrees for 40 to 45 minutes.

Submitted by Mrs. Vaughn G. MacDonald, Carmel, Maine

Pumpkin Pie

¼ cup sugar	1 or 2 eggs, beaten
½ teaspoon salt	1 cup milk
1 teaspoon cinnamon	¼ cup molasses
1 teaspoon ginger	2 cups strained pumpkin
2 tablespoons flour	

Mix the dry ingredients. Add the beaten eggs, milk and molasses to the pumpkin. Combine liquid mixture to dry ingredients and pour into pastry lined pie plate. Bake at 450 degrees for 10 minutes, then lower temperature to 350 degrees and bake about 50 minutes.

Submitted by Mrs. Wanita Lunn, Augusta, Maine

Cream Cheese Cherry Pie

1 large package cream cheese	½ pint whipping cream or
½ cup sugar	1 pint of Cool Whip
1 teaspoon vanilla	1 can cherry pie filling

Combine 1 large package cream cheese, ½ cup sugar, 1 teaspoon vanilla. Add the whipped cream to the above mixture. Spread this mixture over cooled pie shell, saving ¾ cup for topping. Spread 1 can cherry pie filling over this and top with remaining white mixture. Refrigerate overnight.

Submitted by Jean Overlock, Warren, Maine

Paper-bag Apple Streusel Pie

Large brown paper bag
½ cup sugar
2 tablespoons flour

¼ teaspoon nutmeg
5 or 6 apples (about 2 pounds)

STREUSEL

½ cup sugar
½ cup flour

¼ lb. butter or oleo

Unbaked 9-inch flaky pastry pie shell. Make high fluted edge. For baking the pie, we use a big brown paper bag such as groceries come in. It needs to be large enough for the pie plate to fit into in roomy fashion.

To prepare the bag, place the bottom of a 9-inch pie plate over the middle of one side of the bag and mark around the plate; cut around the mark (just on one side of the bag) and reserve the cutout piece. The use of the cutout assures the crust browning.

In a large mixing bowl, stir together ½ cup sugar, 2 tablespoons flour, and nutmeg. Pare apples, core and cut in 1-inch cubes. There should be about 6 cups. Toss apples with the sugar mixture until well coated and turn into pie shell. Stir together ½ cup sugar, ½ cup flour, cut in ¼ lb. butter or oleo until mixture is fine and crumbly. Sprinkle over top of pie.

Place the pie in the middle of the prepared paper bag so you can see its top through the cutout. Fold the open ends of the bag, using drugstore fold, and fasten with paper clips. Carefully place on cookie sheet. Put the cutout back in place over the top of the pie. Bake in 400 degree oven for 30 minutes; remove cutout and continue baking for 30 minutes or until apples are tender. Remove from bag. Delicious served warm.

Submitted by Mrs. Elsie Wortman, East Thorndike, Maine

Leona's Apple Pie

Apples
1 cup sugar
½ teaspoon cinnamon

½ teaspoon nutmeg
Butter

Make pastry for a 2 crust, 9-inch pie. Fill bottom crust with pared, sliced apples. Combine spices with sugar and put on top of apples. Dot with butter. Cover with top crust. Bake at 350 degrees until crust is set and nicely browned. Then lower heat to 300 degrees so juices will not bubble over. Cook until apples are tender when tested with a knife.

Submitted by Mrs. Leona Starrett, Thomaston, Maine

Apple Blush Pie

5 large apples
1 cup crushed pineapple
(drained)
¼ cup cinnamon drops
1 teaspoon lemon juice

½ cup sugar
2 tablespoons flour
⅛ teaspoon salt
2 tablespoons butter

Peel and slice apples, add pineapple, cinnamon candies, and all dry ingredients. Mix well and let stand while preparing crust. Dot filling with the butter before covering with top crust.

Submitted by Nancie Bond, Jefferson, Maine

Apple Pie Filling

Apples to fill a 9-inch pie
shell
½ cup sugar
¼ cup molasses

Pinch of salt
½ teaspoon cinnamon
2 tablespoons butter or oleo

Lightly dust the bottom crust with flour. Add the sliced apples to fill the pan. Sprinkle on the sugar, salt and cinnamon. Pour the molasses over all. Dot with the butter and cover with top crust. Bake in a 425 degree oven for about 45 minutes.

I worked this recipe up myself to give the molasses flavor without using too much of it. I used Northern Spy apples and this amount made it plenty sweet.

Submitted by Joyce Prentice, Freedom, Maine

Pineapple Meringue Pie

1 cup sugar
2 tablespoons flour
3 eggs
1 teaspoon butter

1 can (16 or 17 oz.)
crushed pineapple
¼ cup water

MERINGUE

3 egg whites
¼ teaspoon cream of tartar

6 tablespoons sugar
½ teaspoon flavoring

Line a 9-inch pie pan with piecrust — build up a fluted edge. Cream sugar, flour, egg yolks and butter. Stir in pineapple and water. Mix well and pour into the unbaked pie crust. Bake at 425 degrees for 15 minutes, then bake at 350 degrees for 30 minutes. Cool and apply meringue.

To mix meringue, beat egg whites and cream of tartar until frothy. Gradually add sugar and flavoring. Beat until stiff. Bake 8 minutes at 400 degrees temperature.

Submitted by Mrs. Ruth S. Dow, Dover-Foxcroft, Maine

Rhubarb Dream Pie

1 well beaten egg
½ cup honey
½ cup sugar
1 cup chopped rhubarb (raw)

½ cup macaroon crumbs
½ cup chopped dates
2½ tablespoons butter
¼ teaspoon salt

Mix egg, sugar, and honey. Add rhubarb and other ingredients. Mix well. Pour into pastry-lined pie pan. Cover with strips of pastry and bake in hot oven 400 degrees for 10 to 15 minutes. Reduce heat to 300 degrees and bake until done, about ¾ hour.

This is very nice with a meringue instead of the pastry strips. Make and add meringue after pie is done and put pie in 400 degree oven for 12 to 15 minutes or until meringue is done. Keeps well and improves in flavor.

Submitted by Mrs. Leona Murphy, Mount Desert, Maine

Rhubarb Pie

3 cups cut-up rhubarb
¾ cup sugar
½ teaspoon nutmeg

2 egg yolks, beaten
3 level tablespoons flour
1 tablespoon butter

MERINGUE

2 egg whites
¼ teaspoon salt

4 tablespoons sugar
½ teaspoon lemon flavoring

Mix rhubarb, ¾ cup sugar, nutmeg, egg yolks, flour, and butter together and pour into a 9-inch unbaked pie shell and bake in a 450 degree oven for 10 minutes; then reduce heat to 325 and bake until filling thickens about 30 minutes. Just before it has finished baking, put the meringue on top and put back in oven to brown for 12 to 15 minutes.

To make the meringue, beat the egg whites and salt 'till frothy. Beat in 4 tablespoons sugar, 1 at a time. Beat until the meringue is stiff and glossy and will hold a point and yet look moist. Add ½ teaspoon lemon flavoring and pile on top of pie and bake.

Submitted by Mrs. R. Fred Harmon, Caribou, Maine

Chocolate Cream Pie

1 square chocolate	1 cup evaporated milk
4 tablespoons flour	1 cup water
6 tablespoons sugar	2 egg yolks, well beaten
¼ teaspoon salt	1 teaspoon vanilla

Melt the chocolate over hot water, add flour, sugar and salt. Combine milk and water and add slowly, stirring constantly, to chocolate mixture. Cook over hot water until thick and smooth. Add beaten egg yolks and cook 5 minutes longer, stirring constantly. Cool. Add vanilla and pour into baked pastry shell. Use the 2 egg whites to make meringue. Bake in slow oven 325 degrees for 20 minutes.

Submitted by Mrs. Wanita Lunn, Augusta, Maine

Custard Crunch Mince Pie

1 9-inch unbaked pie shell	3 eggs, slightly beaten
1 cup sugar	¼ cup butter, melted
2 tablespoons flour	½ cup chopped walnuts
⅛ teaspoon salt	1 cup mincemeat

Blend dry ingredients and slowly add to eggs. Add remaining ingredients and mix well. Pour into pie shell and bake in hot oven at 400 degrees for 15 minutes. Reduce heat to 325 degrees and bake 30 minutes.

Submitted by Ruth Duncan, Washburn, Maine

Quick Mince Pie

½ cup hamburg	1 tablespoon molasses
1½ cups chopped apple	2/3 cup sugar
½ cup seedless raisins	2 tablespoons water
2 tablespoons butter	2 tablespoons vinegar
½ teaspoon cinnamon	½ teaspoon salt
¼ teaspoon cloves	

Mix together the ingredients above and put in a pastry lined tin. Place a crust on top and bake in 425 degree oven for 15 minutes, then turn heat down to 350 degrees and bake about 45 minutes until center of pie is well cooked. This is a delicious quick pie.

Submitted by Mrs. Mahlon Salsbury, Ellsworth Falls, Maine

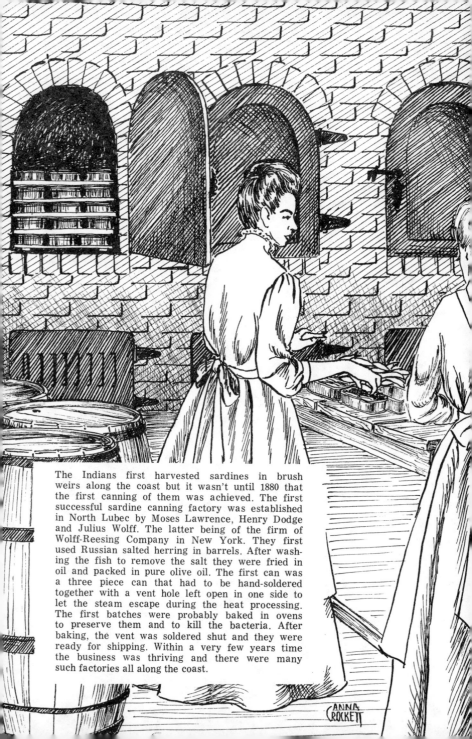

The Indians first harvested sardines in brush weirs along the coast but it wasn't until 1880 that the first canning of them was achieved. The first successful sardine canning factory was established in North Lubec by Moses Lawrence, Henry Dodge and Julius Wolff. The latter being of the firm of Wolff-Reesing Company in New York. They first used Russian salted herring in barrels. After washing the fish to remove the salt they were fried in oil and packed in pure olive oil. The first can was a three piece can that had to be hand-soldered together with a vent hole left open in one side to let the steam escape during the heat processing. The first batches were probably baked in ovens to preserve them and to kill the bacteria. After baking, the vent was soldered shut and they were ready for shipping. Within a very few years time the business was thriving and there were many such factories all along the coast.

ANNA CROCKETT

Old-Fashioned Strawberry Pudding
(Dated 1911)

1 egg yolk
1 cup milk
2 teaspoons cream of tartar

1 teaspoon soda
2 cups flour

Put in bowl the egg yolk, milk and dry ingredients and mix all together by hand as it is rather thick. Put in steamer and steam for about 50 minutes. Serve hot with strawberry sauce.

STRAWBERRY SAUCE

1 cup sugar
½ cup butter

1 cup strawberries
White of egg, beaten

Mix together and cook in double boiler over low flame for 30 minutes. Serves about 6.

Submitted by Mrs. Horace Yeaton, East Wilton, Maine

Xmas Pudding
(Over 100 years old)

½ cup light brown sugar
3 eggs, well beaten
½ cup butter, melted
¾ cup molasses
½ cup milk
3¼ cups sifted flour (scant)
1 teaspoon soda

¼ teaspoon salt
¼ teaspoon cinnamon
¼ teaspoon nutmeg
¼ teaspoon cloves
½ cup salt pork, ground
½ cup seeded raisins

Mix together the first 5 ingredients. Sift flour with soda and seasonings. Add the pork and raisins to the flour mixture and mix into the sugar and egg mixture, beat well. Steam for 3 hours. Serve warm with hard sauce.

Submitted by Mrs. Wyman Russon, N. Chelmsford, Mass.

Coffee Souffle

1½ cups brewed coffee
1 tablespoon plain gelatin
1/3 cup sugar
½ cup milk

1/3 cup sugar
¼ teaspoon salt
Vanilla
3 eggs, separated

Combine coffee, gelatin, 1/3 cup sugar and milk in double boiler and heat. Beat egg yolks slightly, add remaining 1/3 cup sugar and salt and mix well. Add to coffee mixture in double boiler and cook until it thickens. Add whites of eggs beaten stiff and the vanilla. Put into mold, chill and serve with whipped cream.

Submitted by Mrs. Walter E. Edwards, Skowhegan, Maine

Steamed Pudding
(100 years old)

3 cups flour
1½ teaspoons soda
1 teaspoon cinnamon
1 teaspoon ginger

1 cup fat salt pork, ground
1 cup molasses
2 cups buttermilk
1 cup raisins, chopped

Sift flour, soda, cinnamon and ginger together. Rub pork into the dry mixture. Add molasses and buttermilk, mix thoroughly. Fold in raisins last. (½ cup fat may be substituted for salt pork but not as good.) Steam in basin or coffee can for 3 hours, less time in coffee can.

SAUCE

1 heaping tablespoon flour
2 tablespoons butter
1 cup sugar
½ cup cold water

1½ cups boiling water
1 egg, well beaten
¼ teaspoon nutmeg

Rub the flour into butter, add the sugar and the cold water. Put into double boiler with the 1½ cups boiling water and stir until thickened. Add egg and nutmeg and cook a few minutes longer.

Submitted by Melvina W. Johnson, Gorham, Maine

Viola's New England Suet Pudding

3½ cups flour
1 teaspoon soda
1 teaspoon salt
2 teaspoons cinnamon
1 cup milk, sweet or sour

1 cup molasses
1 cup suet (ground)
1 cup dates or figs (chopped)
1 cup raisins

Sift dry ingredients, add milk and molasses, stir. Fold in suet and fruits. Steam 3 hours. This makes 3 1-pound coffee tins. Double this recipe and store in freezer. When needed, bring out and steam ½ hour. Use with the ready mixed toppings for emergency or serve with the following sauce.

SAUCE

½ cup butter
1 cup powdered sugar

1 cup cream, whipped
Vanilla or almond flavoring

Cream the butter and sugar over hot water, take from stove and add the whipped cream and flavoring. Stir until smooth. Serve immediately.

Submitted by Inga J. Chase, Glen Cove, Maine

John's Delight

2 cups dry bread crumbs
½ cup melted butter (scant)
1 cup sweet milk
1 egg, beaten
1 teaspoon soda
½ cup molasses
1 teaspoon cassia
1 teaspoon cloves
1 teaspoon salt
½ cup regular seeded raisins
½ cup golden seeded raisins
1 teaspoon vanilla

Mix melted butter with the bread crumbs. Combine milk, egg, soda, molasses and seasonings with the bread mixture and mix well. Fold in raisins, add vanilla. Steam 2 hours in a greased tin. Serve with the following sauce.

SAUCE

1 cup sugar
1 egg, separated
1 cup cream, whipped
½ teaspoon nutmeg or
1 teaspoon lemon extract

Beat egg yolk, add sugar and beat well. Fold in egg white stiffly beaten and stiffly beaten cream. Add flavoring last.

Submitted by Mrs. Wendell Higgins, Dexter, Maine

Blueberry Crisp Pudding

4 cups fresh blueberries
1/3 cup granulated sugar
2 teaspoons lemon juice
4 tablespoons butter or margarine
1/3 cup brown sugar, packed
1/3 cup sifted all-purpose flour
¾ cup quick cooking oats

Place blueberries in 1½ quart baking dish, sprinkle with sugar and lemon juice. Cream butter, add brown sugar gradually, blend in flour with a fork. Mix in oats. Spread this over the blueberries and bake in a 375 degree oven 35 to 40 minutes or until done.

Submitted by Miss Laura Hemphill, Presque Isle, Maine

Blueberry Dessert

1 quart frozen or fresh blueberries
3 tablespoons minute tapioca
1 cup sugar
1½ cups water

Put blueberries, tapioca, sugar and water in pan. Set for 5 minutes. Cook over medium heat stirring occasionally until it comes to a boil. Pour into a dish and chill. Serve with a little whipped cream as a topping. Makes six servings.

Submitted by Mrs. William Hamel, Greenville, Maine

Blueberry Souffle
With
Custard Sauce

1 pint fresh blueberries
2 tablespoons lemon juice
3 tablespoons sugar
⅛ teaspoon salt

2 tablespoons cornstarch
4 egg whites
⅛ teaspoon cream of tartar
¼ cup sugar

Crush the blueberries and mix with lemon juice. Combine the 3 tablespoons sugar, salt and cornstarch and stir into the berries. Cook until clear and thickened. Cool.

Beat egg whites until frothy and add cream of tartar; beat until they stand in soft peaks. Gradually beat in the ¼ cup sugar and fold into cooked berries. Turn into 6-cup casserole. Place in a pan of hot water. Bake in a preheated 325 degree oven for 45 minutes or until done. Serve with custard sauce.

CUSTARD SAUCE

¼ cup sugar
1 tablespoon cornstarch
1/16 teaspoon salt

3 egg yolks
1½ cups milk
1 teaspoon vanilla

Combine sugar, cornstarch and salt in a saucepan. Gradually beat in egg yolks and milk. Cook over low heat or hot water until mixture coats a metal spoon, stirring constantly. Remove from heat. Cool. Add vanilla.

Submitted by Mrs. Ernest L. Young, Northeast Harbor, Maine

Blueberry Buckle

½ cup shortening
½ cup sugar
1 egg, beaten
2 cups flour

½ teaspoon salt
½ cup milk
2½ cups blueberries

Cream shortening with sugar, add egg and beat. Sift flour with salt and add to the creamed mixture alternately with the milk. Spread in a 8" x 8" pan and spread blueberries over top. Cover with the following topping.

TOPPING

½ cup sugar
½ cup flour

½ cup margarine
¾ teaspoon cinnamon

Bake at 375 degrees 45 minutes.

Submitted by Ruth Duncan, Washburn, Maine

Blueberry Dessert

2 teaspoons sugar
½ cup butter, melted
2 cups blueberries (fresh or frozen)

10 graham crackers
½ cup sugar
2 heaping tablespoons flour

Roll graham crackers fine, add sugar and melted butter. Mix well. Combine blueberries, sugar and flour. Spread in pan putting cracker mixture over top and bake 30 minutes at 350 degrees. Top with whipped cream.

Submitted by Mrs. Roy Barteaux, Brewer, Maine

Cooperstown Pudding

1 pint boiling milk
3 tablespoons flour (even)
1 tablespoon cornstarch
4 tablespoons cold milk
1 teaspoon butter
4 egg yolks, beaten separately

4 egg whites, beaten stiff
1 cup sugar
½ cup butter
1 egg, well beaten
½ cup hot milk
1 teaspoon vanilla

Make a paste with the flour, cornstarch and cold milk. Stir into the pint of boiling milk. Mix well. Remove from heat and cool. Add the well beaten egg yolks, and fold in the stiffly beaten egg whites. Pour into a baking dish and place in a pan of hot water. Bake 45 minutes or until set like custard. Serve with a warm sauce as follows: Cream together the cup of sugar and half cup of butter, add the beaten egg. Stir in the hot milk and vanilla. Mix well.

This recipe was taken from an old cookbook and signed "Thorndike House."

Submitted by Mrs. Maud Patterson, Rockland, Maine

Cherry Surprises

1½ cups icing sugar
1½ cups butter (room temperature)
1½ cups fine coconut

1 teaspoon vanilla
Graham cracker crumbs
1 large jar maraschino cherries

Beat together sugar, butter and coconut. Add vanilla. Roll a small amount of dough around each cherry, and roll in graham cracker crumbs. Keep in a cool place.

Submitted by Mrs. Steve McKenney, Fort Fairfield, Maine

Bread Pudding

1 quart milk
½ cup sugar
¼ teaspoon nutmeg
¼ teaspoon cinnamon
½ teaspoon salt

4 slices bread
2/3 cup molasses
3 eggs, slightly beaten
¼ cup melted butter
1 teaspoon vanilla

Scald milk, sugar, nutmeg, cinnamon and salt together until all are dissolved. Add bread broken in pieces and let soak 15 minutes. Then add molasses, beaten eggs and mix thoroughly. Last add melted butter and vanilla. Pour into greased baking dish. Set in a pan which contains a little warm water and bake in 325 degree oven for 1 hour. Test with silver knife as for custards. Serves 6.

Submitted by Mrs. Mabel Pinkerton, Rockland, Maine

Bread Pudding

1 cup brown sugar
½ cup dark or light Karo
3 slices buttered bread
2 eggs, well beaten

2 cups milk
½ teaspoon vanilla
Pinch salt
Dash of cinnamon

Grease a casserole well with margarine. Put into this the brown sugar, Karo and the bread cut up into cubes. Next add the eggs, milk, vanilla and salt with a generous dash of cinnamon over the top. Do not stir. Set the casserole in a pan of hot water and bake 40 minutes in a 350 degree oven. The Karo syrup is added to make more sauce.

Submitted by Mrs. Frank Rowe, Warren, Maine

Bread Pudding

6 slices day-old bread
2 tablespoons butter
½ cup moist raisins
¼ teaspoon salt

½ cup sugar
3 eggs, beaten
3 cups milk, scalded
¼ teaspoon cinnamon

Toast the bread and spread with the 2 tablespoons of butter while still hot. Arrange toast in a buttered pan and sprinkle with the raisins. Beat the eggs, add salt and all but 2 tablespoons of sugar. Add the milk and stir to mix. Pour over the toast and let stand for 10 minutes. Press the toast down so that it soaks up most of the milk mixture. Mix the cinnamon with 2 tablespoons of sugar and sprinkle over the top. Bake in a 350 degree oven about 25 minutes, until top is brown. Serves 5 or 6.

Submitted by Mrs. Esther Hensler, Presque Isle, Maine

Old-Time Indian Pudding

5 tablespoons yellow cornmeal
1 quart sweet whole milk
2 tablespoons butter
¾ cup molasses
1 scant teaspoon salt
¾ teaspoon cinnamon
½ teaspoon ginger
2 eggs, well beaten
1 cup cold milk

Scald the cornmeal with the quart of milk, add the butter, molasses, salt and spices. Mix well with the two beaten eggs. Pour into a well buttered casserole. Last add the cup of cold sweet milk, (do not stir again). Bake for one hour at 350 degrees.
Submitted by Mrs. Doris B. Jordan, Portland, Maine

Indian Pudding

1 pint milk (skim or whole)
1 egg, well beaten
1 cup molasses
2 level tablespoons cornmeal
⅛ teaspoon salt
½ teaspoon cinnamon
¼ teaspoon ginger
½ cup raisins

Scald the milk in a double boiler. Mix all the other ingredients and add to the scalded milk. Steam in the double boiler 1½ to 2 hours. Stir several times the first hour. This is delicious served with cream, whipped or plain, or with the prepared whips now on the market.
Submitted by Mrs. Carroll M. Curtis, Bethel, Maine

Old-Fashioned Indian Pudding

2 quarts of sweet skim milk
2 cups cornmeal
1 1/3 cups molasses
1 teaspoon salt
1 teaspoon cinnamon
Raisins may be added
1 teaspoon allspice
1 teaspoon ginger
Dash of cloves
1 quart cold milk
2 tablespoons butter

Heat the 2 quarts of skim milk in a double boiler. Add the cornmeal mixed with molasses. Stir until thick. Remove from heat and add salt, cold milk, spices and butter. Add raisins if desired. Mix well and pour into a large casserole. Bake at 325-350 degrees for 3 or 4 hours. Serve with whipped cream, ice cream or topping while still warm.

This recipe is as old as the hills and excellent for a large family.
Submitted by Mrs. Ruth Wade, Nordica Homestead, Farmington, Me.

Apple Indian Pudding

¼ cup cornmeal
½ cup cold water
1 teaspoon salt
3 cups scalded milk
1 cup diced apple

2 eggs, beaten
¼ cup sugar
½ cup molasses
1 tablespoon butter
1 teaspoon cinnamon

Mix together cornmeal, water and salt. Stir into the scalded milk and cook over low heat for 10 minutes, stirring constantly. Add the diced apple. Beat together eggs, sugar, molasses, butter and cinnamon. Blend into cornmeal mixture. Pour into a buttered 1½ quart baking dish which is set in a pan of water and bake about 45 minutes to 1 hour at 325 degrees. Serve with cream. Serves 6.

Submitted by Mrs. Alice Robinson, Buckfield, Maine

Passamaquoddy Bay Indian Pudding

1 cup cornmeal
1 cup molasses
3 cups boiling water
½ cup brown sugar
2 tablespoons white sugar
½ teaspoon salt

½ teaspoon ginger
1 quart milk
2 eggs, well beaten
Raisins (optional)
1 pint cold milk

Combine the cornmeal and molasses, add the boiling water and cook until the mush comes to a boil. Add to this the brown sugar, white sugar, salt, ginger, quart of milk, eggs and raisins. Bake at 300 degrees 1½ hours then add, without stirring, the pint of cold milk and bake 1½ hours longer. Serve hot or cold, plain or with ice cream, whipped cream or sour cream. Yields 12 generous servings.

Submitted by Ethel M. Hilton, Cape Neddick, Maine

Old-Fashioned Indian Pudding

1 quart milk, scalded
1/3 cup cornmeal
1 cup brown sugar
2 cups diced sweet apples or
  raisins

Butter, size of a walnut
½ teaspoon ginger
1 cup cold milk

Add the cornmeal to the scalded milk and cook until thick. Then add the sugar, apples, butter and ginger and mix well. Add cold milk last and bake slowly for 4 hours.

Submitted by Mrs. Irl McKusick, Dexter, Maine

Indian Pudding

1 quart skim milk
3 tablespoons rice
1 beaten egg
½ cup butter or oleo
½ teaspoon ginger

½ teaspoon salt
2/3 cup molasses
1 tablespoon sugar
Little cold milk

Mix first 8 ingredients together and bake 2 hours in a beanpot or casserole in a moderate oven, then pour in the cold milk and bake 1 hour longer. Stir 2 or 3 times.

This is a recipe of my mother's. She is now 104 years old.
Submitted by Edith M. Ames, Caribou, Maine

Indian Bread Pudding

3 cups scalded milk
1 tablespoon margarine
6 slices whole wheat bread
½ cup seedless raisins
1 egg

½ teaspoon ginger
¼ teaspoon salt
2/3 cup sugar
2 tablespoons molasses
Grated rind 1 lemon

Scald the milk and margarine together, trim crusts from bread and crumble the bread into the scalded milk. Add raisins and simmer a few minutes. Combine lightly beaten egg with remaining ingredients and add to the bread mixture. Pour into greased casserole. Set into a pan of hot water and bake at 375 degrees for 50 to 60 minutes. Serve hot or cold. This may be varied by adding orange or lemon marmalade or candied fruit.
Submitted by Elsie F. Holt, Topsham, Maine

Rhubarb Puffs

1/3 cup shortening
1/3 cup sugar
1 egg, well beaten
2/3 cup sweet milk

1½ cups flour
1½ teaspoons baking powder
1/3 teaspoon salt
Stewed rhubarb, sweetened

Beat shortening and sugar together until light, add the well beaten egg, then milk. Sift flour, baking powder and salt together and add to the shortening sugar mixture. Grease individual glass cups. Put 2 tablespoons of sweetened stewed rhubarb in each one, then cover with 2 tablespoons of batter. Bake in a moderately hot oven, 350 degrees for about 25 minutes. Serve with additional rhubarb sauce or any sweet sauce.
Submittd by Mrs. Glen Goodrich, Skowhegan, Maine

Rhubarb Pudding

2 cups flour
2 teaspoons baking powder
½ teaspoon salt
1 tablespoon shortening

1 cup milk
1 cup rhubarb, cut-up
Sugar

Sift dry ingredients together, cut in shortening, add milk and make into dough. Mix in the rhubarb and spread in pan, sprinkle with a handful of sugar. Bake 20 minutes in hot oven.

SAUCE

1 cup sugar
2 cups hot water
2 tablespoons vinegar or lemon juice

¼ teaspoon salt
2½ tablespoons cornstarch
2 tablespoons butter
1 teaspoon lemon extract

Combine sugar, hot water, vinegar and salt in a saucepan and bring to a boil. Thicken with the cornstarch which has been dissolved in a little cold water. Add the butter and lemon extract. Apples or cranberries may be used instead of rhubarb.

Submitted by Faith Pert, Sedgwick, Maine

Apple Dumplings Deluxe

1 egg
¾ cup sour cream
2 cups flour
¼ teaspoon soda
3 teaspoons baking powder

¾ teaspoon salt
2 tablespoons sugar
4 tart apples, cut in thin slices
Margarine, sugar, cinnamon
   and nutmeg, to spread

Beat the egg and the cream, stir in sifted dry ingredients. Toss onto a floured board and roll into an oblong ¼ inch thick. Spread lightly with soft margarine, cover the dough with sliced apple and sprinkle with sugar, cinnamon and nutmeg. Roll up like a jelly roll and cut into inch slices. Place cut side up in a deep baking dish, pour over them the following sauce:

¾ cup white sugar
¾ cup brown sugar
1 cup hot water

2 tablespoons of cornstarch
1½ tablespoons margarine

Combine the ingredients and pour over the apple slices. Bake in a 375 degree oven about 25 minutes.

Instead of sour cream, in above recipe, I sometimes use sour milk and 2 tablespoons of oleo.

Submitted by Mrs. Eula N. Goodwin, Anson, Maine

Apple Crispy

6 cooking apples
1 tablespoon white sugar
¼ teaspoon cinnamon
1 cup flour
½ cup brown sugar
½ cup butter

Peel apples and cut into eighths. Spread bottom and sides of deep pie pan generously with butter. Place apples in rows as close as possible in pan. Mix white sugar and cinnamon and sprinkle over apples. Put flour in bowl, add brown sugar and remaining butter and rub to crumbs. Sprinkle over and between apples and pat smooth. Cover and bake at 275 degrees for 1½ hours. Uncover and bake 15 to 20 minutes longer. Serve with cream or hard sauce.

Submitted by Mrs. Marion Calligan, Grand Lake Stream, Maine

French Apple Cobbler

5 cups peeled, sliced apples
¾ cup sugar
2 tablespoons flour
½ teaspoon cinnamon
¼ teaspoon salt
1 teaspoon vanilla
¼ cup water

Mix together and place in 9 x 9 pan. Dot with butter.

TOPPING

½ cup sifted flour
½ cup sugar
½ teaspoon baking powder
¼ teaspoon salt
2 tablespoons soft butter
1 egg, slightly beaten

Beat together with wooden spoon until smooth. Drop by spoonfuls over filling in pan. Bake 35 to 40 minutes. Makes 9 portions.

Submitted by Mrs. Leon M. Eaton, Deer Isle, Maine

Apple Brown Betty

½ cup sugar
¼ cup lard
1/3 cup molasses
½ teaspoon cinnamon
6 slices bread, cubed
4 apples, diced

Mix in order given and press into greased baking dish. Bake at 375 degrees for ½ hour with the cover on and ¾ hour without cover. Serve with whipped cream or non-dairy topping.

Submitted by Mrs. Dorien Conologue, Newport, Maine

Apple Grunt

1 quart flour	Apples, sliced
1 teaspoon baking soda	Cinnamon
2 teaspoons cream of tartar	Molasses
1/2 teaspoon salt	Butter
2 tablespoons shortening	Scalded milk or warm water
Sweet milk	

Sift flour, baking soda, cream of tartar and salt in a bowl. Cut in the shortening. Then mix altogether with enough sweet milk to make it slightly sticky. Put on floured board and knead lightly then roll to about 1/2 inch thickness. Cut dough in pieces with a sharp knife and place in a kettle in which a small amount of water has been brought to a boil. Add first a layer of sliced apples and then a layer of dough slices. Sprinkle top generously with cinnamon and molasses. Add a large piece of butter. Then add enough scalded milk or warm water to come well up to top of mixture. With kettle covered, cook until dumplings are done. This can be served as is, as it makes its own sauce. It can also be served with thin cream. We prefer it hot but it can be served cold.

Submitted by Irma W. Benner, South Harpswell, Maine

Apple Crunch

4 cups apples, sliced	1/2 cup brown sugar
1/2 cup water	3/4 cup flour
1 teaspoon cinnamon	1/2 cup butter
1/2 cup white sugar	

Arrange the apples in a deep buttered baking pan. Add the water and sprinkle with the cinnamon and 1/2 of the sugar. Blend the flour, remaining sugar and butter. Pack firmly over apples. Bake in 350 degree oven until apples are tender and the crust is brown, about 30 minutes. Serve warm with milk, thin cream or whipped cream. Serves 6 or 8.

Submitted by Mary Muffler, Caribou, Maine

Coffee Mallow

16 large marshmallows	1 cup heavy cream
1/2 cup hot coffee	1/2 teaspoon vanilla

Cut marshmallows in quarters with wet scissors, add coffee. Cook in double boiler until melted. Cool. When beginning to thicken fold in cream beaten stiff and add vanilla. Serves 4.

Submitted by Cora L. Hopkins, Bass Harbor, Maine

Potatoes are one of the largest agricultural crops in the State of Maine. They are grown and shipped from all over the state but the largest potato growing area in the world is located in Aroostook County in the northern part of the state. The climate and soil are ideally suited to growing an exceptionally fine spud with good texture, flavor and cooking qualities. Mile after mile of vast potato fields march across the rolling country as far as the eye can see and when the fields are in bloom it is really a sight to behold. Potatoes form the basis for a good many native dishes and can be found in a variety of dishes served at our public suppers. When one sees the red, white and blue label that says "State of Maine Potatoes" he knows that he is in for some very fine eating.

ANNA CROCKETT

Applesauce Puff Pudding

½ cup grapenuts
1 jar applesauce (15 ounces or 1 2/3 cups)
3 tablespoons brown sugar or granulated sugar
1 teaspoon vanilla
¼ cup chopped pecans
2 egg whites

Combine the cereal, applesauce, sugar, vanilla and pecans and mix well. Beat egg whites until stiff peaks form. Fold into applesauce mixture. Spoon into a greased 1½ guart casserole. Bake in a slow oven, 325 degrees for 40 minutes. Serve warm with fluffy lemon sauce, custard sauce or cream. Makes 6 servings.
Submitted by Marjorie A. Mahar, Calais, Maine

Railroad or Suet Pudding

1 cup molasses
1 cup sweet milk
1 cup chopped salt pork or suet
3 cups flour
1 teaspoon soda
1 teaspoon cinnamon
1 teaspoon cloves
½ teaspoon ginger (optional)
1 teaspoon salt
Chopped nuts (optional)
1 cup raisins (or raisins and dates)

Beat together the molasses and milk with the pork or suet. Sift flour, soda, cinnamon, cloves, ginger and salt together and add to the molasses mixture. Fold in nuts and raisins last. Steam for 3 hours and serve with whipped cream or hard sauce.
This pudding recipe has been used in our family for years. Mother always made it for Christmas and Thanksgiving.
Submitted by Ellen Perry, Carmel, Maine

Suet Pudding

3 cups sifted flour
1 teaspoon cinnamon
½ teaspoon cloves
½ teaspoon salt
1 teaspoon soda
1 egg, beaten
1 cup molasses
1 cup milk
1 cup ground suet
1 piece citron
Candied ginger
1 cup raisins

Sift dry ingredients together, beat the molasses, egg and milk together and add to the flour mixture. Stir in the suet, citron, ginger and raisins and steam 3 hours.
Submitted by Nellie Craig, Charlotte, Maine

Apple Walnut Cobbler

½ cup sugar
½ teaspoon cinnamon
¾ cup walnuts, chopped
4 cups thinly sliced apples or
   1 No. 2 can pie apples
1 egg, beaten
½ cup evaporated milk

1/3 cup butter or margarine,
   melted
1 cup flour
1 cup sugar
1 teaspoon baking powder
¼ teaspoon salt

Mix ½ cup sugar, cinnamon and half the nuts. Place apples in baking dish and sprinkle with the cinnamon mixture. Combine egg, milk and butter. Sift together the dry ingredients and add to the egg mixture. Mix until smooth. Pour over apples and sprinkle with the remaining nuts. Bake in a slow oven.

Submitted by Mrs. John Pearse, Hope, Maine

Apple Tapioca

¾ cup sugar
3 tablespoons tapioca
1 cup water

1 teaspoon cinnamon
Pinch salt
Apples

Fill a 2-quart casserole 2/3 full of sliced cooking apples (peeled and cored). Dot with butter. Boil together the tapioca, sugar, water, cinnamon and salt for 3 to 4 minutes to cook tapioca. Pour over apples adding more water if necessary as apples cook. Stir occasionally. Bake at 350 degrees for 45 minutes.

Submitted by Mrs. Hans Meier, Mt. Desert, Maine

Cranberry Pudding
(83 years old)

2 cups fresh cranberries
1 egg
½ cup molasses

1/3 cup hot water
1 2/3 cups flour
2 teaspoons baking powder

Cut each cranberry in half. Beat egg, add hot water and molasses. Sift flour with the baking powder, add to the egg mixture and combine with the cranberries. Pour into greased pan. Steam 1½ hours. Serve with the following sauce.

½ cup butter
1 cup sugar

½ cup sweet cream

Boil together until slightly thick. Flavor with vanilla. Serve warm.

Submitted by Mrs. Ernest Bliss, West Baldwin, Maine

Vegetable Pudding

1 cup raw potato	1 cup sugar
1 cup raw carrots	1 teaspoon nutmeg
1 cup bread crumbs	1 teaspoon cinnamon
1 cup raisins	1 teaspoon cloves
1 cup oleo	1 teaspoon soda
1 cup flour	1 tablespoon hot water

Grind first four ingredients and set aside. Sift together the flour, sugar and spices and mix with the oleo. Add to this the soda which has been dissolved in the hot water. Put all together and mix well. Place in greased pan and steam 3 hours. Make sure water is boiling at all times. Serve with the following sauce.

SAUCE

1½ cups sugar	½ teaspoon salt
2 tablespoons flour	1½ cups boiling water
1/3 cup butter	1 teaspoon vanilla

Mix sugar, flour, butter and salt together and heat in pan, stirring constantly (as this burns very easily) until dissolved. Add the boiling water and stir until thickened. Remove from stove and add the vanilla. This is a delicious pudding and will serve 10.

Submitted by Mrs. Lillian Burke, Newport, Maine

Cranberry Duff

3 cups sifted all-purpose flour	1 teaspoon salt
1 cup sugar	1/3 cup shortening
2 teaspoons cream of tartar	1½ cups milk
1 teaspoon soda	2 cups whole cranberries

Sift the dry ingredients together. Cut in the shortening until the mixture is mealy. Add the milk all at once and mix lightly until all the flour is moistened. Add cranberries and mix. Pour into one large well-greased mold and cover tightly. Place on a rack over boiling water. Cover the steamer and steam two hours. Serve warm with the following Molasses Sauce:

MOLASSES SAUCE

½ cup sugar	1 cup hot water
1 cup molasses	1 tablespoon butter
1 tablespoon flour	½ teaspoon vanilla
¼ teaspoon salt	¼ teaspoon nutmeg

Cook the above five ingredients until slightly thickened. Add vanilla, nutmeg and butter. Keep hot until ready to serve.

Submitted by Mrs. William R. Hopkins, Rockland, Maine

Pumpkin Cottage Pudding

1/3 cup soft shortening
½ cup sugar
2 eggs
1 small can pumpkin
½ cup light molasses
1 tablespoon grated orange peel
1 2/3 cups sifted pastry
flour
½ teaspoon salt
1 teaspoon soda
1 teaspoon cinnamon
½ teaspoon cloves
½ teaspoon nutmeg
¼ teaspoon ginger
1/3 cup orange juice
2 3 oz. packages cream cheese
2 tablespoons milk

Cream shortening and sugar. Beat in eggs, one at a time. Stir in pumpkin, molasses and orange peel. Mix and sift dry ingredients. Blend into pumpkin mixture alternately with orange juice. Mix cream cheese with the milk and fold in last. Turn into greased and waxpaper lined 9-inch square cake pan. Bake at 350 degrees from 30 to 35 minutes.

Submitted by Mrs. Pearl M. Smith, Presque Isle, Maine

Steamed Date Crumb Pudding

2 cups crumbs (cake, cookie or
bread)
1 cup milk
1/3 cup shortening
1 egg, beaten
½ cup molasses
¼ cup flour
½ teaspoon salt
½ teaspoon cinnamon
½ teaspoon allspice
½ teaspoon nutmeg
1 teaspoon soda
1 cup dates, cut-up

Soak crumbs in milk for a few minutes, add shortening, egg and molasses. Sift dry ingredients together and add to the crumb mixture. Stir in dates and steam for 2 hours. Serve with whipped cream or the following sauce.

FOAMY SAUCE

3 tablespoons butter
1 cup powdered sugar
2 eggs, separated
½ cup cream, whipped
1 teaspoon lemon or vanilla

Cream butter and sugar, add egg yolks and beat over hot water. Add well beaten egg whites and whipped cream. Add flavoring. Cool and serve over warm pudding.

Submitted by Isabel T. Howard, Dover-Foxcroft, Maine

Quick Rice Pudding

2 cups uncooked rice
6 cups water
1 teaspoon salt
1½ cups milk
1¼ cups sugar

1 teaspoon vanilla
½ teaspoon cinnamon
¼ teaspoon nutmeg
1 egg

Combine the rice, water and salt. Cook until rice is tender and drain. Blend milk, sugar, vanilla, spices and egg. Add to the rice. Cook over low heat until slightly thickened. Remove from heat, cool slightly and serve with cream or topping.

Submitted by Madeline Tice, Athens, Maine

Lemon Sauce Pudding

1 tablespoon butter
1 cup sugar
2 eggs
3 tablespoons flour

Juice of one lemon, or 1/3 cup
   real lemon juice
1 cup milk

Cream butter and sugar, add flour, lemon juice, beaten egg yolks, and milk. Fold in stiffly beaten egg whites. Cook in baking dish set in pan of water for 35 minutes at 350 degrees. The batter forms a cake on top, thus making pudding and sauce in one dish.

Submitted by Mrs. Doris Foster, Limestone, Maine

Heirloom Chocolate Rice Pudding

¼ cup uncooked rice
2 cups milk
1 teaspoon salt
2 eggs, separated
2 tablespoons butter
½ cup sugar

2 squares unsweetened chocolate,
   melted
2 teaspoons vanilla
¾ cup seeded raisins
½ cup cream
Meringue

Soak rice in milk ½ hour in top of double boiler, add salt. Then cook over hot water until rice is tender, stirring often. Beat egg yolks lightly, add a little hot rice mixture to yolks and return to double boiler, cook and stir for a few minutes. Blend butter and sugar, stir in melted chocolate and vanilla, stir in raisins, add to the rice mixture. Whip cream, fold in. Beat egg whites well and fold in. Turn into buttered baking dish. Bake in slow oven until pudding is set. For the meringue, beat 2 egg whites to stiff peaks and add ¼ cup sugar. Pile on pudding and cook 15 minutes in 325 degree oven. Serve warm or cold.

Submitted by Mrs. Albion Raynes, Bowdoinham, Maine

Chocolate Pudding

½ cup sugar
1 egg
1 tablespoon butter
Pinch salt
2 cups flour

1 teaspoon soda
1 heaping teaspoon cream tartar
1 cup milk
2 squares chocolate, melted

Cream sugar, egg, butter and salt together. Sift flour with soda and cream tartar. Add alternately with the milk to the creamed mixture. Stir in chocolate last. Steam 1 hour in a covered dish. Serve with a vanilla sauce.

SAUCE

½ cup sugar
1 tablespoon cornstarch
1 cup boiling water

3 tablespoons butter
1 teaspoon vanilla

Combine sugar and cornstarch, add water, butter and vanilla and cook over low heat until clear and thick.

Submitted by Mrs. Vinal R. McNeal, Bar Harbor, Maine

Date Pudding

1 cup sour milk
1 heaping teaspoon soda
1 teaspoon salt
½ cup molasses

1 cup graham flour
Pastry flour
½ cup dates, cut in pieces

Combine milk and soda, add salt and molasses. Mix in graham flour and enough pastry flour to make rather stiff. Fold in dates and steam for two hours.

Submitted by Mrs. Bessie Dunklee, Vernon, Vermont

Coconut Date Surprise

1 quart milk
1 cup brown sugar
4 tablespoons minute tapioca
2 tablespoons cornmeal

4 tablespoons grated coconut
½ teaspoon salt
1 cup dates, stoned and cut fine
Marshmallows

Heat the milk in a double boiler. Mix together the remaining ingredients except the marshmallows and add to the hot milk. Pour into a covered greased baking dish and bake in a 350 degree oven for 45 minutes. Remove from oven and cover with marshmallows. Return to oven to brown. Makes a splendid sauce. Serves 8.

Submitted by Mrs. Marion Holbrook, North Anson, Maine

Angel Food Delight

1 tablespoon plain gelatin	Juice of 1 lemon
3 tablespoons cold water	1 cup sugar
1 cup boiling water	½ pint cream, whipped
1 cup orange juice	1 large angel cake

Dissolve the gelatin in the cold water, add to the cup of boiling water and dissolve thoroughly. Mix together the orange and lemon juice with the sugar and add to the gelatin mixture. Let cool. Fold in the whipped cream. Break the angel cake in pieces. Put a layer of cake in bottom of pan and cover with gelatin mixture, another layer of cake etc., using last a layer of gelatin mixture. Do not press down. Let stand at least 48 hours in refrigerator. Serve with whipped cream and a cherry. A good dish to use for this is a square pyrex dish. Will serve 9.

Submitted by Mrs. Juanita B. Allen, Bryant Pond, Maine

Lemon Meringue Pudding

1 pint milk	1 cup sugar
1 cup bread crumbs	1 lemon
2 eggs, separated	½ cup sugar

Heat milk and pour over the bread crumbs, let set for a few minutes. Beat yolks of eggs slightly, add 1 cup sugar and grated lemon rind, mix and add to the hot milk mixture. Bake in moderate oven until firm in center. Remove from oven, allow to cool slightly and cover with the following meringue. Beat egg whites until very stiff, beat in the ½ cup sugar alternately with the lemon juice. Put on pudding and cook in slow oven 15 to 20 minutes until delicately browned.

Submitted by Edith Knox, Fryeburg, Maine

Grapenut Pudding

3½ tablespoons minute tapioca	½ cup Grapenuts
2½ cups boiling water	½ cup walnuts
1 cup brown sugar	¼ teaspoon salt
1 cup seedless raisins	1 teaspoon vanilla

Mix the tapioca with the boiling water in top of double boiler and cook until clear, then add the brown sugar and the raisins and cook 10 minutes longer. Remove from heat and add the Grapenuts, walnuts, salt and the vanilla. Serve when cold with cream.

Submitted by Arlene Guptill, Addison, Maine

Old New England Sauce

2 tablespoons flour
1 cup sugar
2 cups boiling water
1 tablespoon butter

1 teaspoon nutmeg
1½ tablespoons vinegar
Pinch of salt

Mix salt, flour and sugar together in an iron frying pan. Add boiling water gradually, stirring continuously. Add butter and cook for 5 minutes. Remove from the stove and add nutmeg and vinegar.

This sauce is excellent on bread pudding or plain cake.

This recipe was given to me many years ago by my grandmother, and was her mother's before that.

Submitted by Mrs. Iza M. Schmieks, Auburn, Maine

Brown Sugar Sauce

1 cup brown sugar
½ cup white sugar
2½ cups water

1 tablespoon butter
4 tablespoons cornstarch
1 teaspoon vanilla

Mix the two sugars with water and butter in a saucepan and bring to a boil. Stir a little water into the cornstarch and add to the sugar water mixture and cook until slightly thick. Cool and add vanilla.

Submitted by Nellie Stetson, Bethel, Maine

Orange Sauce

1 tablespoon cornstarch
½ cup sugar
¼ teaspoon salt
¼ teaspoon cinnamon

2 teaspoons grated orange peel
1 cup orange juice
2 tablespoons butter

Combine cornstarch, sugar, salt and cinnamon in saucepan. Add orange peel gradually and stir in orange juice. Cook over medium heat, stirring constantly until mixture thickens and comes to a boil. Remove from heat and stir in the butter.

Submitted by Pearl M. Smith, Presque Isle, Maine

Butter Sauce

½ cup butter
1 cup sugar

½ cup cream

Heat in double boiler, do not boil.

Submitted by Beverly Perkins, Bangor, Maine

Cream Puffs
(Cold Oven Method)

1 cup boiling water
1 stick margarine or butter

1 cup sifted flour
4 eggs, unbeaten

Bring water to a boil. Melt oleo in water. Add flour all at once — turn off heat as you do this. Stir until water, oleo and flour forms a big ball in the saucepan. Remove pan from stove and add the eggs, one at a time. The important thing is to be sure the mixture is very stiff after the addition of each egg. Form mixture in rounds. This will make 12 good-sized puffs. The fun part of this is — put them on a cookie sheet in a cold oven. Turn temperature to 400 degrees and bake about 50 minutes.

OLD-FASHIONED CREAM FILLING

2 cups milk
1/3 cup flour
½ teaspoon salt

2/3 cup sugar
2 eggs
1 teaspoon vanilla

Scald the milk in top of double boiler. Mix flour, sugar and salt. Beat the eggs and combine with flour mixture. Add a small amount of the hot milk to the egg mixture, stir well, and turn into the hot milk. Cook until the mixture thickens. Allow to cook a few minutes more and remove from heat. Cool and add flavoring. Fill cooled cream puffs.

Submitted by Mrs. Thelma W. Everett, Thomaston, Maine

Dump Bars

1 stick of margarine
1 pound light brown sugar
1 teaspoon vanilla
½ teaspoon salt
4 eggs

2 cups sifted all-purpose flour
1 teaspoon baking powder
1 package chocolate bits
(6 ounces)
½ cup chopped nuts

Into top of the double boiler, dump the margarine, sugar, vanilla, salt and eggs. Having dumped these ingredients in the top of double boiler, place over boiling water. Stir so that the eggs are well mixed into the other ingredients. Do not cook chocolate bits. Heat and stir until the margarine is melted. Remove from the heat and dump in the flour and baking powder sifted together. Add the chocolate bits and the nuts. Beat together well and put in a greased 9 x 13 pan. Bake at 325 degrees for 40 minutes.

Variations in place of chocolate bits and nuts: 1 cup coconut and ½ cup cut-up dates; or coconut and butterscotch bits.

Submitted by Mrs. James Tinker, Rockland, Maine

Pecan-Raisin Tarts

2 bars margarine
2 packages cream cheese
(3-ounce size)

2 cups flour

FILLING

2 eggs
1½ cups brown sugar
2 tablespoons melted margarine
Dash salt

¼ teaspoon vanilla
½ cup pecans, broken
½ cup golden raisins

Soften the 2 bars of margarine, add the cream cheese and mix well. Add flour in fourths and work well with fingers into a smooth dough. Pinch off small pieces and shape into balls about 1¼ inches in diameter. Put each ball in the cup of small muffin pans and with thumb, press dough against bottom and sides, lining cup evenly with dough. Sprinkle coarsely chopped pecans and raisins in the tart shells. Beat the eggs with a fork, add brown sugar gradually, and mix well. Add salt, vanilla and melted margarine. Spoon this mixture into tarts — have half full. Bake at 350 degrees for about 20 minutes, until filling is set and firm. Cool. Remove carefully from pans.

Submitted by Mrs. Norman Hilyard, Cushing, Maine

Crunchy Top Bars

1/3 cup butter
1 egg
½ teaspoon vanilla
1 1/3 cups flour
½ teaspoon nutmeg
½ teaspoon salt
2/3 cup sugar

2/3 cup apple sauce
¾ teaspoon soda
1 teaspoon cinnamon
¼ teaspoon cloves
½ cup seedless raisins
½ cup chopped nuts

TOPPING

1/3 cup crushed corn flakes
1 tablespoon butter

¼ cup chopped nuts
2 tablespoons sugar

Cream butter and sugar, add the egg and beat until fluffy. Mix apple sauce and vanilla. Sift flour with salt, soda and spices in a bowl. Add the nuts and raisins to the flour. Mix well and blend into the creamed mixture. Spread batter in an 8 x 8 pan. Combine the corn flakes, butter, nuts and sugar for the topping. Sprinkle over the top of batter. Bake at 350 degrees for 30 minutes. Cool, cut in bars. Can use a larger pan for thinner bars.

Submitted by Brenda Hemphill, Presque Isle, Maine

Mincemeat Bars

½ cup margarine
1 cup brown sugar
1½ cups rolled oats (dry)
1½ cups sifted flour
½ teaspoon soda

1 teaspoon cream of tartar
2 cups mincemeat
½ cup white sugar
4 tablespoons flour
1 teaspoon vanilla

Cream margarine and brown sugar. Add rolled oats and flour sifted with soda and cream of tartar. Blend well together, making a crumb mixture. Pack half of it into an 8 x 8 pan. Cover bottom of pan and press down well. Mix the mincemeat with the sugar, flour and vanilla. Cook over medium heat until thick. Cool slightly. Spread over the crumb mixture in the pan. Top with the rest of the crumb mixture. Bake in a 350 degree oven for 20 minutes. Cool. Cut into bars.

These bars are delicious when green tomato mincemeat is used.
Submitted by Mrs. Florence Vanidestine, Monroe, Maine

Peanut Chewy Bars

1/3 cup shortening
½ cup peanut butter
¼ cup light brown sugar
(firmly packed)
1 cup sugar
1 teaspoon vanilla

2 eggs
1 cup unsifted flour
1 teaspoon baking powder
¼ teaspoon salt
1 1/3 cups coconut

Cream together the shortening, peanut butter, sugars, vanilla and eggs. Sift the flour, salt and baking powder. Combine creamed mixture, flour and coconut. Mix well. Spread in a 13 x 9 lightly greased pan. Bake for 25 minutes at 350 degrees. Cool. Cut in bars.
Submitted by Mrs. Jeanne Farrar, Sangerville, Maine

Cranberry Crunch

1 cup quick cooking oats
½ cup flour
1 cup brown sugar

½ cup margarine
1 can whole cranberry sauce

Mix well together the oats, flour, sugar and margarine. Spread ½ of this crumb mixture on a greased 8 x 8 pan. Cover with the cranberries and spread the rest of the crumb mixture on top. Bake about 30 minutes at 350 degrees until golden brown. Serve hot or cold with ice cream or whipped cream.
Submitted by Mrs. Elizabeth Tate, Biddeford, Maine

Apple Squares

1 egg
¾ cup sugar
¼ cup evaporated milk
1 teaspoon vanilla
¾ cup flour
1 teaspoon baking powder

½ teaspoon cinnamon
¼ teaspoon salt
1 cup chopped raw apple
½ cup nut meats
2 tablespoons sugar
½ teaspoon cinnamon

Beat egg, milk, sugar and vanilla together. Add the flour sifted with baking powder, cinnamon and salt. Add the apple and nut meats. Spread in a 9 x 9 greased pan. Mix the 2 tablespoons of sugar and cinnamon, spread on top of the batter. Bake in a 350 degree oven for 35 minutes. Cool in the pan and cut in squares.

Submitted by Mrs. Maude Smith, Caribou, Maine

Toffee Bars

1 cup margarine
1 cup light brown sugar
1 teaspoon vanilla
2 cups flour

1 egg yolk
1 chocolate candy bar
½ cup chopped nuts

Mix together the margarine, sugar, egg yolk, vanilla and flour. Press into a 9 x 9 lightly greased pan and bake for 15 minutes at 300 degrees. Soften the chocolate bar and spread on top of the bars as soon as removed from the oven, while still warm. Sprinkle with chopped nuts. Cool and cut in one inch squares.

Submitted by Mary M. Berry, Medway, Maine

O.K. Squares

½ cup sugar
½ cup white corn syrup
¾ cup peanut butter
3 cups Special K cereal
½ cup coconut flakes

½ small package chocolate bits
½ small package of butterscotch bits

Cook together the sugar and corn syrup; allow to come only to a boil, no longer.

Butter the sides of a big mixing bowl and add the peanut butter, cereal and coconut. Pour over this the sugar-syrup mixture and stir well. Spread in a 9 x 9 pan and press down. Melt the bits together and spread on top. Cool. Cut in squares.

Submitted by Miss Helen Moyes, Limestone, Maine

A comparative newcomer on our list of marketable foods is shrimp. Always known along the Maine coast as a delicate and flavorful food, shrimp has just begun to come into prominence as an exportable product along with sardines, lobster, clams and other shellfish. Caught in nets all along the coast during the winter and early spring months these tiny, pink shellfish can be used in all manner of ways. In recent years factories have opened up all along the coast to process and market them and have provided steady winter employment during the off-season for the herring industry. The advantage of Maine shrimp over other varieties is that they need no deveining which cuts down a lot of tedious preparation work for the cook.

Date Squares

1 cup dates, cut up
1 teaspoon soda
1 cup boiling water
1 cup sugar
4 tablespoons shortening
1 egg, beaten
1 2/3 cups flour
½ teaspoon salt

½ teaspoon vanilla
TOPPING
4 tablespoons butter
4 tablespoons cream or top milk
10 tablespoons brown sugar
1 cup grated coconut

Pour boiling water over dates and soda. Let cool. Cream sugar and shortening. Add beaten egg. Mix in the date mixture, add flour, salt and vanilla. Bake in a greased 9 x 13 inch pan for 25 minutes at 375 degrees. Remove from the oven. Mix the ingredients for the topping and spread on the cooked squares. Return to the oven until well browned. (Chocolate bits and chopped nuts may be used as topping, put on before baking.)

Submitted by Mrs. Jennie L. Bugbee, Presque Isle, Maine

Date And Nut Bars

1 cup sugar
½ cup butter or margarine
2 eggs
¼ teaspoon salt
1 teaspoon vanilla
1½ cups sifted flour

1 teaspoon baking powder
1 cup chopped dates
1 cup chopped nut meats
2 egg whites
1 cup brown sugar

Cream the butter and the sugar, add the eggs, salt and vanilla and beat until fluffy. Mix in the flour which has been sifted with the baking powder. Spread this mixture in a greased baking pan 15½ x 10½ x 1. Scatter the chopped dates and nuts over the batter (or stir them in the batter). Beat the 2 egg whites stiff and add the cup of brown sugar. Drop this or spread it over the top of dates and nuts. Bake in a 350 degree oven for 20 minutes. Remove from oven and cut into bars.

Submitted by Mrs. Doris Crawford, Exeter, Maine

Spicy Fruit Bars

1 cup pared chopped apple
1 cup cut-up dates
1/3 cup molasses
¼ cup butter
¼ cup orange juice
2 cups flour
½ teaspoon salt
½ teaspoon soda

1 teaspoon cinnamon
¼ teaspoon cloves
¼ teaspoon nutmeg
⅛ teaspoon ginger
1½ cups light brown sugar
2 eggs
1 teaspoon vanilla

Combine in a saucepan the apple, dates, molasses and orange juice and butter. Cook over medium heat until thick. Cool. Combine sugar, eggs and vanilla in large bowl and beat until well blended. Stir in the fruit mixture. Sift the flour with salt, soda, cinnamon, cloves, ginger and nutmeg. Add to the blended mixture gradually and mix well. Turn into a 10 x 15 buttered pan. Bake at 350 degrees for 30 to 35 minutes. Cool and cut in bars.

Submitted by Mrs. Harold Bonney

Dream Bars

1 cup flour
½ cup white sugar
½ cup butter
2 eggs
1 cup brown sugar
2 tablespoons flour

¼ teaspoon soda
6 dates, cut thinly
½ teaspoon salt
1 teaspoon vanilla
½ cup walnuts
1 cup coconut

Blend together the cup of flour, ½ cup of white sugar and ½ cup of butter. Pat in a 9 x 9 baking pan and bake for 15 minutes at 350 degrees until light brown.

Combine the eggs, brown sugar, 2 tablespoons of flour, soda and salt. Add vanilla, dates, walnuts and coconut. Pour this mixture over the baked crust. Bake 20 to 25 minutes in a 350 degree oven. Cool and cut in bars.

Submitted by Mrs. Stanley Lazore, Fort Kent, Maine

Jim's Tarts

PASTRY

2 cups sifted flour
½ teaspoon salt

2/3 cup shortening
4-6 tablespoons water

FILLING

¼ cup shortening
¼ cup sugar
1 egg
2 teaspoons lemon juice
½ teaspoon lemon rind

¾ cup sifted flour
1 teaspoon baking powder
¼ teaspoon salt
Raspberry Jam

Sift flour and salt together. With pastry blender, work in shortening until it is the consistency of coarse corn meal. Gradually add the 4 to 6 tablespoons water, stirring with a fork until mixture holds together. Roll dough on slightly floured board and line 12 muffin pans with pastry. Cream shortening and sugar. Beat in egg, lemon juice and rind. Sift flour, baking powder, and salt together. Blend into creamed mixture. Place heaping teaspoon raspberry jam in each pastry shell. Cover with a spoonful of cake mixture. Roll leftover pastry very thin, cut into very narrow strips. Place a pastry spiral on top of each tart. Bake in 400 degree oven 10 to 15 minutes or until golden brown. Makes 1 dozen tarts.

Submitted by Mrs. Ethel Ellingson, Milo, Maine
Dedicated to her son Jim, who was killed in Vietnam, Jan. 1969.

Raspberry Jam Squares

1 cup flour
½ teaspoon salt
1 teaspoon baking powder
½ cup butter
1 egg, beaten
1 tablespoon milk

Raspberry jam
1 egg, beaten
1 cup sugar
1 tablespoon melted butter
2 cups shredded coconut

Sift the 1 cup of flour with the salt and baking powder. Rub in the butter and add the beaten egg and milk. Mix well and spread in a 9 x 9 pan, making it a little thinner at the edges. Spread this batter with raspberry jam. Cover with a topping, made by combining the beaten egg with the sugar, melted butter and coconut. Bake in a 350 degree oven about 25 minutes. Cut in squares while warm.

Submitted by Mrs. Robert C. Chamberlain, Clinton, Maine

Marshmallow Fudge Squares

1 package semi-sweet
chocolate bits
1 cup evaporated milk
2 cups sugar
¼ teaspoon salt
½ package small marshmallows

or 24 large marshmallows,
cut-up
1 tablespoon butter
1 teaspoon vanilla
3 cups graham cracker
crumbs

Combine chocolate and milk in saucepan and place over low heat until chocolate is melted, add sugar and salt, stir until dissolved. Cook until mixture reaches soft ball stage, 230 degrees. Remove from heat. Add marshmallows, butter, vanilla and graham cracker crumbs. Press into greased shallow pan 11 x 7. Chill 8 to 12 hours.

Submitted by Nellie M. Lawton, Rockport, Maine

Mincemeat Bars

½ cup margarine
1 cup sugar
1 egg
1 cup moist mincemeat
1 cup chopped nuts

3 cups flour
1 teaspoon baking powder
1 teaspoon cinnamon
½ teaspoon salt
½ teaspoon soda

Cream margarine and sugar. Add egg and beat well. Add mincemeat and nuts. Mix until thoroughly blended. Sift together the dry ingredients and add to the above mixture. Chill at least 1 hour. Divide the dough into 4 pieces. Roll each one on a lightly floured board into strips about 1 inch wide and ½ inch thick. Bake on a greased cookie sheet in a 370 degree oven for 20 minutes. Cut into 1-inch diagonal strips.

Submitted by Mrs. Edith R. Richards, New Vineyard, Maine

Date-Nut-Marshmallow Roll

1 pound graham crackers
1 pound dates
60 marshmallows

1 cup chopped nuts
¾ cup orange juice

Crush all but 4 of the graham crackers. Cut up marshmallows, dates and nuts. Add to the crushed crackers, moisten with orange juice and form into a roll. Crush the 4 crackers and use to coat the roll. Refrigerate, and when real cold, slice and serve, with or without whipped cream. Stored in refrigerator, it will keep a long time.

Submitted by Mrs. Verna Young, Old Town, Maine

Date Pinwheels

1 cup brown sugar   1 cup white sugar
1 cup shortening   3 eggs
3½ cups flour   1 teaspoon soda
1 teaspoon cinnamon   ¼ teaspoon salt

Cream sugar and shortening. Add unbeaten eggs and beat well. Add remaining dry ingredients. Chill dough for 20 minutes. Divide into thirds. Roll out and spread with date mixture. Roll as for jelly roll. Wrap in waxed paper and chill thoroughly or freeze. Slice and bake in a 350 degree oven 12 to 15 minutes.

FILLING

1 cup finely chopped dates   ½ cup water
½ cup sugar   1 cup chopped nuts

Cook dates, sugar, and water until thick. Cool and add chopped nuts.

Submitted by Hester Pullen, North Anson, Maine

Chocolate Syrup Brownies

1 cup sugar   ¼ teaspoon soda
½ cup oleo   ¾ cup chocolate syrup
2 eggs   1 teaspoon vanilla
1 cup flour   ¾ cup chopped nuts

Cream together the sugar and oleo until light and fluffy. Add the eggs one at a time, beat well after each addition. Sift flour and soda. Add alternately with the chocolate syrup to the creamed mixture. Add and blend in the vanilla and chopped nuts. Pour into a 9 x 9 pan and bake at 350 degrees 40 to 45 minutes. Cut in squares.

Submitted by Mrs. Maud H. Donnelly, Bangor, Maine

Apple Brownies

1 cup sugar   ¼ teaspoon salt
¼ pound oleo (1 stick)   ½ teaspoon baking powder
1 egg   ½ teaspoon soda
1 teaspoon vanilla   3 apples, chopped fine
1 cup flour   ½ cup chopped nuts

Cream sugar and oleo. Add the slightly beaten egg and vanilla. Sift flour with salt, baking powder and soda. Add to the creamed mixture with the chopped apple and the nuts. Bake in an 8 x 8 pan at 350 degrees until done, about 25 minutes.

Submitted by Mrs. Thelma Squiers, Hampden, Maine

Chocolate Sponge Roll

3 large eggs
1 cup sugar
5 tablespoons water
1 teaspoon vanilla

1 square of melted chocolate
1 teaspoon baking powder
¼ teaspoon salt
1 cup sifted flour

Beat eggs until thick, gradually beat in sugar and add water. Sift flour, salt and baking powder, and add. Beat in the melted chocolate, and vanilla until smooth. Pour into a greased and floured jelly roll pan, 15½ x 10½. Bake in a 375 degree oven 12 to 15 minutes or until done. Loosen the edges and immediately turn upside down on a towel sprinkled with confectioner's sugar. If pan was lined with paper or foil, quickly and carefully pull it off. Roll up in the towel until cool. Fill with whipped cream and store in the refrigerator. THE KIDS LOVE IT.

Submitted by Mrs. Fern Cummings, Edinburg, Maine

Nut Goodies

1 cup sugar
½ cup butter or oleo
2 egg yolks
1½ cups flour
1 teaspoon baking powder
½ teaspoon salt

¾ cup milk
1 teaspoon flavoring
1 cup chopped nut meats
2 egg whites
1½ cups brown sugar
¼ cup chopped nuts

Cream the butter with the sugar and add egg yolks. Sift together flour, baking powder and salt. Add dry ingredients alternately with the milk and flavoring to the creamed mixture. Add 1 cup chopped nuts. Spread in a sheet cake pan. Beat the egg whites with the brown sugar and spread all over the cake. Sprinkle with nut meats and bake at 375 degrees about 25 minutes, until done. Cut in squares while warm.

Submitted by Mrs. Gladys King, Hampden Highlands, Maine

Whoopie Filling

3 tablespoons flour
¾ cup sweet milk
¾ cup sugar

1 teaspoon vanilla
¾ cup shortening
½ cup butter or margarine

Cook flour and milk together over medium heat until thick. Stir often. Cool. Add the sugar, vanilla, shortening and butter. Whip altogether until creamy.

Submitted by Mrs. Theresa Shorey, Dexter, Maine.

Chocolate Peanut Butter Squares

1 cup sifted flour
1 teaspoon baking powder
¼ teaspoon baking soda
¼ teaspoon salt
2 tablespoons butter

1 cup sugar
1 egg
½ cup peanut butter
1 square melted chocolate
¼ cup milk

Sift together flour, baking powder, soda and salt. Beat together butter, sugar, egg, peanut butter and melted chocolate. Gradually stir in the flour alternately with the milk. Bake in an 8 x 8 greased pan in a 375 degree oven for about 15 to 20 minutes. Cut in squares.

Submitted by Shirley Beauchemin, Ellsworth, Maine

Delicious Squares

2 cups graham crackers, crushed
½ cup brown sugar
½ cup melted butter
1 package whipped topping

1 8-ounce package of cream cheese
1 cup confectioner's sugar
1 small bottle maraschino cherries

Mix well together the graham crackers, sugar and melted butter. Press into an 8 x 8 pan and place in the refrigerator to set. Mix the package of whipped topping as directed on the package, except a little less milk. Mix together until fluffy the topping, the cream cheese and the confectioner's sugar. Spread over the cooled graham cracker mixture and top with the cherries. Cut in squares and serve well cooled.

Submitted by Mrs. Elosia Marshall, East Corinth, Maine

Lemonade Cookies

1 cup oleo
1 cup sugar
2 eggs
3 cups flour

1 teaspoon soda
1 can frozen lemonade concentrate (6 ounce)

Cream sugar and oleo. Add eggs, one at a time. Sift flour and soda together, and stir into the creamed mixture alternately with ½ cup of lemonade. Drop by spoonfuls, 2 inches apart on an ungreased cookie sheet. Bake about 8 minutes or until cookie is slightly browned on the edges. Remove from oven and brush top with rest of the lemonade and sprinkle with sugar. Place on a rack to cool. Makes 7 dozen cookies.

Submitted by Mrs. Herbert Dunham, Bryant Pond, Maine

Date Brambles

CRUST

2 cups flour
2/3 cup lard

1 teaspoon salt
Ice water

Combine flour, lard and salt and mix with pastry blender until consistency of coarse meal. Add ice water a little at a time until mixture clings together. Divide dough in half and roll out quite thin on floured board. Fit one half into a 9 inch square pan, reserving other half for top covering.

DATE FILLING

1 cup cut-up dates
½ cup water
½ cup sugar

1 tablespoon butter
Nuts (optional)
1 egg, beaten

Boil together until thick the dates, water, sugar and butter. Add beaten egg and cook one minute longer, being careful not to burn. Add nuts if desired. Cool. Turn into bottom crust in pan and cover with top crust. Cook at 350 degrees until top crust is golden brown, approximately 35 minutes.

Submitted by Mrs. Annie Rogers, Thomaston, Maine

Old-Fashioned Oatmeal Cookies

1 cup raisins (small ones)
1 cup water
¾ cup shortening
1½ cups sugar
2 eggs
1 teaspoon vanilla
2½ cups flour (measure
   loosely)

½ teaspoon baking powder
1 teaspoon soda
1 teaspoon salt
1 teaspoon cinnamon
½ teaspoon cloves
2 cups rolled oats (quick
   cooking)
½ cup nuts (optional)

Simmer raisins and water in saucepan over low heat until raisins are plump — 20-30 minutes. Drain raisin liquid into measuring cup and add enough water to make ½ cup of liquid.

Mix shortening, eggs, sugar and vanilla. Stir in raisin liquid. Stir together, flour, baking powder, soda, salt and spices. Blend in. Add rolled oats, nuts and raisins. Drop rounded teaspoons of dough about 2 inches apart on ungreased baking sheet. Bake 10 minutes in 400 degree oven. Makes 6 dozen.

Submitted by Rita Grindle, South Penobscot, Maine

Apple Sauce Cookies

1 cup shortening
2 cups sugar
1 egg
3 cups flour
1 teaspoon cinnamon
½ teaspoon cloves

1 teaspoon salt
1 teaspoon soda
1 cup unsweetened apple sauce
1 cup chopped nuts
½ cup seedless raiains
1 teaspoon vanilla

Cream shortening, add sugar gradually and cream until fluffy and light. Add egg, beat thoroughly. Sift flour, measure and sift dry ingredients together. Fold in first batter. Add apple sauce, nuts and raisins, then vanilla. Mix into a stiff batter. Drop from teaspoon onto greased cookie sheet. Bake 15-20 minutes in a moderate hot oven of 375 degrees.

Submitted by Mrs. W. Ross Harmon, Milltown, Maine

Soft Molasses Cookies

1 cup shortening
1 cup brown sugar
1 cup molasses
1 cup sour milk
2 teaspoons soda

1 teaspoon ginger
1 teaspoon cinnamon
Pinch of salt
2 teaspoons vinegar
6 cups flour

Mix ingredients in order given. Add 6 cups flour, a little at a time to get the right consistency. Add only enough flour to make the dough as soft as can be handled. Roll out on floured board about ½ inch thick, cut with cookie cutter. Bake on ungreased cookie sheet in 350 degree oven about 10 minutes or until cookie is springy at the touch, not too long or it makes them a hard cookie and not a soft one.

Submitted by Mary Silvernail, Hudson, New York

Snowballs

2¼ cups sifted flour
2 sticks oleo
½ cup confectioner's sugar

1 cup finely chopped nuts
1 teaspoon vanilla

Combine all the ingredients and form into balls the size of a walnut. If dough is too stiff, add 1 tablespoon water. Bake in 350 degree oven for 20 minutes. Roll in confectioner's sugar after baking. Makes 3 dozen.

Submitted by Dolores Reglin, Orrington, Maine

Filled Drop Cookies

1 cup shortening
2 cups brown sugar
2 eggs
½ cup warm water
1½ teaspoons soda
1 teaspoon salt
1 teaspoon vanilla
4 cups sifted flour

Cream shortening and sugar, add eggs and beat well. Dissolve soda in warm water and add to mixture. Stir in vanilla, add dry ingredients sifted together. Drop by dessert spoon onto cookie sheet. Make dent in center of each with back of spoon, place teaspoon of filling, then teaspoon of dough on top. Bake in 400 degree oven for 10 minutes.

FILLING

1 cup chopped dates or raisins
1 cup water
½ cup sugar
1 tablespoon lemon juice
2 tablespoons flour
½ cup chopped nuts

Cook until thickened.

These cookies are delicious and freeze well.

Submitted by Mrs. Carroll Bumps, South China, Maine

Crinkles Chocolate Cookies

½ cup shortening
1 2/3 cups sugar
2 teaspoons vanilla
2 eggs
2 1-ounce squares unsweetened chocolate
2 cups flour
2 teaspoons baking powder
½ teaspoon salt
1/3 cup milk
½ cup nuts

Put all together and mix. Add nuts. Mixture will be quite thick. Chill about 1 hour before baking off. Roll in small balls, then roll the balls in confectioner's sugar. Bake on greased cookie sheet at 350 degrees about 15 minutes and no longer.

Submitted by Mrs. Jeanne M. Frost, Hampden Highlands, Maine

Maine Crunchies

2 cups sugar
3 tablespoons cocoa
¼ pound margarine
½ cup milk
1 teaspoon vanilla
½ cup peanut butter
3 cups dry quick cooking oatmeal

Mix together sugar, cocoa, margarine and milk. Bring to a boil and boil hard for one minute (no more). Remove from fire and add vanilla, peanut butter and oatmeal. Mix well and drop on waxed paper with teaspoon.

Submitted by Mrs. Helen Thomson, York Beach, Maine

Chocolate Banana Cookies

2¼ cups flour
2 teaspoons baking powder
½ teaspoon salt
¼ teaspoon soda
2/3 cup shortening
1 cup sugar
2 eggs
1 package chocolate bits
(6 ounce)
1 teaspoon vanilla
1 cup mashed bananas

Blend together shortening and sugar. Add eggs, one at a time, beating after each addition. Stir in thoroughly chocolate bits and vanilla. Sift flour, baking powder, salt, soda together and add alternately with the mashed bananas. Drop by teaspoon onto ungreased cookie sheet. Bake in 350 to 375 degree oven for 12-15 minutes.

Submitted by Mrs. Harold Haines, Presque Isle, Maine

5-Minute Chocolate Cookies (unbaked)

2½ cups dry quick cooking
oatmeal
½ cup cocoa
1 cup coconut (1 small
package)
Dash salt
Nuts if desired
1 stick margarine
½ cup evaporated milk,
undiluted
2 cups sugar
Vanilla

Place the oatmeal, cocoa, coconut and salt in large bowl. Cook margarine, milk and sugar for 3 minutes. Add vanilla and pour over oatmeal mixture, stir and drop on waxed paper to cool.

These cookies are also good if cocoa is omitted and about ½ cup peanut butter is added to cooked ingredients just before it is added to dry ingredients.

Submitted by Mrs. Charles J. Doyle, Calais, Maine

Sugar Cookies With Filling

1 cup sugar
¼ cup butter
1 egg
1 cup sour milk
3¼ cups flour
1 teaspoon baking powder
¼ teaspoon salt
1 teaspoon vanilla

Cream sugar and butter, add egg, sour milk and vanilla. Sift flour with salt and baking powder. Add to above mixture. Roll very thin and bake in a 350 degree oven until a delicate brown, about 10 minutes. Use jelly or your favorite filling to put in these cookies. (Put two cookies together.)

Submitted by Mrs. Jeanette Fall, Lincoln, Maine

Applejacks

1 cup light brown sugar
½ cup shortening (1 stick oleo)
1 egg
1½ cups sifted flour
½ teaspoon soda
½ teaspoon salt
½ teaspoon nutmeg
1 cup chopped apples (unpeeled if new, older apples need the skins removed)

Cream sugar and shortening, beat in egg. Add dry ingredients, beating until well blended. Stir in apples, beat until the dough is fairly soft, as this blending makes the difference in the texture of the cookies. Drop on a greased pan. Bake 12-15 minutes in 375 degree oven. Optional: As soon as cookies are out of the oven, sprinkle each cookie with 4 or 5 drops of rum extract.

Submitted by Mrs. Edna G. Norton, Bangor, Maine

Coconut Cookies

½ cup shortening
½ cup white sugar
½ cup brown sugar
1 egg
¾ cup flour
½ teaspoon soda
1 teaspoon baking powder
⅝ cup rolled oats
¾ cup coconut
½ teaspoon salt

Cream shortening and sugars well. Add egg, mix well. Sift dry ingredients together then add to cream mixture. Stir in coconut. Make balls by teaspoonfuls, press with fork. Bake in 350 degree oven 8 to 10 minutes or until golden brown.

Submitted by Mrs. L. Allan Wood, Woodland, Maine

Chocolate Chip Cookies

1 cup sifted flour
½ teaspoon soda
¼ teaspoon salt
½ cup butter or oleo
4 teaspoons liquid Sucaryl
½ teaspoon vanilla
1 egg, beaten
½ cup semi-sweet chocolate pieces

Preheat oven to 375 degrees. Sift together the dry ingredients. Cream butter, add Sucaryl, vanilla and egg, blending well. Add flour mixture and beat well. Stir in chocolate pieces. Drop by teaspoonfuls onto a lightly greased baking sheet. Bake 8 to 10 minutes.

Submitted by Mrs. Florence Allen, Matinicus, Maine

ANNA CROCKETT

Lobstering has been going on in Maine since the beginning. Early fishermen set and hauled their traps from small boats such as dories but in this age of power the work is done from boats with comparative ease and mechanical assistance. Even so, the lobsterman's life is a hard one, fraught with danger and bringing little in the way of great wealth. The hours are long. When not hauling he must spend most of his time repairing or replacing the damaged and worn out traps from his average string of about two hundred. When storms hit he is apt to lose over half of his string washed up on beaches or litterally torn apart by the force of the sea. The wooden lathe trap is still the most commonly used gear although in recent years a lightweight smaller trap made of wire has been introduced. This new trap is having relatively slow acceptance. When one tastes a Maine lobster fresh from the sea it is very obvious that it is worth all of the work involved in raising it out of the ocean depths.

Molasses Cookies

1 cup sugar
¾ cup oleo
¼ cup molasses
1 egg
2 cups all-purpose flour
½ teaspoon salt

1½ teaspoons soda
1 teaspoon cinnamon
½ teaspoon cloves
¼ teaspoon nutmeg
1½ teaspoons ginger

Cream sugar and oleo, add molasses, beat well. Add egg, beat. Add sifted flour, soda, salt and spices, mix well. Roll in balls and dip in sugar. Flatten balls with tumbler, covered with a wet cloth. Bake at 375 degrees for 8-15 minutes.

Submitted by Helen Orbeton, Augusta, Maine

Gram's Hermits

2 cups sugar
1 cup butter and lard (mixed)
2 eggs
1 teaspoon soda (scant)
¼ cup hot water
1 teaspoon cinnamon

½ teaspoon allspice
1 teaspoon salt
1 cup chopped raisins
½ teaspoon nutmeg
4 cups flour (may need a little less)

Beat together the sugar, shortening and eggs. Dissolve the soda in the hot water and add with the flour sifted with salt and spices. Add raisins. Roll ¼ inch and cut in desired size. Bake at 350 degrees for 20 to 25 minutes.

Submitted by Alice Hahn, Thomaston, Maine

Country Raisin Gingersnaps

1½ cups seedless raisins
¾ cup shortening
1 cup sugar
1 egg
2¼ cups sifted flour
2 teaspoons soda

½ teaspoon salt
1 teaspoon ginger
¼ cup molasses
½ teaspoon cinnamon
½ teaspoon cloves

Chop raisins, as this makes the cookie chewy as well as crunchy. Beat together shortening, sugar, and egg. Blend in molasses. Blend in flour sifted with soda, salt and spices. Mix in raisins. Chill dough. Shape dough into small balls and roll in additional sugar, if desired. Place on lightly greased baking sheet. Bake in moderately hot oven 375 degrees, 8-10 minutes. Remove to cooling rack. Makes about 3 dozen cookies.

Submitted by Helen Hobert McLeod, Dixfield, Maine

Molasses (Filled) Cookies

1 cup sugar
1 cup molasses
1 egg
¾ cup shortening, melted and cooled
¾ cup hot water
4 teaspoons soda

1 teaspoon cream of tartar
1 teaspoon ginger
1 teaspoon cinnamon
1 teaspoon vanilla
¼ teaspoon salt
5 cups flour

Mix sugar and shortening. Add molasses and egg; soda and cream of tartar dissolved in hot water; spices and vanilla. Add sifted flour and salt. Batter will be thin but do not add more flour. Let set in refrigerator until cool — about 1 hour. Roll and bake in 375 degree oven for 12 minutes. Cool and fill with filling.

FILLING

1½ cups dates
¼ cup white sugar

½ cup water

Cook over low heat until thickened, about 10 minutes. Then cool a little.

Submitted by Mrs. Markie Day, Medway, Maine

Generation Hermits

1 cup sugar
¾ cup shortening
2 eggs
1 cup molasses
1 cup raisins
1 teaspoon cinnamon
1 teaspoon soda

½ teaspoon cloves
½ teaspoon nutmeg
½ teaspoon baking powder
3 to 3½ cups flour
¼ cup sour milk (can use sweet milk and ⅛ teaspoon vinegar)

Cream together the sugar and shortening, beat in the eggs and molasses. Mix together the spices, soda and baking powder. Stir into the creamed mixture with the raisins. Thoroughly stir in the flour and milk, using enough flour to make a fairly stiff dough. Spoon the dough on a lightly greased cookie sheet, lengthwise, making 3 strips about 2 inches wide. Bake at 375 degrees for 10 to 15 minutes until golden brown and firm to touch. Cut in desired size.

Submitted by Mrs. Marion A. Peterson, Saco, Maine

Old-Fashioned Soft Molasses Cookies

1 cup molasses
1 cup sugar
1 cup melted shortening
1 egg
1 cup milk
2 teaspoons baking soda

1 teaspoon salt
½ teaspoon cinnamon
½ teaspoon cloves
½ teaspoon nutmeg

Add the following ingredients in order given: molasses, sugar, shortening, egg, and milk. Sift soda, salt, cinnamon, cloves, and nutmeg in 1 cup flour and add to other mixture. Add 4 more cups flour and mix well. Turn onto floured board and roll quite thick. Place on cookie sheet and bake 10-12 minutes only, in 350 degree oven.

Submitted by Mrs. Beverly Lothrop, Rockland, Maine

Old-Fashioned Soft Molasses Cookies

1 cup sugar
1 cup melted shortening (scant)
1 egg
4 teaspoons soda
1 cup molasses
2/3 cup hot water

1 teaspoon cream of tartar
(heaping)
1 tablespoon ginger
Salt
4¾ cups flour

Mix in order given. Use a 3-inch cutter. Bake in 350 degree oven 12-15 minutes. The secret is, be sure and roll thick.

Submitted by Mrs. Mabel D. Brewer, Presque Isle, Maine

Peanut Butter Round Ups

1 cup shortening
1 cup white sugar
1 cup light brown sugar
2 eggs
1 cup peanut butter

2 cups flour
2 teaspoons soda
½ teaspoon salt
1 teaspoon vanilla
1 cup uncooked rolled oats

Beat shortening and sugars together. Add eggs and beat well. Add peanut butter and beat again. Sift flour, soda and salt and add to creamed mixture. Stir in oats. Add ¼ cup milk if mixture is dry. Add vanilla last. Roll a small amount of dough in hands to form a ball the size of a golf ball. Place on ungreased cookie sheet. Press down with fork dipped in flour. Bake 12 minutes in 350 degree oven.

Submitted by Gwen Church, Port Clyde, Maine

Molasses Coconut Cookies

½ cup shortening
¾ cup sugar
¼ cup molasses
1 egg
1½ cups sifted all-purpose
flour

¾ teaspoon soda
½ teaspoon salt
½ cup moist coconut
½ cup nut meats

Cream shortening and sugar. Beat in egg. Stir in molasses. Mix and sift together flour, salt and soda. Stir into creamed mixture. Add coconut and nut meats or use 1 cup of coconut and omit nut meats. Drop batter on greased cookie sheet and bake in a moderately hot oven, 375 degrees for 8 to 10 minutes. Remove from pan and cool on rack. Store in jar with tight cover.

Submitted by Mrs. Agatha McGuire, Cutler, Maine

Candy Cookies
(Unbaked)

2 cups sugar
3 tablespoons cocoa
½ cup milk
¼ cup oleo
3 cups oatmeal

½ cup peanut butter
1 teaspoon vanilla
Nuts and/or coconut may be
added

Boil sugar, cocoa, milk and oleo for 2 minutes. Add the oatmeal, peanut butter, and vanilla. Mix well. Add nuts or coconut if desired. Drop on waxed paper and cool.

This is an easy recipe for the young people.

Submitted by Miss Lisa Ludden, Brooks, Maine

Oatmeal Cookies

1 cup flour
1 teaspoon baking powder
½ teaspoon salt
½ teaspoon ginger
1 cup brown sugar (packed)

1 cup rolled oats
¼ cup vegetable oil
2 tablespoons milk
1 egg
¾ cup chopped nuts

Stir together in a bowl the flour, baking powder, salt and ginger. Add the brown sugar and rolled oats. Mix in thoroughly the vegetable oil, milk and egg. Stir in the walnuts. Bake 10 minutes in 375 degree oven. Makes 3 dozen cookies.

Submitted by Rose Marie Salameda, Los Altos, California

Soft Molasses Cookies

(Won $50.00 Prize in 1896, this was my grandmother's recipe.)

½ cup molasses
½ cup sugar
1/3 cup butter
1/3 cup lard
1 egg, beaten
2 tablespoons cold water

1 tablespoon vinegar
1 heaping teaspoon ginger
1 heaping teaspoon salt
2 teaspoons soda
3 cups sifted flour

Add soda to molasses and let foam for 5 minutes. Cream sugar and shortening with spices and salt. Then add the beaten egg, water and vinegar, beat well. Add flour. Roll out and bake 10-20 minutes in 350 degree oven.

Submitted by Mrs. Hazel C. Chambers, Grand Lake Stream, Maine

Old-Fashioned Cookies

1 cup brown sugar
1 cup molasses
1 cup melted shortening
1 cup undiluted canned milk
5 cups sifted flour
1 tablespoon lemon extract

4 teaspoons baking soda
½ teaspoon salt
2 tablespoons vinegar
¼ teaspoon cinnamon
¼ teaspoon ginger

Melt shortening. Mix sugar and molasses thoroughly, add melted shortening. Make sour milk by adding 2 tablespoons vinegar to 1 cup undiluted canned milk. Add to above ingredients. Beat well. Add lemon extract. Sift flour with other dry ingredients. Add to above mixture beating as you add until the mixture is just soft enough to handle. Roll ½ inch thick. Cut and bake 8-10 minutes in 375 degree oven. Do not over bake.

Submitted by Mrs. Forrest F. Fowle, Newport, Maine

Molasses Cookies

1 cup molasses
1 cup sugar
1 cup lard
2 teaspoons salt
1 teaspoon ginger
1 teaspoon cloves

1 teaspoon cinnamon
1 cup water
2 teaspoons cream of tartar
4 teaspoons soda
Flour to roll

Bake in 400 degree oven.

This makes a large batch of cookies. There are no eggs in this recipe. This one goes back to the 1850s and 60s.

Submitted by Mrs. Marion Calligan, Grand Lake Stream, Maine

Filled Molasses Cookies

1 cup molasses
1 cup sugar
2/3 cup butter and shortening (half and half)
2 eggs, beaten
¼ cup cold water
2 tablespoons vinegar

1 teaspoon ginger
2 teaspoons cinnamon
2 teaspoons salt
4 teaspoons soda
2 teaspoons vanilla
6 cups sifted flour

Add soda to molasses and let foam for five minutes. Cream sugar and shortening with salt and spices, add to molasses and soda mixture. Add the beaten eggs, water and vinegar, beat well. Stir in the six cups flour. Roll cookies ½ inch thick on a floured board. Cut with large cutter. Bake at 350 degrees until done, 10-12 minutes. Cool and fill with the following filling. This filling is also good used in layer cakes.

FILLING

1 egg white
1 cup white sugar

¼ cup boiling water
1 cup chopped seeded raisins

Boil water and sugar until it threads then take from stove. Stir in egg white, beaten stiff. Add ½ teaspoon vanilla. When cool stir in the raisins.

Submitted by Jannie Wiers, St. Albans, Maine

Orange Peanut Butter Cookies

½ cup shortening
½ cup peanut butter
½ cup granulated sugar
½ cup brown sugar, firmly packed
1 egg
2 tablespoons orange juice

1 tablespoon grated orange rind
2¼ cups sifted all-purpose flour
½ teaspoon baking soda
¼ teaspoon salt
½ cup walnuts, chopped very fine

Place shortening, peanut butter, sugars, egg, orange juice and rind in large mixing bowl. Beat thoroughly. Sift together flour, baking soda and salt. Add half of the dry ingredients to the shortening mixture, blend, and add the remaining ingredients and mix thoroughly. Add nuts and mix well. Knead dough with hands until smooth. Pack firmly in 2 bars (1½ x 1½ inches square). Wrap in waxed paper. Place in refrigerator; chill until very firm. Cut in ⅛ inch slices; place on greased baking sheet. Bake in 400 degree oven for 8 to 10 minutes. Makes about 75 cookies.

Submitted by Elsie Swanson, Bar Harbor, Maine

Dreamies

40 small chocolate covered
  peanut butter cup candies
¼ cup creamy peanut butter
1/3 cup firmly packed brown
  sugar
1 package (9 ounce) pie
  crust mix

1 egg, well beaten
½ teaspoon vanilla
1 cup (3 ounce can) crushed
  chow mein noodles

Combine pie crust mix, brown sugar and peanut butter. Add vanilla and egg. Crush noodles with rolling pin and add to mixture. Shape into 1 inch balls. Place 2 inches apart. With back of spoon, make deep indentation in each. Bake at 370 degrees for 8 minutes. Remove from oven and press a candy in each center. Return to oven for about 1 minute. Remove to rack to cool.
Submitted by Julia Burgess, Waldoboro, Maine

Banana Nuggets

½ cup shortening
1 cup sugar
1 egg
1½ cups flour
1 teaspoon soda
1 teaspoon salt

¼ teaspoon nutmeg
¾ teaspoon cinnamon
1 cup mashed bananas
1¾ cups rolled oats
1 small package chocolate bits

Cream shortening and sugar, add egg and mix well. Sift flour with soda, salt, nutmeg and cinnamon. Mix into the egg mixture. Add the mashed banana and rolled oats, mixing well. Stir in the chocolate bits. Drop by teaspoon on a greased cookie sheet. Bake at 375 degrees for 15 to 20 minutes.
Submitted by Mrs. Theresa Shorey, Dexter, Maine

Sighs

3 egg whites
1 cup sugar
½ teaspoon lemon juice

½ cup slivered blanched
  almonds, packaged or canned

Beat egg whites until stiff. Add sugar gradually and then lemon juice while continuing to beat. Fold in almonds. Line baking sheets with foil. Drop meringue mixture by teaspoonfuls on foil. Bake in 350 degree oven for 12 minutes or until delicately browned. Makes about 4 dozen.
Submitted by Mrs. Stanwood H. King, Southwest Harbor, Maine

Cooked Oatmeal Drop Cookies

1 cup sugar
1 cup cooked oatmeal
1 egg
½ cup shortening
½ teaspoon salt
½ teaspoon nutmeg
1 teaspoon cinnamon

¼ teaspoon cloves
2 teaspoons vanilla
1 cup raisins ground
1 teaspoon soda
1 teaspoon baking powder
2½-3 cups flour
Nuts may be used

Mix sugar, cooked oatmeal, shortening and egg. Sift flour with soda, baking powder, salt and spices. Add to first mixture. Add raisins and vanilla.

A neighbor of ours, when bringing up her family, said they had oatmeal for breakfast each morning and many times some was left over. She didn't want to waste it, so created this recipe. It is very good.

Submitted by Mrs. Arthur Hussey, Seboeis, Maine

Oatmeal Macaroons

1 cup shortening
1 cup brown sugar
1 cup white sugar
2 eggs
1½ cups flour

1 teaspoon soda
1 teaspoon salt
½ teaspoon cinnamon
1 teaspoon vanilla
3 cups oatmeal (uncooked)

Cream butter and sugar. Add beaten eggs and vanilla. Sift together flour, soda, salt, and cinnamon. Mix together with first mixture. Add 3 cups uncooked oatmeal (quick cooking). Bake at 350 degrees 10 minutes. Leave on pan a minute or two before removing. Makes 5 dozen cookies.

Submitted by Mrs. Clarence Booker, Bangor, Maine

Tropical Oatmeal Cookies (Drop)

½ cup granulated sugar
½ cup brown sugar
½ cup shortening
1 egg, beaten
1 cup crushed pineapple
1½ cups oatmeal

1 cup flour
½ teaspoon soda
½ teaspoon salt
½ teaspoon cinnamon
⅛ teaspoon nutmeg

Mix ingredients in the order given and drop by spoonfuls onto greased cookie sheet. Bake at 375 degrees for 15 minutes.

Submitted by Mrs. Elva Stanley, Howland, Maine

Filled Cookies

2 cups sugar
1 cup shortening
2 eggs, beaten
½ teaspoon salt
2 heaping teaspoons cream of tartar
2 heaping teaspoons soda
1 teaspoon vanilla
1 cup milk
Flour to roll, just firm enough to handle and roll thin.

Cream sugar and shortening together. Add remaining ingredients. Flour to roll just firm enough to handle and roll thin. Cut with round cookie cutter. Spread filling on cookie cover with another cookie and pinch edges together. Bake in moderate oven 15-20 minutes.

FILLING

1 package chopped raisins
2 heaping tablespoons flour
1 cup sugar
Butter, size of small egg
Water to cover.

Cook until thick and cool before using.

Submitted by Miss Ruth L. Fickett, Lubec, Maine

Caramel Nut Cookies

½ cup butter
1 cup brown sugar (packed)
2 eggs
1½ cups flour
1 teaspoon soda
½ teaspoon salt
1 teaspoon vanilla
½ cup chopped nuts
½ cup chopped raisins
1 tablespoon vinegar

Cream butter and brown sugar. Beat in eggs, vanilla and vinegar. Sift flour with soda and salt and stir into the creamed mixture. Add nuts and raisins. Drop by teaspoon on a greased cookie sheet. Bake at 375 degrees for 8 to 10 minutes. These cookies freeze very well.

Submitted by Elizabeth Chute, Charleston, Maine

Cherry Surprise

½ cup butter
2 cups confectioner's sugar
1 tablespoon cream or top of milk
¼ teaspoon vanilla
½ teaspoon almond extract
Cherries
Graham cracker crumbs

Mix together the butter, sugar, cream and flavorings. Roll into balls. Drain the cherries and coat with the butter-sugar mixture. Roll in cracker crumbs. Store in cool place.

Submitted by Mrs. Francina Pelletier, Calais, Maine

Cool-as-a-Cucumber Shrimp Salad

1 package of lime gelatin
1 No. 2 can crushed pineapple
2 medium cucumbers
¼ cup lemon juice
1 pound of fresh cooked
shrimp

          or
2 (5 oz.) cans
¼ cup sweet or sour cream
Salad greens
Dash of paprika

DRESSING

2 teaspoons salt
2 teaspoons sugar
¼ teaspoon pepper

2/3 cup salad oil
¼ cup vinegar

Combine the ingredients for the dressing and beat or shake well. Marinate the shrimp in 1/3 cup of the dressing. Set in refrigerator to chill.

Mix gelatin according to directions, using the juice from the can of pineapple and the lemon juice instead of cold water (about 1 cup). Chill until slightly thickened. Peel the cucumbers and put through the food chopper with the pineapple and add to the slightly thickened gelatin. Turn into an oiled ring mold. Chill until set. Unmold, put a few salad greens in center of salad and pile the marinated shrimp on top of greens. Use a dash of paprika. Salad greens around the outside of the ring really dresses it up. Combine the remainder of the dressing with the cream and use as a dressing when you serve the salad.

Submitted by Capt. Mary Sue Emery, Rockland, Maine

Angel Hash Salad

1 lb. can crushed pineapple
1 lb. can fruit cocktail
2 tablespoons cornstarch
¼ cup sugar
1 cup heavy cream, whipped

¼ cup chopped walnuts or
pecans
2 cups miniature marshmallows
2 bananas, sliced if desired
2 egg yolks, beaten

Drain well the pineapple and fruit cocktail. Combine cornstarch and sugar in a saucepan and mix well. Add the egg yolks and juice from the fruits. Cook over medium heat, stirring constantly, until mixture comes to a boil and thickens. Remove from heat. Cool thoroughly at room temperature.

Fold in whipped cream and nuts, marshmallows, crushed pineapple and fruit cocktail. Chill overnight or for 2 to 3 hours.

Just before serving you may add 2 bananas, sliced. Serve on crisp lettuce.

Submitted by Mrs. Christopher Richardson, Wytopitlock, Maine

Apricot Salad

1 No. 2½ size can apricots (cut-up)
1 No. 2½ size can crushed pineapple
2 cups hot water
2 packages orange Jello
1 cup juice, from apricot and pineapple mix
¾ cup miniature marshmallows
½ cup granulated sugar
2 tablespoons flour
1 egg, slightly beaten
1 cup remaining fruit juice
2 tablespoons butter
1 cup cream or Dream Whip
¾ cup grated American cheese

Drain juice of both apricots and crushed pineapple and mix fruit. Prepare Jello with hot water and juice. Let cool. Add fruits and marshmallows. Set in ring mold.

After this has set, remove from mold and top with the following dressing: Cook sugar, flour, egg and 1 cup of remaining fruit juice over low heat until thick. Add 2 tablespoons butter. Cool. Whip 1 cup cream (or Dream Whip), mix with dressing and spread on Jello. Top with ¾ cup finely grated cheese.

Submitted by Mrs. Vesta Libby, Belgrade, Maine

Holiday Salad

1 package lime gelatin
2 cups boiling water
1 package lemon gelatin
1 cup boiling water
1 cup marshmallows (cut fine)
1 large can crushed pineapple
1 small package cream cheese
1 cup heavy cream
1 package cherry gelatin
2 cups boiling water

Dissolve lime gelatin in 2 cups of water and pour into a three quart mold. Refrigerate and let set.

Dissolve lemon gelatin in 1 cup boiling water and pour into a double boiler. Add marshmallows and melt. Cool. Add pineapple and juice, cream cheese and whipped cream. Pour into mold over first layer. Refrigerator and let set.

Dissolve cherry gelatin in 2 cups of boiling water. Pour over second layer, refrigerate and let set.

This red and green salad is attractive for Christmas. At Easter I substitute grape gelatin for the cherry gelatin and at Thanksgiving I use orange gelatin in place of the cherry gelatin. This yields 12 servings.

Submitted by Mrs. Albert W. Blasenak, Littleton, N. H.

Apple Sauce-Peach Jellied Salad

1 package of lemon or orange
gelatin (3 ounce)
1¼ cups boiling water
1 cup apple sauce

1 can peaches (No. 2)
halves or slices
1/3 cup pecans, broken in
small pieces

Substitute some of the peach juice for part of the 1¼ cups of boiling liquid. Pour the boiling liquid over the gelatin in a bowl and mix until dissolved. Pour one half of the dissolved gelatin in a mold and set in refrigerator until firm. Keep the other half at room temperature. As soon as the first half starts to thicken add the apple sauce, pecans and peach halves or slices. Spread the apple sauce, sprinkle on the pecans and arrange the peaches on top. Pour the rest of gelatin mixture on top. Chill until firm. Serves 8.

Submitted by Mrs. Janet Bouchard, Old Town, Maine

Club Salad

3 small packages of cream
cheese
1 can pimientos (chopped)
1 can crushed pineapple

1½ packages lemon gelatin
1 pint hot water
1 teaspoon dry mustard
½ cup cream, whipped

Mash the cheese with one tablespoon of cream. Add pineapple and well drained pimiento. Add the whipped cream and the dry mustard.

Add 1 pint of hot water to the gelatin. Cool, and when it is almost set, fold in the creamed mixture. Cool until firm. Serve with fruit salad dressing. This will easily serve 12.

Submitted by Mrs. Mabel Wilson, Tenants Harbor, Maine

Cranberry Salad

2 cups fresh cranberries
1½ cups water
1 cup sugar

1 package raspberry Jello
½ teaspoon salt
Celery and nuts

Cook cranberries and water for 10 minutes. Add 1 cup sugar and cook for 5 more minutes. Stir in 1 package of raspberry Jello while hot. Add the salt.

Cool and add celery and nuts.

Submitted by Mrs. Blanche Goodwin, Kingfield, Maine

Deep sea fisheries form a vital part of the State's economy and employ a great many people. Men catch the fish and women work in packing plants preparing the fish for market. Frozen fish portions and fillets are popular everywhere and in this day of high prices on red meats, make a very tasty, nourishing and economical meal. Most of the fishing is done from large draggers and trawlers that go out on the banks bordering the New England coast. The freshly caught fish are iced and brought to the packing plant soon after being caught. There they are cleaned and cut up into the finished product and quick frozen for shipment all over the country. Quick handling and attractive packaging have made a product of high quality and dependability. Several varieties are processed but the most popular is Ocean Perch.

Cranberry-walnut Salad

2 cups cranberries
¾ cup water
1½ cups sugar
1 package lemon Jello

½ cup boiling water
1 cup diced celery
½ cup chopped walnuts

Combine the cranberries and ¾ cup water. Cook until skins break open. Add the sugar, cook 3 minutes longer. Combine the Jello and boiling water, stir until dissolved. Combine Jello and berries. Chill until syrupy. Add the celery and nuts to the Jello mixture and pour into a 1-quart mold and chill.

Submitted by Mrs. D. F. London, Houlton, Maine

Cabbage Salad

3 lbs. cabbage (large head)
1 large onion
¾ cup vinegar
1 teaspoon salt

⅛ teaspoon pepper
¾ cup salad oil
1 cup sugar

Peel off outside leaves of cabbage and onion. Grate the two together and place in a large bowl. Mix well.

In a saucepan, combine vinegar, salt, pepper, oil, and sugar. Bring to a boil and pour boiling hot over the vegetables. DO NOT STIR. Allow to set undisturbed for 1½ hours. Then toss and mix. Store in refrigerator at least 12 hours before serving.

Submitted by Mrs. Ruby Hussey, Old Town, Maine

Pyramid Salad

Red jelly
Pineapple slices
Lettuce

Mayonnaise
Whipped cream

Cut a circle of red jelly a little larger than a slice of pineapple. Place jelly on a lettuce leaf, pineapple slice on top. Mix mayonnaise and whipped cream. Pile on top of the pineapple, leaving a good margin of pineapple. Top this individual serving with a red cherry.

Submitted by Mrs. Gertrude Mitchell, Weeks Mills, Maine

Green Ribbon Salad

2 packages lime Jello
1 package lemon Jello
½ pint heavy cream (whipped)
2 cups cottage cheese (sieved)

1 large can pineapple (drain)
½ cup celery cut fine
½ cup chopped nuts

This is made in layers. The first layer: 1 package lime Jello — dissolve in 1½ cups hot water and ½ cup pineapple juice. Set to cool until syrupy, then add ½ cup pineapple, ¼ cup nuts, and ¼ cup celery. Divide and put into two round molds. (This is 1st layer.)

The second layer: 1 package lemon Jello dissolved in 1 cup hot water. Cool and when syrupy, stir in the whipped cream, cottage cheese, 1 cup pineapple. Divide and put on top of first layer.

The third layer is the same as first.

I set my Jello all at the same time. The first layer doesn't want to be firm when the second layer is added and the same with third. If too firm, they will separate when unmolded. Grease molds with cooking oil.

Submitted by Meridith M. Fisher, St. Albans, Maine

Sweet and Sour Salad

1 No. 2 can bean sprouts,
  drained
1 No. 2 can sauerkraut
2 cups diced celery

1 cup diced onion
½ cup green pepper
2 cups sugar
1 cup water

Mix bean sprouts, sauerkraut, celery, onion and green pepper together. Let set and fix the syrup. Bring the sugar and water to a boil. Cool. When cold, add to the first mixture and let set for 48 hours. This is very good with cold meat or baked beans.

Submitted by Reta Charest, East Wilton, Maine

My Favorite Salad

1 package lemon flavored
  gelatin
1 cup boiling water

1 tablespoon brown sugar
1 cup crushed pineapple
2 carrots grated

Mix boiling water and the gelatin, stir in the brown sugar and the crushed pineapple. Pour into a salad mold and sprinkle the grated carrots on top. Do not stir. Serve with the carrot side down.

Submitted by Mrs. N. L. Witham, Rockland, Maine

Lake House Cole Slaw

1 cabbage, about the size of a
   grapefruit

1 medium sized onion, minced
   fine

DRESSING

2 tablespoons salad oil
1 tablespoon vinegar
2 heaping tablespoons of
   mayonnaise
¼ cup milk

1 heaping tablespoon granulated sugar
½ teaspoon prepared mustard
½ teaspoon salt
Dash of cayenne pepper

Grate cabbage as fine or as coarse as desired. Add finely minced onion. Mix thoroughly.

Put sugar, prepared mustard, salt, cayenne pepper, salad oil, and vinegar in a bowl and mix well. Add mayonnaise and milk. Beat mixture with beater. The dressing should be similar to heavy cream. If it is too thick, add a little more milk; if it is too thin, add a little more mayonnaise. Pour dressing over cabbage and onion mixture.

For larger sized cabbages, just multiply the ingredients to make as much dressing as desired.

This can be kept in a jar in the refrigerator for an indefinite length of time.

Submitted by Mrs. Charles Adams, Decatur, Georgia

Salad Dressing

¾ cup cider vinegar
2 eggs
¾ cup sugar

1 teaspoon dry mustard
1 cup all-purpose cream

In a medium saucepan, bring to a boil the ¾ cup of vinegar. Set aside to cool. In a bowl, beat the eggs and add the sugar. Blend well. In a cup, put the mustard and add a little of the cream to make a smooth paste. Gradually add all of the cream. Add to the egg-sugar mixture and mix well. Pour into the pan of vinegar and cook over medium heat, stirring occasionally, until thick (not too thick). Remove, cool and refrigerate.

Note: Taste as you cook, if too sweet, add more vinegar, if too tart, add more sugar. This dressing is excellent for potato, salmon, tuna, Waldorf salads as well as a combination of lettuce and tomato.

Submitted by Mrs. Ethel Kinderman, Belfast, Maine

Cabbage Dressing (Cole Slaw)

1 egg, beaten
Pepper
Salt
1 tablespoon prepared mustard

1 tablespoon butter
1 teacup of vinegar
Sugar

Mix egg, little pepper, salt, mustard, butter, vinegar and a little sugar in a saucepan and let it come to a boil. Cool and then pour over cabbage which must be chopped *very fine*. Two teaspoons of celery seed improves the flavor.

Submitted by Mrs. Ethel M. Hilton, Cape Neddick, Maine

Aunt Alice's Salad Dressing (very old)

1 egg
1/3 cup vinegar
½ cup milk
1 dessert spoon dry mustard

½ teaspoon salt
1 tablespoon flour
1 tablespoon sugar
Small piece of butter

Mix the dry ingredients thoroughly and add to well beaten egg. Heat milk in double boiler, add butter, then stir in the egg and mustard mixture. Stir in the vinegar as the last ingredient.

Submitted by Arthur J. Cummings, Bethel, Maine

Tomato French Dressing

2 tablespoons sugar
2 teaspoons dry mustard
1 teaspoon salt
½ teaspoon pepper
1 can condensed tomato soup

½ soup can vinegar plus 2 tablespoons
½ soup can salad oil plus 2 tablespoons
2 tablespoons minced onions

Combine dry ingredients in a one quart jar, add remaining ingredients and shake well. Shake well again before using.

Submitted by Mrs. Sara C. Wilson, Rockland, Maine

Sweet Salad Dressing

5 tablespoons sugar
½ tablespoon mustard
½ tablespoon salt

2 eggs, beaten
3 tablespoons vinegar
1 cup sweet or sour cream

Cook in double boiler until thick. Use with whipped cream for fruit salad.

Submitted by Mrs. Grace Irvine, Warren, Maine

Fruit Salad Dressing

1 can pineapple
¾ cup sugar
2 eggs, separated

2 tablespoons butter
3 heaping tablespoons flour
½ pint cream, whipped

Drain juice from pineapple (about 1 cup). Cream sugar and egg yolks, then cream in butter and flour. Beat egg whites very stiff and add to the creamed mixture. Heat juice in double boiler, stir in above mixture and cook until thick. When ready to serve add the cream.

Submitted by Rita H. Ellis, Skowhegan, Maine

Pineapple Fruit Salad Dressing

2/3 cup pineapple juice
½ cup sugar

2 eggs, well beaten
1 cup cream, whipped

Heat the pineapple juice and sugar together, add beaten eggs and cook until thick, beat smooth. Cool and when used, add the cream.

Submitted by Etta Beverage, North Haven, Maine

Strawberry Jam

6 cups strawberries
6 cups sugar

½ cup fresh lemon juice

Wash the berries, lifting them from the water to drain. Remove the hulls. Leave the berries whole. Place the berries in a shallow pan; pour boiling water over them just to cover; let stand for three minutes. Drain. In a kettle, combine the drained berries and 3 cups sugar, mix. Bring to boiling point and boil for 8 minutes, stirring constantly. Add the remaining 3 cups sugar and the lemon juice, boil for 10 minutes, stirring constantly. Pull the kettle to the back of the stove and stir and skim for two minutes. Pour the jam into a shallow platter or glass baking dish. Let the jam set overnight. In the morning, fill hot sterilized jars with the cold jam and seal.

This is a soft jam which is just right to go on hot biscuits or toast.

(Small baby food jars make good containers for jams or jellies because they can be sealed and do not need to be waxed if the rubber gasket is still in the cover of the jar.) Sterilize the jars and covers before using.

Submitted by Mildred B. Schrumpf, Orono, Maine

Rhubarb-Strawberry Jam

5 cups chopped rhubarb   2 packages strawberry Jello
5 cups sugar

Mix rhubarb and sugar in a saucepan and set overnight. In the morning, boil the mixture for 2 minutes. Add 2 packages of Jello. Boil 10 minutes, and mash while it is cooking to break up rhubarb. Pour into sterilized, hot jars, cover and wax.

Submitted by Mrs. Hans Meier, Mt. Desert, Maine

Pear Harlequin

½ peck of pears (about 6½ pounds)
1 medium sized can of crushed pineapple
2 oranges

¾ cup of sugar for each cup of fruit
1 8-ounce bottle maraschino cherries

Peel pears and slice thin. Grate the rind of the oranges, then put them, rind and all, through the food chopper. Add the pineapple, juice and all the pears. Add the grated and chopped oranges. For each cup of fruit add ¾ cup of sugar. Mix together well and let stand overnight. In the morning, add the maraschino cherries, cut up small. Stir well and cook slowly until thick, then bottle and seal.

Submitted by Mrs. Charlotte Wiers, St. Albans, Maine

Christmas Marmalade

1 orange
1 lemon
1 grapefruit

Sugar
Enough water to cover fruit

Wash and peel orange, lemon and grapefruit; cut into thinnest possible slices. Cut pulp into chunks; cover with water and simmer 5 minutes. Let stand overnight. Cook very slowly until skins are tender, cool. Measure and add 1 cup sugar for each cup of fruit and juice. Cook to jellying point. Pour into hot glasses. Seal at once.

Submitted by Elsie Swanson, Bar Harbor, Maine

Rhubarb Marmalade

3 pounds rhubarb
3 pounds sugar
1 box of raisins

2 large oranges or 3 small ones

Put sugar in rhubarb at night. Do not add water. Heat in the morning, then add raisins and ground oranges, and cook to right consistency. Bottle and seal.

Submitted by Mrs. Frank Rowe, Warren, Maine

Quince Honey

5 large quinces
5 pounds of sugar

1 pint boiling water

Stir the sugar into the boiling water and stir over heat until sugar is dissolved. Pare and grate the quinces; add to the sugar syrup and cook 15 or 20 minutes. The grated quince may be strained out or left in. Turn into hot sterilized jars. When cold, it should be about the color and consistency of honey.

Submitted by Mrs. Joy Warren, Pittsfield, Maine

Ripe Cucumber Relish

12 large ripe cucumbers, peeled and seeded, put through food grinder — coarse blade
2 cups chopped onion
½ cup salt
3 cups vinegar

1 cup flour
6 cups sugar
1 teaspoon tumeric
1 teaspoon celery seed
1 teaspoon dry mustard
1 cup vinegar

Add salt to vegetables and let set overnight. Drain in the morning. Heat 3 cups vinegar. In bowl, mix flour, sugar, tumeric, celery seed, mustard, and 1 cup vinegar, to make paste. Add to hot vinegar and cook, stirring constantly until thick. Add cukes and onions, cook slowly 10 minutes. Bottle. This is very good with baked beans.

Submitted by Mrs. Nola Sawtelle, Corinna, Maine

Pepper Relish

12 green hot peppers
12 sweet red peppers
12 medium sized onions

2 cups sugar
4 tablespoons salt
1 quart vinegar

Chop peppers and onions, or put through food grinder. Cover with boiling water and let stand for 5 minutes. Drain. Add sugar, salt and vinegar. Boil for 20 minutes. Put in jars. This relish will keep indefinitely.

Submitted by Mrs. Edna Keyes, Thomaston, Maine

Pickled Beans

4 quarts string beans
3 pounds sugar
1 tablespoon celery seed
½ cup dry mustard
½ cup flour
1 tablespoon tumeric
3 pints vinegar

Take 4 quarts beans, wash, string and cut in 1" lengths. Boil in salted water until tender. Drain well.

Make dressing of sugar, celery seed, dry mustard, flour, tumeric, and vinegar. Boil until thick, pour over beans. Mix well and put in jars.

Submitted by Katherine F. Crockett, Machias, Maine

Marinated Beans

1 can green beans
1 can wax beans
1 can kidney beans
1 can lima beans
½ cup celery (cut in small pieces)
1 big onion, sliced
¾ cup sugar
1/3 cup oil
2/3 cup wine vinegar
1 teaspoon salt

Combine beans, add the celery and onion, toss lightly. Make a sauce with the sugar, oil, vinegar and salt. Bring the sauce to a boil, then cool. Put beans in a tightly covered dish and pour the sauce over them. Shake the container of beans several times during the next two or three days.

Submitted by Mrs. Ervin Knowlen, Holden, Maine

Bread and Butter Pickles

1 gallon cucumbers, sliced thin
8 small onions, sliced thin
1 green pepper, sliced thin
1 quart crushed ice
½ cup salt
5 cups vinegar
5 cups sugar
1½ teaspoons tumeric
1 teaspoon ground cloves
1 teaspoon celery seeds
2 teaspoons mustard seeds

Cover cucumbers, onions, and pepper with 1 quart of crushed ice and ½ cup salt. Let stand at least 3 hours.

Combine vinegar, sugar, tumeric, ground cloves, celery seeds and mustard seeds. Add the drained cucumber mixture and bring to boiling point. Pack in sterilized jars. Let stand at least 30 days.

Submitted by Mrs. Granville Green, Fairfield, Maine

Hot Dog Relish

5 cups diced cucumbers,
  seeds removed
3 cups onions, cut up
3 cups celery, cut up
2 red peppers, cut up
2 sweet red or green peppers

¾ cup salt
1½ pints water
1 quart vinegar
3 cups sugar
2 teaspoons mustard seed

Prepare vegetables and cover with salt and water. Let stand overnight. Drain the next morning. Heat the vinegar, sugar, and mustard seed and add to the vegetables. Boil slowly for 10 minutes. Seal hot.

Submitted by Arlene Spencer, Hartland, Maine

Sweet Tomato Pickles

1 peck green tomatoes
1 cup salt
1 quart vinegar

4 pounds brown sugar
1 tablespoon cloves
½ cup broken cinnamon

Slice tomatoes and sprinkle salt over each layer. Let stand overnight. In the morning, drain off water and cook slowly in water and vinegar in the proportion of 3 parts water to 1 of vinegar. When tender, drain and put in stone jar. Boil vinegar, sugar, and spice and pour over tomatoes. Let stand 2 days. Drain off vinegar and boil down 1/3. Pour over pickles. These don't have to be sealed. These are delicious.

Submitted by Mrs. Kermit K. Bailey, Caribou, Maine

Chopped Pickle

1 quart chopped cabbage
2 quarts green tomatoes
6 large onions
3 red peppers, or a can of
  pimentos
1 tablespoon celery seed

¼ cup white mustard seed
1 tablespoon tumeric
4 cups white sugar
¼ cup salt
1½ cups vinegar

Combine all ingredients and boil 20 minutes. Put in hot jars and seal. I do all my "chopping" by just cutting on a breadboard because we like the pieces big.

Submitted by Frances Taylor, North Anson, Maine

Apple Relish

1 quart vinegar
1 cup white sugar
2 cups brown sugar
1 tablespoon mustard seed
12 apples with peelings

3 large onions
6 green tomatoes
1 teaspoon salt
1 teaspoon ground cloves
1 cup raisins

Chop all ingredients and cook in the vinegar. Fill jars and seal tightly.

Submitted by Beatrice S. Barrett, Mars Hill, Maine

Pickled Eggs

12 hard-boiled eggs (peeled and pricked)
1 medium onion, sliced
1 cup water

1 cup vinegar
1 teaspoon salt
1 teaspoon mixed pickling spice

Pack eggs in a jar, alternating with onion slices. Heat water, vinegar, salt and spices to boiling point. Pour hot solution over eggs. Store in refrigerator for 36 hours before eating.

Submitted by Arlene Guptill, Addison, Maine

Chili Sauce (1896)

6 ripe tomatoes
2 green peppers or ¼ teaspoon red pepper
4 medium onions

1 tablespoon salt
2 scant cups sugar
2 cups vinegar

Boil 1 hour and bottle.

Submitted by Mrs. Mary Bancroft, Norway, Maine

Spiced Beet Pickles

2 cups white sugar
2 cups water
2 cups vinegar

1 teaspoon whole cloves
1 teaspoon allspice
1 tablespoon cinnamon

Boil small beets until tender and then peel. Make a syrup of the sugar, water, vinegar, cloves, allspice, and cinnamon. Pour over beets and simmer 15 minutes. Pack into jars and seal.

Submitted by Mrs. Stella Hollister, Hartland, Maine

Garden Special

4 quarts ripe tomatoes	6 sweet peppers
1 quart celery	3 tablespoons salt
1 quart onions	2 tablespoons sugar
1 quart water	

Dice peppers, onions, and celery, add water and cook together for 20 minutes. Add tomatoes, which have been peeled and cut up, and seasonings. After it all comes to a boil, put into hot jars and process in hot water bath for 30 minutes.

To Use For A One-dish Meal

1 pint Garden Special	2 cups cooked spaghetti, rice
½ pound hamburg steak or	or cold diced potato
scraps of cold meat	

Put in layers in baking dish and cook in oven until well heated through. This makes four large or six small servings.

I have found this very useful for a "hurry-up" meal in a parsonage!

Submitted by Mrs. Charles R. Monteith, Rockland, Maine

Mincemeat

2 bowls of chopped meat	1½ bowls of oleo
4 bowls of chopped apple	½ bowl vinegar
1 bowl of sugar	Spices and salt to taste
1 bowl of molasses	2 boxes of raisins
1 bowl of chopped suet, or	

Mix ingredients together and simmer for at least 3 hours. Stir frequently to prevent burning. I generally use venison in this recipe.

Submitted by Mrs. Roger Stanley, Bernard, Maine

Grammie's Mincemeat

2 pints chopped beef	3 level tablespoons nutmeg
5 pints chopped apple	3 level tablespoons cinnamon
1 pint chopped suet	2 level tablespoons ground
1 pint raisins	cloves
1 pint currants	3 pints sugar
1 cup cider or vinegar	1½ cups molasses
3 level tablespoons salt	

Mix in the above order (add more cider or vinegar if more liquid is needed); cook slowly one hour. Be careful not to burn. This makes a number of pies or may be put into hot jars and sealed for future use.

Submitted by Mrs. Eaino Heikkenine, South Paris, Maine

Green Tomato Mincemeat

6 quarts chopped tomatoes
1 teaspoon fat
1 cup vinegar
2 cups brown sugar
1 pound seeded raisins,
  ground

1 pound seedless raisins
1 pound citron, optional
1 teaspoon cloves, ground
1 teaspoon cinnamon
1 teaspoon nutmeg
Salt to taste

(Note: Any leftover jelly or fruit juice, boiled cider, etc., may also be added.)

Rinse the chopped tomatoes until water is clear. Stew ½ hour, rinse and drain. Add remaining ingredients. Cook slowly until tender. Pack and seal while hot. Makes 3 quarts.

(Instead of packing into canning jars, this mincemeat may be packed into freezer containers and frozen.)

Use as is in pies or any recipe calling for mincemeat.

Submitted by Blanche Glover Hammond, Albion, Maine

Mincemeat

5 quarts of meat, ground
2 cups molasses
3 pounds raisins or 1 of currants and 2 of raisins
3 dozen apples
1½ cups vinegar
1 tablespoon salt

½ teaspoon allspice
1 teaspoon cinnamon
½ teaspoon cloves
½ teaspoon nutmeg
2 cups sugar
1 cup ground suet or ½ cup
  butter

Grind meat and apples. Add rest of ingredients and simmer or bake 2 hours. Put into jars. Seal while hot.

Submitted by Mrs. Leona Sutherland, Ashland, Maine

Mom's Deer Mincemeat

1 bowl deer meat, ground
2 bowls apples, ground
1/3 bowl suet, ground
  (may use butter)
1/3 bowl sugar
1/3 bowl molasses

1/3 bowl coffee
1/3 bowl raisins
2/3 bowl sweet cider
Salt, cinnamon, cloves and
  nutmeg to suit your taste

Mix all ingredients together well. Simmer slowly, stirring from the bottom often as it burns very easily. Simmer 3 to 4 hours. Can in hot sterilized jars.

Submitted by Mrs. Constance Butler, Sanford, Maine

234

Smothered Rabbit with Onions

1 rabbit (or more)
Flour
Salt
Paprika
3 tablespoons drippings or
    butter

Sliced onions
½ teaspoon salt
1 cup thick, sour cream

Clean and cut rabbit into pieces. Season with salt and paprika and dredge with flour. Melt drippings or butter in a skillet and saute rabbit until brown. Cover thickly with sliced onions, sprinkle with salt. Pour over them, 1 cup thick sour cream. Cover skillet closely and simmer for 1 hour, or place in a 325 degree oven and bake until tender, about 1 hour. Remove the meat and add water and flour to make gravy, if desired. Add seasonings to taste.

Submitted by Mrs. W. G. Glover, Dover-Foxcroft, Maine

Rabbit Pie

1 or 2 rabbits
Crust for a 2-crust pie

Sliced potatoes
Sliced onions

Parboil rabbits. Make a good pie crust and line a 9 x 9 inch baking pan. Put in a layer of thinly sliced potatoes, one of rabbit, and one of thinly sliced onions. Repeat until dish is full. Pour over all the liquor rabbit was cooked in and sprinkle with your favorite herbs or seasonings. Add the top crust. Bake in a 350 degree oven for 2 hours.

Submitted by Mrs. Leola Peaslee, North Edgecomb, Maine

Beans and Venison

1½-2 cups red kidney beans
¼ cup sugar
Salt and pepper
¼ teaspoon dry mustard

Small onion
Venison chunks (beef short
    ribs or stew beef)
Salt pork or bacon fat

Soak beans as usual, add salt pork or bacon fat, sugar, salt and pepper, dry mustard, small whole or sliced onion, venison chunks. Cover with water and bake all day. Meat may be thawed or used directly from freezer.

Submitted by Mrs. Owen H. Grant, East Waterboro, Maine

Hunter's Stew

2 pounds cut-up deer meat
¼ cup flour
1½ teaspoons salt
¼ teaspoon pepper
¼ cup butter
1 large onion, sliced

2 cups diced carrot
2 cups diced celery
8 medium potatoes
   (quartered)
3 cups milk
1 cup diced cheese (optional)

Cut the meat in 1½-inch cubes, dredge with the flour, salt and pepper. Melt the butter in a heavy pan, brown the meat, add the onions and cook until tender. Peel potatoes and quarter, add with the carrots and celery to the meat during the last half of cooking. Gradually add the milk. Can thicken stew with 2 tablespoons of flour in ¼ cup of milk for each cup of gravy. Top with the diced cheese or doughboys. Makes 8 servings.

Submitted by Mrs. Roy Lilley, Houlton, Maine

Steak for the "I hate to fuss camper"

1 pound piece chuck steak,
   ¾-inch thick
2 potatoes, thick slices

1 onion, sliced
Salt and pepper to taste

Place steak in a hot fry pan and brown on both sides. Add water to partially cover and cover with potatoes and onions. Add salt and pepper to taste, while cooking. Allow to simmer slowly, about 10 minutes. Cover and cook until potatoes are done. Additional water may be necessary while cooking, depending on the heat of the campfire.

Submitted by W. A. Lindquist, Camden, Maine

Pheasant en Casserole

1 pheasant
1 can cream of celery soup

½ soup can fresh milk
Salt to taste

Clean and wash pheasant thoroughly. Cut in half. Put in a buttered casserole dish (depending on size of bird). Add the celery soup and milk, be sure the bird is completely covered. Bake covered in a slow oven, 300 to 325 degrees, so milk won't darken or curdle, for 2 hours. Can use cream of mushroom soup, but celery soup is more flavorful.

Submitted by Mrs. Harriet Keenan, Owls Head, Maine

Baked Eider Ducks

4 Eider ducks
1 large onion
¼ cup cooking oil
3 tablespoons Worcestershire sauce
2 tablespoons prepared mustard
2 teaspoons salt
½ teaspoon pepper
1/3 cup lemon juice
1½ cups dandelion wine
Onion and celery for stuffing

The ducks are skinned and cleaned. Soak overnight in salt and water, standard procedure for sea ducks. Make a barbecue sauce by simmering the onion, cut-up, in the salad oil, until onion is soft. Add the sugar, Worcestershire sauce, mustard, salt, pepper and lemon juice. Simmer another 15 minutes.

Combine the simmered mixture with the dandelion wine and pour this mixture over the ducks in a small crock. Leave ducks in the crock at least 24 hours, turning occasionally and dipping the barbecue sauce over them.

When ready to bake the ducks, stuff loosely with whatever desired. Cut-up onion and celery is adequate as these birds are small. Wrap each duck in a piece of foil, bring it up around each bird but leave a small opening at the top. This prevents the bird from being baked too dry. Add the barbecue sauce over each duck and start in a 450 degree oven for the first 45 minutes then turn down to 350 degrees for rest of cooking time. I baste the birds a few times during baking. They are simply delicious.

Submitted by Mrs. Dorothy Stewart, Castine, Maine

Partridge Fillet

Breast meat from partridge
¼ cup butter
1 tablespoon lemon juice
Very fine bread crumbs
1 egg, beaten
Deep fat

Remove the meat from partridge breast and cut in finger-size pieces, about 8 pieces per bird. Melt the butter and add the lemon juice. Dip the partridge pieces in butter mixture and spread out on a plate to congeal the butter. Then roll each piece in the very fine bread crumbs. Dip in beaten egg and roll in crumbs again. Fry in deep fat until done, about 5 minutes.

Submitted by Mrs. Stanley Knowlton, Harmony, Maine

Wild Birds and Dumplings
Down East Version

Bird(s)
2 small slices salt pork
¼ teaspoon pepper
2 teaspoons salt (about)
Diced turnip

Whole potatoes
1 pint flour
1 teaspoon salt
2 teaspoons baking powder
Milk

Cut up the bird or birds and just barely cover with water. Add the salt pork and pepper. Cook slowly for 3 hours. Watch them and add more water as needed, but not too much, so as to make brown gravy. Add 2 teaspoons of salt 1 hour after the birds start cooking. Add diced turnip and whole potatoes (amount needed for your meal) 1 hour before bird will be done. To make dumplings, sift together salt, flour and baking powder and mix with milk so they will drop from spoon. Cover and cook undisturbed for 20 minutes. Serve while dumplings are piping hot.

These birds (depends on the kind) are so small we always speak of cooking a pair of birds.

Submitted by Mrs. Juanita B. Allen, Bryant Pond, Maine

Corned Beef Casserole

1 package macaroni (6 ounce)
1 can corned beef (12 ounce)
¼ pound cheese, cubed
1 cup milk

½ cup chopped onion
1 can condensed cream of chicken soup
Buttered crumbs

Cook macaroni in boiling salted water, drain and rinse. Cube the corned beef and add with the onion and cheese to the macaroni. Combine the soup and milk and add. Pour into a 2-quart casserole. Top with the buttered crumbs. Bake in a 350 degree oven for 1 hour.

Submitted by Mrs. John Workman, Prospect Harbor, Maine

Barbecue Sauce

1 teaspoon prepared mustard
3 tablespoons vinegar
1/3 cup water

3 tablespoons brown sugar
¾ cup catsup
Dash of Tabasco (optional)

Combine all ingredients and cook over low heat ½ hour.

Submitted by Mrs. Ferne Sanborn, Bangor, Maine

Low Sodium Bread

¼ cup lukewarm water
1 cake compressed yeast or 1
package granular yeast
2 cups hot water

2 teaspoons sugar
2 tablespoons unsalted
shortening
6 cups flour (approximately)

Soften yeast with ¼ cup of lukewarm water. Pour the 2 cups of hot water over the sugar and shortening. Cool to lukewarm. Add the yeast and flour to make a stiff batter. Beat well. Add more flour to make a soft dough. Turn out on board. Knead until light and elastic and until dough does not stick to the board. Place in a warm greased bowl. Grease top of dough lightly. Cover. Keep in a warm place. When doubled in bulk (about 2 hours) punch down, round up and let rise again to double in bulk (1½ hours). Shape into loaves. Place on a greased pan, grease top lightly. Let rise again to double in bulk. Bake in a 400 degree oven for 40 to 50 minutes.

Submitted by "Chef" Henry Tremblay, Windsor, Maine

Diabetic Mincemeat

1 quart ground cooked beef
(Small piece of suet,
ground with beef)
3 quarts ground apples
1 bottle diabetic pancake syrup
2 tablespoons liquid sweetener
2 teaspoons cloves

2 teaspoons nutmeg
2 teaspoons cinnamon
4 cups vinegar
1 teaspoon salt
2 cups liquid in which meat
was cooked

Add all ingredients together and cook slowly for 3 or 4 hours.

Submitted by Mrs. Leon Beal, Waterboro, Maine

Father John's Diabetic Cookies

1¼ cups shortening
½ cup sugar
3 eggs
1 tablespoon vanilla
1½ tablespoons sugar substitute,
or the equivalent of ¾ cup
sugar
2¾ cups flour

1 heaping teaspoon baking
powder
½ teaspoon salt
¾ cup milk
½ cup raisins
1/3 cup chocolate-mint
morsels

Drop onto a tin and bake in 410 to 425 degree oven for about 10 minutes.

Submitted by Mrs. Marjorie Wilder, Norridgewock, Maine

Diabetic Banana Pie

1½ cups milk
2 eggs, separated
1 envelope gelatin
3 (¼ gram) saccharin
¼ teaspoon salt

¼ cup cold water
½ teaspoon vanilla
Cooked pie shell or graham
    cracker crust

Heat milk in top of double boiler, add salt and dissolved saccharin. Add small amount of hot milk to beaten egg yolks, then stir into milk mixture until it coats the spoon. Dissolve gelatin in cold water. Add to hot milk mixture and stir until dissolved. Remove from stove and cool. When it begins to thicken, fold in stiffly beaten egg whites. Cover bottom of crust with egg mixture, then a layer of sliced bananas. Alternate bananas and egg mixture until crust is full, ending with egg mixture. Serve with whipped cream sweetened with saccharin. Serves 6.

Submitted by Mrs. Arline Harris, Newport, Maine

Sugar-free Fruit Delight

1 envelope raspberry
    (D-Zerta)
1 cup boiling juice
1 cup sugar-free, crushed
    pineapple
1 cup fresh or frozen straw-
    berries, thawed

1 envelope (D-Zerta) whipped
    topping
2 tablespoons finely ground
    walnuts (if desired)

Drain crushed pineapple and strawberries and add enough water or sugar-free juice of any kind to make 1 cup of liquid. Bring to boil and dissolve gelatin, then chill to consistency of egg whites. Whip topping according to package directions. Fold pineapple, strawberries, nuts and whipped topping into the gelatin. Pour into serving dishes or mold and chill a few hours. Yield 6-8 servings.

Submitted by Virginia M. Phippen, Southwest Harbor, Maine

Diabetic Cookies

¾ cup biscuit mix
1 egg
1 package low calorie dessert
    pudding (butterscotch)

2 tablespoons Wesson oil
1/3 cup chopped dates
½ teaspoon maple flavoring
    or vanilla

Mix all together and form into small balls. Put on cookie sheet, flatten, and bake at 350 degrees for 8 minutes.

Submitted by Mrs. Roy Lilley, Houlton, Maine

Diabetic Salmon Loaf

¼ cup canned salmon
1 teaspoon butter
2 teaspoons vinegar
1 tablespoon water

1 egg, beaten
¼ cup skimmed milk
½ teaspoon gelatin
Salt substitute

Flake the salmon, add beaten egg, melted butter, milk and vinegar and salt. Cook in top of double boiler, stirring constantly until the mixture thickens. Soak gelatin in the cold water and add to salmon mixture. Fill mold, chill and serve.

Submitted by Mrs. Leon Beal, Waterboro, Maine

Custard Pie
(Dietetic)

3 cups scalded milk (if you use dry skim milk or canned milk, you need not scald)
3 eggs, slightly beaten
¼ teaspoon salt

Artificial sweetener to taste (amount to equal ½ cup sugar)
1 teaspoon vanilla
Nutmeg to taste

Line a pie plate with your favorite pastry. Pour this filling in. Bake as usual for custard pie.

Submitted by Mrs. S. H. Lord, Ellsworth, Maine

Saccharin Pickles

2 quarts cold vinegar
¼ cup salt
½ cup horseradish
1½ teaspoons cassia
½ teaspoon cloves

½ teaspoon allspice
2 teaspoons alum, powdered
2 teaspoons saccharin, powdered
3 tablespoons dry mustard

Wash and pack cucumbers in jars. Mix all other ingredients together. Cover cucumbers in jars. Cucumbers may be cut length-wise, if large. If vinegar is too strong, it may be diluted. These pickles may be eaten by dietetics.

Submitted by Edith Knox, Fryeburg, Maine

Slippery-Elm Bark Tea

Break the bark into bits, pour boiling water over it, cover and let it infuse until cold. Sweeten, ice and take for stomach disorders, or add lemon juice and drink for a bad cold.

Submitted by Mrs. Ada M. Spencer, Bradley, Maine

Diabetic Mincemeat

1 cup cooked beef, ground
3 cups apples, ground
1 cup raisins
2 cups meat stock or water
½ cup sweet cider
¼ cup vinegar
½ stick margarine
1 teaspoon cloves
½ teaspoon allspice
1 teaspoon cinnamon
¼ teaspoon nutmeg
3 tablespoons sucaryl

Simmer together until thick in consistency and the apples are well done.

Submitted by Dora V. Williams, Thomaston, Maine

Low Calorie Ice Cream

1 14½ ounce can of evaporated
skim milk
1 tablespoon liquid sweetener
1 tablespoon vanilla or any
flavoring

Pour skim milk into freezing tray. Freeze until solid. Beat until fluffy. Add sweetener and flavoring. Stir until mixed. Return to freezer. Remove 10 minutes before serving. Makes 1 pint.

Submitted by Elaine Dutil, Lewiston, Maine

Macaroni and Cottage Cheese
(Dietetic)

2 cups elbow macaroni
1 pound small curd cottage
cheese
6 slices American cheese
1 egg
2 cups skim milk
4 tablespoons oleo
Salt to taste

Add macaroni to rapidly boiling salted water. Stir once to prevent sticking, and boil for about twenty minutes. I use three quarts of water in a ten-quart aluminum kettle.

Prepare a large casserole (3-quart or two, 1½ quarts) in the following manner. Cut the butter in ¼ inch slices. Place one in the bottom of casserole and the rest around the edge of sides. Add the cottage cheese and cut up (coarsely) American cheese. Drain the macaroni and add immediately to the cottage and American cheeses and toss to mix. Add egg which has been beaten with the skim milk and salt to taste (about 1 teaspoon). Cover and place in a pan of water. Cook for one and a half hours in a 225 degree oven, covered. I sometimes cut up cubes of bread and add to the mixture by placing them around the top. This is optional, however, but looks rather nice, but, of course, adds calories.

Submitted by Christine B. Duke, Southport, Maine

WEIGHTS and MEASURES

Dash *equals* less than ⅛ teaspoon
3 teaspoons *equal* 1 tablespoon

4 tablespoons *equal* ¼ cup
5⅓ tablespoons *equal* ⅓ cup
8 tablespoons *equal* ½ cup
10⅔ tablespoons *equal* ⅔ cup
12 tablespoons *equal* ¾ cup
14 tablespoons *equal* ⅞ cup
16 tablespoons *equal* 1 cup

2 tablespoons *equal* 1 fluid ounce
1 cup *equals* 8 ounces

1 cup *equals* ½ pint (liquid)
2 cups *equal* 1 pint
4 cups *equal* 1 quart
4 quarts *equal* 1 gallon

8 quarts *equal* 1 peck
4 pecks *equal* 1 bushel

16 ounces *equal* 1 pound

FOOD EQUIVALENTS

BUTTER or MARGARINE, CHOCOLATE
¼ stick *equals* 2 tablespoons
½ stick *equals* 4 tablespoons or ¼ cup
1 stick *equals* ¼ pound or ½ cup
4 sticks *equal* 1 pound or 2 cups
1 square chocolate *equals* 1 ounce
SUGAR
1 pound granulated *equals* 2 cups
1 pound brown sugar *equals* 2¼ cups (firmly packed)
1 pound confectioner's *equals* 3½ cups (sifted)
1 pound powdered *equals* 2⅓ cups

FLOUR

1 pound all-purpose *equals* 4 cups, sifted
1 pound cake flour *equals* 4½ cups, sifted
1 pound unsifted graham flour *equals* 3½ cups
1 pound cornmeal *equals* 3 cups

FRUITS and VEGETABLES

1 15 ounce package seedless raisins *equals* 3 cups
1 15 ounce package seeded raisins *equals* 3¼ cups
Juice of 1 lemon *equals* 3 to 4 tablespoons
Grated rind of 1 lemon *equals* 1½ to 3 teaspoons
Juice of 1 orange *equals* 6 to 7 tablespoons
Grated rind of 1 orange *equals* about 1 tablespoon
1 medium apple, chopped *equals* 1 cup
1 medium onion, chopped *equals* ½ cup

CHEESE and EGGS

4 cups grated American cheese *equal* 1 pound
6 tablespoons white cream cheese *equal* 3 ounce package
16 tablespoons (1 cup) white cream cheese *equal* ½ pound
    package
12 to 14 egg yolks *equal* 1 cup
8 to 10 egg whites *equal* 1 cup

CRUMBS

12 graham crackers *equal* 1 cup fine crumbs
22 vanilla wafers *equal* 1 cup fine crumbs
1 slice bread *equals* ½ cup soft crumbs
20 salted crackers *equal* 1 cup fine crumbs

NUTS and MARSHMALLOWS

16 marshmallows *equal* ¼ pound
1 pound walnuts in shell *equals* 2 cups shelled
¼ pound chopped nuts *equals* about 1 cup

SUBSTITUTIONS

1 tablespoon cornstarch *equals* 2 tablespoons flour
1 square (1 oz.) chocolate *equals* 3 tablespoons cocoa plus 1 teaspoon butter
1 whole egg *equals* 2 egg yolks plus 1 tablespoon water (in cookies, etc.)
1 whole egg *equals* 2 egg yolks (in custards and such mixtures)
1 cup sour milk *equals* 1 tablespoon lemon juice or vinegar plus sweet milk to make 1 cup
1 cup milk *equals* ½ cup evaporated milk plus ½ cup water
1 cup less 2 tablespoons all-purpose flour *equals* 1 cup cake flour

OVEN TEMPERATURES

Slow	250 to 300 degrees
Slow Moderate	325 degrees
Moderate	350 degrees
Quick Moderate	375 degrees
Moderate Hot	400 degrees
Hot	425 to 450 degrees
Very Hot	475 to 500 degrees

SIZE OF CANS

No. 1 *equals* 2 cups or 16 ounces
No. 2 *equals* 2½ cups or 20 ounces
No. 2½ *equals* 3½ cups or 28 ounces
No. 3 *equals* 4 cups or 32 ounces
No. 10 *equals* 13 cups or 6 pounds, 10 ounces

Breads

BISCUITS
Angel 34
Buttermilk 35
Easy 34
Mile High 34
Nice and Light 35

BREADS
Apple Cranberry 45
Banana Nut 43
Cape Cod Tea 48
Carrot Loaf 46
Carrot Nut 46
Cherry 49
Cranberry 45
Five Islands Tea Cake 48
Grapenut 44
Kernel Corn 37
Irish Treacle 48
Lemon Tea 44
Orange 50
Peanut Butter 45
Peggy's Prune 46
Pineapple Pecan 44
Pumpkin 49

BROWN BREADS
Brown, Plain 33
Evaporated Milk 33
Old-Fashioned 33

COFFEE CAKES
Blueberry 47
Cinnamon 47
Coffee Ring 37
Rhubarb 47

DOUGHNUTS
Applesauce, Wheat Flour .. 112
Brown Sugar 114
Buttermilk 113
Chocolate 112
Chocolate 115
Maine Potato 112
Molasses 115
Never Fail 113
Plain 114
Raised 115
Squash 114
Sugar 113
Sugarless 114

GRIDDLECAKES
Corn 35
Cornmeal 36

JOHNNY CAKE
Aunt Gertie's 32
Molasses 32
Spider 32

MUFFINS
Blueberry 39
Cream Style Corn 39
French Breakfast 38
Ginger 38
Graham Apple 38
Graham Cracker 37
Maine Cranberry 40
Mother's Bran 40
Squash 40

MISCELLANEOUS
Batter for Fish Sticks 31
Dumplings 50
Golden Waffles 51
Popovers 35

PANCAKES
Mashed Potato 31
Plain 31
White Flour 31

ROLLS
Cinnamon 36
Graham Buns 43
Old-Fashioned Graham 39
Ten Minute Gems 43

YEAST BREAD
All Bran 50
Finnish Coffee 56
Oatmeal 54
Oatmeal 55
Rolled Oats 54
Shredded Wheat 54

YEAST ROLLS
Buttermilk 52
Delicious Raised 51
Drop Feather 55
One Hour 52
Overnight 51
Icebox 55
Parker House 52
Parker House 53
Raised Corn 56
Refrigerator 53

Cakes

CAKES

Aaron's Bundles	95
Almond	97
Apple, Danish	66
Apple, Dutch	69
Apple, Grated	76
Apple Loaf	68
Apple, Molasses	67
Apple, Nobby	69
Apple, Raw	66
Apple Sauce	67
Apple Sauce	67
Apple Sauce	68
Blueberry	69
Blueberry	70
Blueberry	70
Blueberry	74
Blueberry, Old-Fashioned Molasses	70
Blueberry Pudding Cake	73
Brown Sugar Cupcakes	86
Butter, Golden	95
Butterscotch Sundae	96
Carrot	80
Cheesecake	76
Cheesecake, Lemon Apple	75
Cheesecake, Refrigerator	75
Cherry Nut, Easy	74
Chocolate	90
Chocolate, Cheap	89
Chocolate, Date	94
Chocolate, Deluxe	92
Chocolate, Fudge	91
Chocolate, Fudge	91
Chocolate, Molasses	92
Chocolate, Never Fail	92
Chocolate, Plain	93
Chocolate, Potato	90
Chocolate, Salad Dressing	91
Chocolate, Spanish	93
Chocolate, Throw Together	90
Chocolate "Wowie"	93
Coconut Pound	56
Crumb Cake	81
Crumb, Dark	95
Date, Margarets	77
Date, Aunt Lizzie	77
Date, Golden	78
Fruit, Anna's	64
Fruit, Boiled	63
Fruit, Boiled	64
Fruit, Cream Cheese	63
Fruit, Economical	63
Fruit, French	60
Fruit, Gumdrop	61
Fruit, Harrison	62
Fruit, My Own	62
Fruit, Old Town Raisin	64
Fruit, Orange	61
Fruit, Orange	87
Fruit, Our	60
Fruit, White	59
Fruit Cocktail Easy Fruit	96
Forty Day	88
Gingerbread	100
Gingerbread, Bride's	103
Gingerbread, Grandma's	100
Gingerbread, Great-Great-Grandmother's	103
Gingerbread, Hardtack	98
Gingerbread, Molasses	99
Gingerbread, Nellie's	103
Gingerbread, Old-Fashioned	103
Gingerbread, Old-Fashioned Hard	100
Gingerbread, Spiced	99
Gingerbread, Sugar	99
Hungry Cake	97
Jelly, Grandma Joy's	81
Martha Washington	98
Mocha, Oatmeal	86
Mincemeat	87
Nut	78
Nut Loaf Xmas	80
Peanut Butter	94
Pork, Salt	98
Plantation	81
Pumpkin	66
Raisin	65
Raisin	65
Raisin, Boiled	65
Raisin, Shortcake	89
Raspberry, Upside Down	73
Rhubarb, Upside Down	78
Ribbon	88
Sauerkraut	79
Sour Cream, Grandmother's	97
Spice and Frosting	82
Spice, Golden	87
Spice, Spud and Spice	79
Spice, Three Minute	89
Sponge, Ellen's Molasses	85
Sponge, Golden	82
Sponge, Hot Milk	85
Sponge, Josie Barker's	85
Strawberry, My	74

Candy

Caramels	107	Chocolate	108
Caramels, Chocolate	109	Chocolate, Supreme	108
Molasses, Old-Fashioned	110	Divinity	111
Needams	111	Easy Never Fail	108
Pineapple	109	Foolproof	109
Southern Pralines	110	Light	106
Walnut Clusters	107	Peanut Butter	110

FUDGE
Brown Sugar 107

Peanut Butter 110
Three Minute 111

Cookies

Apple Jacks 206
Apple Sauce 203
Banana Nuggets 215

Candy Cookies 212
Caramel Nut 217
Cherry Surprise 217

Chocolate, Banana 205
Chocolate, Chip 206
Chocolate, Crinkles 204

Chocolate, Five Minute 205
Coconut 206
Crunchies, Maine 204

Date Pinwheels 199
Dreamies 215
Filled 217

Filled Drop 204
Filled Molasses 214
Gingersnaps, Country Raisin 209

Hermits, Generation 210
Hermits, Gram's 209
Lemonade 201

Molasses 209
Molasses 213
Molasses, Coconut 212
Molasses, Filled 210
Molasses, Soft 203

Molasses, Old-Fashioned
  Soft 211
Molasses, Soft 213

Oatmeal 212
Oatmeal, Drop 216
Oatmeal, Macaroons 216
Oatmeal, Old-Fashioned ... 202
Oatmeal, Tropical 216
Old-Fashioned 203
Peanut Butter, Orange 214
Peanut Butter, Roundups .. 211

Sighs 215
Snowballs 203
Sugar with Filling 205

MISCELLANEOUS
Chocolate Sponge Roll 200
Cream Puffs 189
Date-Nut Marshmallow
  Roll 198
Jim's Tarts 197
Pecan Raisin Tarts 190
Whoopie Filling 200

BARS
Crunchy Top 190
Date and Nut 195
Dump 189
Dream 196
Mincemeat 191
Mincemeat 198
Nut Goodies 200
Peanut Chewy 191
Spicy Fruit 196
Toffee 192

SQUARES
Apple 192
Apple Brownies 199
Chocolate Syrup 199
Chocolate Peanut Butter .. 201
Cranberry Crunch 191
Date Brambles 202
Date 195
Delicious 201
Marshmallow Fudge 198
O.K. 192
Raspberry Jam 197

Banana Pie 240	Ice Cream, Low Calorie ... 242
Bread, Low Sodium 239	Macaroni and Cheese 242
Cookies 240	Mincemeat 242
Cookies, Father John's 239	Mincemeat 239
Custard Pie 241	Pickles with Saccharin 241
	Salmon Loaf 241
Fruit Delight, Sugar Free . 240	Tea, Slippery Elm Bark ... 241

FROSTINGS

Butterscotch 105	Michigan Fudge 106
Coffee 105	Never Fail 104
Decorator's 104	Quick Caramel 106
	Seven Minute 105
Frosting 106	Whipped 105

Game

Apple Pie Crumb Topping ... 104	Pineapple Topping 104
Camper's Steak 236	Rabbit Pie 235
Eider Ducks, Baked 237	Rabbit, Smothered 235
Hunter's Stew 236	Pheasant au Casserole 236
	Venison with Beans 235
Partridge Fillet 237	Wild Birds and Dumplings . 238

Main Dishes

BAKED BEANS

Bertha's 143	Swedish Meat Balls 132
Boston 143	Swedish Meat Balls 134
With Maple Syrup 143	Upside Down Pie 134

BEEF

CHICKEN

Baked Heart 136	Apple Scallop 123
Bean Pot Stew 134	Baked Sesame 122
Beef Stroganoff 128	Barbecued 120
Becky's Meat Loaf 135	Busy Day Casserole 120
Burlington Barbecue 133	Chicken A-Go-Go 120
Caracus 130	Chicken Casserole 119
Cedric's Casserole 128	Chicken Casserole 119
Corned Beef Casserole 238	Chicken Casserole 121
Dutch Casserole 142	Chicken Casserole 122
Dutch Meat Loaf 136	Chicken Casserole 122
Hamburg, Barbecued 139	Chicken Easy 116
Hamburg Bean Pot 133	Chicken-Rice Casserole 125
Hamburger Meat Loaf 132	Chicken That's Different .. 124
Hamburg Pie 135	Chuck Wagon Special 127
Hamburg Stroganoff 128	Colonial 124
Meat Balls Deluxe 129	Honey Baked 123
Southern Hamburg 133	Pineapple 125
Spaghetti & Meat Balls 132	Roast 123

Main Dishes

HAM
Asparagus 116
Ham and Cheese Strata ... 130
Slices with Cranberry 116

LAMB
Creamy Lamb Stew 140

LIVER
Chicken Livers 142
Liver and Bacon Loaf 142
Liverwurst 141
Loaf 141

MISCELLANEOUS
Frankfurters, Barbecued ... 135
Lasagne, Quick and Easy . 141
Rice Scallop 119
Sandwich Spread 148
Stuffing, Pennsylvania
   Dutch 121
Stuffing, Sage 129

PORK
Apple 'N Pork Pie 126

Gumbo 127
Pie 126
Sweet and Sour 127
With Apple Stuffing 126

VEAL
Parmesan 140

VEGETABLES
Asparagus, Fried 144
Cabbage Scramble 146
Corn and Cheese Casserole 131
Corn Scallop 139
Eggplant 146
Green Bean Casserole 145
Green Peppers, Stuffed ... 147
Onion and Apple Casserole 145
Onion Rings, French Fried 139
Potato and Egg 131
Potato Puff 147
Potatoes, Scalloped 145
Spinach Pie 146
Tomato Casserole 144
Tomatoes, Fried 147
Zucchini Casserole 144

Pies

Apple, Blush 162
Apple, Leona's 161
Apple, Paper Bag 161
Apple Pie Filling 162
Butter 158
Buttermilk, Grandmother's 158
Blueberry 154
Cherry, Cream Cheese 160
Chocolate Cream 164
Coffee Toffee 159
Cranberry 156
Cranberry, Raisin 156
Crust, 100 Year Old 149
Crust, Mix 149
Crust, with Beaten Egg ... 149
Crust, with Egg Yolk 150
Crust, with Vinegar 149
Custard 157
Custard, Beautiful 157
Lemon, Icebox 153

Lemon, Frozen 153
Lemon, Meringue 150
Lemon, Rhubarb 153
Lemon, Sponge 154
Mince, Custard Crunch ... 164
Mince, Quick 164
Muskmelon 157
Pecan, Southern 154
Pineapple, Meringue 162
Pumpkin 160
Pumpkin, with Eggs 160
Raisin, with Meringue 159
Rhubarb 163
Rhubarb, Dream 163
Squash 155
Squash, New England 155
Squash, without Eggs 155
Strawberry, Cheese 158
Tomato, Green 156

Preserves and Pickles

Beans, Marinated 230
Beans, Pickled 230

Chili Sauce 232
Eggs, Pickled 232

Preserves and Pickles

Garden Special 233
Jam, Strawberry 227
Jam, Rhubarb-Strawberry 228
Marmalade, Rhubarb 229
Marmalade, Xmas 228
Mincemeat 234
Mincemeat, Grammie's 233
Mincemeat, Green Tomato 234
Mincemeat, Mom's Deer .. 234
Mincemeat, Venison 233

Pear, Harlequin 228
Pickles, Bread and Butter 230
Pickles, Chopped 231
Pickles, Spiced Beet 232
Sweet Tomato 231
Quince, Honey 229
Relish, Apple 232
Relish, Hot Dog 231
Relish, Pepper 229
Relish, Ripe Cucumber 229

Puddings

Angel Food Delight 187
Apple, Brown Betty 177
Apple, Crispy 177
Apple, Crunch 178
Apple, Dumplings Deluxe .. 176
Apple, French Cobbler 177
Apple, Grunt 178
Apple, Tapioca 182
Apple, Walnut Cobbler 182
Apple Sauce Puff 181
Blueberry Buckle 170
Blueberry Crisp 169
Blueberry with Graham
  Crackers 171
Blueberry with Tapioca ... 169
Blueberry Souffle 170
Bread with Karo Syrup ... 172
Bread with Molasses 172
Bread with Raisins 172
Cherry Surprises 171
Chocolate 186
Chocolate, Heirloom Rice . 185
Coconut Date Surprise 186
Coffee Mallow 178
Coffee Souffle 167
Cooperstown 171
Cranberry 182

Cranberry Duff 183
Date 186
Date, Crumb Steamed 184
Grapenut 187
Indian 173
Indian 175
Indian, Apple 174
Indian, Bread 175
Indian, Old-Fashioned with
  Brown Sugar 174
Indian, Old-Fashioned 173
Indian, Old-Time 173
Indian, Passamaquoddy ... 174
John's Delight 169
Lemon Meringue 187
Lemon Sauce 185
Pumpkin, Cottage 184
Rhubarb 176
Rhubarb Puffs 175
Rice, Quick 185
Steamed, 100 Years Old 168
Strawberry, Old-Fashioned 167
Suet 181
Suet or Railroad 181
Suet, Viola's New England 168
Vegetable 183
Xmas 167

Salads

Angel Hash 218
Apple Sauce Peach 220
Apricot 219
Cabbage 223
Club 220
Cranberry 220
Cranberry Walnut 223
Dressing, Aunt Alice's 226
Dressing, Cabbage 226
Dressing, Fruit 227
Dressing, Pineapple Fruit . 227

Dressing, Salad 225
Dressing, Sweet 226
Dressing, Tomato French . 226
Green Ribbon 224
Holiday 219
Lake House Cole Slaw 225
My Favorite 224
Pyramid 223
Shrimp Cool as a
  Cucumber 218
Sweet and Sour 224

Sauces

SAUCES, MEAT
Barbecued 238
Brown Sugar for Pancakes 148
Horseradish 148
Meat 148
Spaghetti, My 131

SAUCES, DESSERT
Brown Sugar 188
Butter 188
Old New England 188
Orange 188
Topping for Cake 68

Seafoods

CLAM
Cakes 19
Chowder 17
Corn Casserole 18
Dip 18
Drops 19
Fried Cakes 17
Puffs 18
Souffle 17

CODFISH
Balls 19

CRAB
Cobbler 20
Rolls 20

FLOUNDER
Baked 21

HADDOCK
Baked 24
Baked, Cheese Dressing ... 25
Baked, Sticks 26
Fish Chowder 29
Fish Loaf 25
Gravy, Fish 23
Maine Chowder 26
Salad 24
Souffle 29
Turbot 25

LOBSTER
Baked, Spanish 5
Clara's Fried 5
Casserole 6
Deviled 6
Newburg 6

MISCELLANEOUS
Fish Casserole 30
Mixed Shellfish au Gratin 23

Seafood Melody 26
Seafood Thermidor 24

MUSSEL
Stew 15

OYSTERS
Casino 16
Scalloped 16
Soup 15
Soup 16
Toast 16

SALMON
Curry 22
Rice Casserole 21
Stuffed Slices 22

SCALLOPS
Baked 12
Scalloped 12
Scalloped 15

SHRIMP
Baked Cheese Custard 10
Chowder 8
Cooking Method 10
Creole 8
Curried Creole 7
Espanol 12
Exotica 7
Noodle Casserole 9
Pie 8
Scallops & Shrimp 10
Shrimp & Scallop Gruyere . 9
Sweet & Sour 11

TUNA
Easy Casserole 29
Fish Scallop 30
Hot Tuna Buns 30

Notes

Notes

Notes

Notes